Recommendatory Letter

The following letter from Rev. Andrew Broaddus (Caroline), and Peter Nelson, Esq. (Professor of Wingfield Academy, Hanover), is so gratifying to the feelings of the author that he cannot withhold from publication the recommendation of men so capable of judging of the merits of such a work:

August 30, 1810.

Dear Sir,—The examination of your *History of the Rise and Progress of the Baptists in Virginia* has indeed been to us a pleasing task; not merely as it has afforded us an opportunity of complying with the requisition of a friendship we highly value, but from the manner in which the compilation is executed.

We are far from intending the complimentary style of recommendation when we say that we consider this a truly valuable and well executed work. The style is perspicuous, concise, and well adapted to history; the arrangement clear and happily calculated to prevent confusion; and the matter it contains highly important and interesting to every friend of truth and piety.

We cannot conclude without congratulating *you* on the completion of an undertaking so laborious as this has been, and the *public* on the acquisition of a work calculated, in a considerable degree, to gratify the curious and inform the inquisitive, as well as to promote the cause of true religion.

Accept the assurances of our friendship and esteem.

Peter Nelson.
Andrew Broaddus.

A History

of the
Rise And Progress
of the
Baptists In Virginia

BY
ROBERT B. SEMPLE
1810

Charleston, AR:
COBB PUBLISHING
2019

Publisher's Preface

This book is being republished at the request of some who see in it a usefulness for combatting modern attempts at changing and editing history to promote a false narrative. The only changes made in this edition of *A History of the Rise and Progress of the Baptists in Virginia* are in spelling, punctuation, and formatting. Footnotes from the 1810 edition are generally marked with "*Author's note*" at the end. The remaining footnotes, all of which are to explain a potentially archaic or obscure word or phrase, are new to this edition.

In the Appendix, which contains several letters and addresses, we did not seek to correct any of the spelling or capitalization to modern usage, but left it as in the original.

In some instances, last names were spelled differently throughout the book ("Harriss" and "Hariss," for example). When these were noted, we made them uniform (now they all read "Harriss") in order not to detract from the content of the book.

A History of the Rise and Progress of the Baptists in Virginia, Updated Edition, is copyright © 2019 Cobb Publishing, all rights reserved.

Published in the United States by:
Cobb Publishing
704 E. Main St.
Charleston, AR 72933
CobbPublishing.com
CobbPublishing@gmail.com
(479) 747-8372

ISBN: 979-8-3303-2076-9

Preface to the Original Edition

Unless the compiler is wholly deceived in himself, his attempt to write a history of the Virginia Baptists did not spring either from the love of money or the love of fame. To say that these things never entered his thoughts would be saying what no one would believe. His motive was an ardent wish for the prosperity of truth, which he really thought could be greatly promoted by a plain and simple exhibition of God's dealings towards His people. The rise and rapid spread of the Baptists in Virginia was so remarkable that there are but few who do not believe that some historical relation of them will be productive of real advantage to true religion. So much were our revolutionary reformers persuaded of this that they made arrangements, as early as 1788, to collect materials and publish a history, as may be seen by turning to our history of the proceedings of the General Committee.

If his book does not recommend itself by its polished style, deep erudition or rhetorical flights, he thinks that it possesses qualities that are more valuable in such a work. Candor and simplicity, in church history, appear to the author properties of primary importance. He has faithfully recorded the foibles and failures, as well as the virtues and praises, of his own people.

The documents which were before him were of various sorts. Some were printed, and, of course, rested upon the veracity of the author. Some were old manuscripts gathered from the papers of persons long since dead, and which might have been hastily composed, their authors not expecting their publication and not being alive to give explanations. Some, and indeed many, were furnished by living characters, who doubtless always gave as correct information as they possessed. But from the contradictory statements of the same facts by different persons there must have been many mistakes. The compiler always strove to select from the various statements that which seemed most likely to be correct; yet without doubt he will be found sometimes to have been mistaken. His errors, however, if there are any, are chiefly, if not wholly, respecting matters of secondary importance. To make a satisfactory selection was often extremely difficult indeed, yet the arrangement of materials received was not the most arduous part. An unaccountable backwardness of many to furnish in any way the information possessed rendered the task almost impracticable. All these difficulties considered, with many that cannot be expressed, the reader will do no more than justice to say that however incorrect the work may be in some of its parts, and however deficient in others, it is still a performance that must have cost no inconsiderable labor and solicitude.

Whilst he expresses regret at the backwardness of some, he feels a more than commensurate pleasure in expressing his gratitude for the laudable forwardness of others. These are so numerous and so deserving that he is fearful, whilst he cannot insert the names of all, the sensibility of others might be wounded if he should mention those of the *Rev. William Mason,* of Culpeper; *John Poindexter,* of Louisa; *A. Waller*, of Spotsylvania; *William Brame*, of Richmond; *Benjamin Watkins*, of Powhatan; *William Richards*, of Mecklenburg; *Josiah Osborne* and *John Alderson,* of Greenbrier; *William Howard,* of Montgomery; *John Jenkins*, of Pittsylvania; *Jeremiah Moore,* of Fairfax; and *Mr. Thomas Buck,* of Frederick. From these a prompt and friendly aid was afforded; and, indeed, some exerted themselves above what could have been expected. From the histories of the Kehukee and Ketocton Associations, extracts have been made as to Portsmouth and Ketocton. To their authors he must, therefore, express his obligations. Mr. Leland's *Virginia Chronicle,* his manuscript collection, &c., were the more valuable because they furnished matter which could not have been easily, if at all, obtained elsewhere.

There are some parts of the history, such as treat on churches, &c., which will not be interesting to many readers; yet to others these places may be the most desirable.

The tables prefixed to each Association are designed to exhibit a compendious view of the churches of which they are composed.

In treating on churches and Associations, opportunities are often taken of delineating some living characters, and thereby to hold up for imitation the praiseworthy properties of good men; and, in a few instances, by exhibiting the true characters of bad ones, a warning is offered to the unwary.

Finally, whatever may be the censures of bigots and cynics, the author hopes for the candid and liberal support of the friends of truth and piety; and for these this book is particularly designed.

Notwithstanding great pains have been taken to prevent it, some grammatical and some typographical errors have imperceptibly crept into this work. These, it is believed, seldom, if ever, affect the sense.

Contents

CHAPTER ONE:
Of the Origin of the Separate Baptists.

The Baptists of Virginia originated from three sources. The first were emigrants from England, who, about the year 1714, settled in the southeastern parts of the State. About 1743 another party came from Maryland and formed a settlement in the northwest. Each of these will be treated of in their proper places. A third party, from New England, having acted the most distinguished part, first demands our attention.

By the preaching of Mr. Whitefield through New England a great work of God broke out in that country, distinguished by the name of the *New Light Stir*. All who joined it were called *New Lights*. Many preachers of the established order became active in the work. Their success was so great that numbers of the parish clergy, who were opposed to the revival, were apprehensive that they should be deserted by all their hearers. They therefore not only refused them the use of their meetinghouses, but actually procured the passage of a law to confine all preachers to their own parishes. This opposition did not effect the intended object. The hearts of the people, being touched by a heavenly flame, could no longer relish the dry parish service, conducted, for the most part, as they thought, by a set of graceless mercenaries.

The *New Light Stir* being extensive, a great number were converted to the Lord. These, conceiving that the parish congregations, a few excepted, were far from the purity of the Gospel, determined to form a society to themselves. Accordingly, they embodied many churches. Into these none were admitted who did not profess vital religion. Having thus separated themselves from the established churches, they were denominated *Separates*. Their church government was entirely upon the plan of the in*dependents*, the power being in the hands of the church. They permitted unlearned men to preach, provided they manifested such gifts as indicated future usefulness. They were Pedobaptists in principle, but did not reject any of their members who chose to submit to believers' baptism.

The *Separates* first took their rise, or rather their name, about the year 1744. They increased very fast for several years. About a year after they were organized into a distinct society they were joined by Shubal Stearns, who, becoming a preacher, labored among them until 1751, when, forming acquaintance with some of the Baptists, he was convinced of the duty of believers' baptism. Being a good man, to know his duty was sufficient to induce him to perform it. The same year in which he was baptized he was ordained, and took the pastoral care of a church.

Mr. Stearns and most of the *Separates* had strong faith in the immediate teachings of the Spirit. They believed that to those who sought Him earnestly God gave evident tokens of His will. That such indications of the divine pleasure, partaking of the nature of inspiration, were above, though not contrary to reason, and that following these, still leaning in every step upon the same wisdom and power by which they were first actuated, they would inevitably be led to the accomplishment of the two great objects of a Christian's life—the glory of God and the salvation of men. Mr. Stearns, listening to some of these instructions of Heaven, conceived himself called upon by the Almighty to move far to the westward to execute a great and extensive work. Incited by his impressions, in the year 1754, he and a few of his members took their leave of New England. They halted first at Opeckon, in Berkeley County, Virginia, where he found a Baptist church under the care of Rev. John Garrard, who met him kindly. Here, also, he met his brother-in-law, the Rev. Daniel Marshall, just returned from his mission among the indians, and who after his arrival at this place had become a Baptist. They joined companies and settled for a while on Cacapon, in Hampshire County, about thirty miles from Winchester. Here, not meeting with his expected success, he felt restless. Some of his friends had moved to North Carolina; he received letters from these, informing him that preaching was greatly desired by the people of that country; that in some instances they had ridden forty miles to hear one sermon. He and his party once more got under way, and, traveling about two hundred miles, came to Sandy Creek, in Guilford County, North Carolina. Here he took up his permanent residence. Soon after his arrival, viz., November 22, 1755, he and his companions, to the number of sixteen, were constituted into a church called *Sandy Creek,* and to which Mr. Stearns was appointed pastor. In this little church in the wilderness there were, besides the pastor, two other preachers, viz., Joseph Breed and Daniel Marshall, neither of whom was ordained.

Thus organized they began their work, kindling a fire which soon began to burn brightly indeed, spreading in a few years over Virginia, North and South Carolina, and Georgia.

The subsequent events seem completely to have verified Mr. Stearns's impressions concerning a great work of God in the West.

CHAPTER TWO:
From Their Final Settlement in North Carolina until the Commencement of Legal Persecution.

The natives around about this little colony of Baptists, although brought up in the Christian religion, were grossly ignorant of its essential principles. Having the form of godliness, they knew nothing of its power.

The doctrine of Mr. Stearns and his party was consequently quite strange. To be born again appeared to them as absurd as it did to the Jewish doctor, when he asked if he must enter the second time into his mother's womb and be born again. Having always supposed that religion consisted in nothing more than the practice of its outward duties, they could not comprehend how it should be necessary to feel conviction and conversion. But to be able to ascertain the time and place of one's conversion was, in their estimation, wonderful indeed. These points were all strenuously contended for by the new preachers.

But their manner of preaching was, if possible, much more novel than their doctrines. The *Separates* in New England had acquired a very warm and pathetic address, accompanied by strong gestures and a singular tone of voice. Being often deeply affected themselves while preaching, correspondent affections were felt by their pious hearers, which were frequently expressed by tears, trembling, screams, shouts, and acclamations. All these they brought with them into their new habitation. The people were greatly astonished, having never seen things on this wise before. Many mocked, but, the power of God attending them, many also trembled. In process of time some of the natives became converts, and bowed obedience to the Redeemer's scepter. These, uniting their labors with the chosen band, a powerful and extensive work broke out. From sixteen, Sandy Creek church soon swelled to six hundred and six members, so mightily grew the work of God!

Daniel Marshall, though not possessed of great talents, was indefatigable in his endeavors. He sallied out into the adjacent neighborhoods and planted the Redeemer's standard in many of the strongholds of Satan. At Abbott's Creek, about thirty miles from Sandy Creek, the Gospel prospered so largely that they petitioned the mother church for a constitution and for the ordination of Mr. Marshall as their pastor. Mr. Marshall accepted the call and went to live among them. His ordination, however, was a matter of some difficulty. It required a plurality of elders to constitute a presbytery; Mr. Stearns was the only ordained minister among them. In this dilemma they were informed that there were some Regular Baptist preachers living on Pedee. To one of these Mr. Stearns applied, and requested him to assist him in the ordination of Mr. Marshall. This request he sternly refused, declaring that he held no fellowship with Stearns's party; that he believed them to be a disorderly set, suffering women to pray in public and permitting every ignorant man to preach that chose; that they encouraged noise and confusion in their meetings. Application was then made to Mr. Henry Ledbetter, who lived somewhere in the Southern States, and who was a brother-in-law of Mr. Marshall. He and Mr. Stearns ordained Mr. Marshall to the care of this new church. The work of grace continued to spread, and several preachers were raised in North Carolina. Among others was James: Read, who was afterwards very successful in Virginia. When he first began to preach he was entirely illiterate, not knowing how to read or write. His wife became his instructor, and he soon acquired learning sufficient to enable him to read the Scriptures.

Into the parts of Virginia adjacent to the residence of this religious colony the Gospel had been quickly carried by Mr. Marshall. He had baptized several in some of his first visits. Among them was Dutton Lane, who shortly after his baptism began to preach. A revival succeeded, and Mr. Marshall at one time baptized forty-two persons. In August, 1760, a church was constituted under the pastoral care of Rev. Dutton Lane. This was the first Separate Baptist church in Virginia, and, in some sense, the mother of all the rest. The church prospered under the ministry of Mr. Lane, aided by the occasional visits of Mr. Marshall and Mr. Stearns. They endured much persecution; but God prospered them and in delivered them out of the hands of all their enemies.

Soon after Mr. Lane's conversion the power of God was effectual in the conversion of Samuel Hariss, a man of great distinction in those parts. Besides being burgess of the county and colonel of the militia, he held several other offices. Upon being honored of God, he laid aside all worldly honors and became a laborer in the Lord's vineyard. In 1759 he was ordained a ruling elder. From the time of the commencement of his ministry for about seven years his labors were devoted chiefly to his own and the adjacent counties. Being often with Mr. Marshall in his ministerial journeys, he caught the zeal, diligence, and indeed the manners of Marshall. His labors were crowned with the blessing of Heaven wherever he went.

Stearns, though not as laborious as Marshall, was not idle. He seems to have had the talent of arranging materials when collected. He understood well discipline and church government. Having now constituted several churches, and there being some others that exercised the rights of churches though not formally organized, Mr. Stearns conceived that an association composed of delegates from all these would have a tendency to impart stability, regularity, and uniformity to the whole. For this prudent purpose he visited each church and congregation and explained the contemplated plan, induced them all to send delegates to his meeting-house the ensuing January, which was in the year 1760.

Their regulations and proceedings may be seen in our account of the General Association. Here it may suffice to observe that through these meetings the Gospel was carried into many new places, where the fame of the Baptists had previously spread, for great crowds, attending from distant parts, mostly through curiosity, many became enamored with these extraordinary people, and petitioned the Association to send preachers into their neighborhoods. These petitions were readily granted, and the preachers as readily complied with the appointments. Thus the Association became the medium of propagating the Gospel in new and dark places. They were instrumental in another way in advancing truth. When assembled their chief employment was preaching, exhortation, singing, and conversing about their various exertions in the Redeemer's service and the attendant success. These things so inflamed the hearts of the ministers that they would leave the Association with a zeal and courage which no obstacles could impede.

Mr. Marshall's impressions led him to travel farther south. Of his success in those quarters, see some account in his biography.

Mr. Hariss was destined of God to labor more extensively in Virginia than in any other State. Having done much good in the circumjacent parts, the time had now arrived for him to lengthen his chords. In January, 1765, Allen Wyley,[1] an inhabitant of Culpeper, and who had been baptized by David Thomas, hearing of the *Separate Baptist preachers*, traveled from Culpeper to Pittsylvania in order to get one or more of them to come and preach in Culpeper. He traveled on, scarcely knowing whither he went. An unseen hand directed his course. He providentially fell in with one of Mr. Hariss's meeting. When he came into the meetinghouse Mr. Hariss fixed his eyes upon him, being impressed previously that he had some extraordinary message. He asked him when he came, &c. Mr. Wyley told him his errand. Upon which, after some deliberation, believing him to be sent of God, Mr. Hariss agreed to go. Taking three days to prepare, he started with Wyley, having no meetings on the way, yet exhorting and praying at every house where he went.

Arriving in Culpeper, his first meeting was at Wyley's own house. He preached the first day without interuption, and appointed for the next. He the next day began to preach, but the opposers immediately raised violent opposition, appearing with whips, sticks, clubs, &c., so as to hinder his labors; in consequence of which he left that night over to Orange County, and preached with much effect. He continued many days preaching from place to place, attended by great crowds and followed throughout his meetings by several persons, who had been lately converted or seriously awakened under the ministry of the Regular Baptists, and also by many who had been alarmed by his own labors. When Mr. Hariss left them he exhorted them to be steadfast, and advised some (in whom he discovered talents) to commence the exercise of their gifts and to hold meetings among themselves.

In this ministerial journey Mr. Hariss sowed much good seed, yielding afterwards great increase. The young converts took his advice and began to hold meetings every Sabbath, and almost every night in the week, taking a tobacco house for their meeting-

---

[1] Mr. Wyley is now living, and furnished from under his own hand the above account. He has maintained ever since an upright character as a zealous and pious professor.—*Author's note.*

house. After proceeding in this way for some time they applied to Mr. David Thomas, who lived somewhere north of the Rappahannock, to come and preach for them, and to teach them the ways of God more perfectly. He came, but in his preaching expressed some disapprobation of the preaching of such weak and illiterate persons. This was like throwing cold water upon their flaming zeal. They took umbrage, and resolved to send once more for Mr. Hariss.

Sometime in the year of 1766, and a short time after Mr. Thomas's preaching, three of the parties, viz., Elijah Craig and two others, traveled to Mr. Hariss's house, in order to procure his services in Orange and the adjacent parts, to preach and to baptize the new converts. They found to their surprise that he had not been ordained to the administration of the ordinances. To remedy this inconvenience he carried them about sixty miles into North Carolina to get James Read, who was ordained.

There is something singular in the exercises of Mr. Read about this time. He was impressed with an opinion that he had frequent teachings from God; and, indeed, from the account given by himself, we must either doubt his veracity or admit that his impressions were supernatural.[1] He declares that respecting his preaching in Virginia, for many weeks he had no rest in his spirit. Asleep or awake, he felt his soul earnestly impressed with strong desires to come to Virginia to preach the Gospel. In his dreams he thought that God would often show him large congregations assembled to hear preaching. He was sometimes heard by his family to cry out in his sleep, *O Virginia, Virginia, Virginia!* Mr. Graves, a member of his church, a good man, discovering his anxiety, and believing his impressions to be from God, offered to accompany him. Just as they were fixing to come off, Mr. Hariss and the three messengers mentioned above came for him to go with them. The circumstances so much resemble Peter's call from Joppa to Caesarea, that we can hardly for a moment hesitate in placing implicit confidence in its being a contrivance of divine wisdom.

Mr. Read agreed to go without much hesitation. One of the messengers from Spotsylvania went on to appoint meetings on the way. The two preachers, after filling up some appointments in

---

[1] In a manuscript furnished from his own hand.—*Author's note.*

their own parts, pursued their contemplated journey, accompanied by Mr. Graves and the other two. In about a fortnight they arrived in Orange, within the bounds of Blue Run church as it now stands. When they came in sight and saw a very large congregation they were greatly affected. After a few minutes of prayer and reflection, they recovered their courage and entered upon their great work. They preached with much effect on that day. The next day they preached at Elijah Craig's, where a vast crowd attended. D. Thomas and John Garrard, both preachers of the Regular order, were at this meeting. The ministers on both sides seemed desirous to unite, but the people were against it, the larger part siding with the *Separates.* As they could not unite, both parties held meetings the next day, being Sabbath, but a small distance from each other. Baptism was administered by both. These things widened the breach. Messrs. Read and Hariss, however, continued their ministrations. Mr. Read baptized nineteen the first day and more on the days following. They went through Spotsylvania into the upper parts of Caroline, Hanover, and Goochland counties, sowing the seed of grace and peace in many places. So much were they inspirited by these meetings that they made appointments to come again the next year. In their second visit they were accompanied by the Rev. Dutton Lane, who assisted them in constituting and organizing the first *Separate Baptist church* between the Rappahannock and James Rivers. This took place on the 20th of November, 1767. The church was called *Upper Spotsylvania,* and consisted of twenty-five members, including all the *Separate Baptists* north of James River. This was a mother to many other churches. Read and Hariss continued to visit these parts for; about three years with wonderful effect. In one of their visits they baptized seventy-five at one time, and in the course of one of their journeys, which generally lasted several weeks, they baptized upwards of two hundred.

It was not uncommon at their great meetings for many hundreds of men to camp on the ground, in order to be present the next day. The night meetings, through the great work of God, continued very late. The ministers would scarcely have an opportunity to sleep. Sometimes the floor would be covered with persons struck down under conviction of sin. It frequently happened that when they would retire to rest at a late hour they would be under the necessity of arising again through the earnest cries of the penitent. There were instances of persons traveling more than one hundred miles to one of these meetings; to go forty or fifty was not uncommon.

On account of the great increase of members, through the labors of Messrs. Read and Hariss, aided by a number of young preachers, it was found necessary to constitute several other churches. Accordingly, on the 2nd day of December, 1769, *Lower Spotsylvania church* was constituted, with 154 members, who chose John Waller for pastor. He was consecrated to this office June 2, 1770. Lewis Craig was consecrated pastor to the mother church November, 1770. *Blue Run church* was constituted December 4, 1769, and choosing Elijah Craig for their pastor, he was consecrated May, 1771.

Read and Hariss, particularly the latter, were men of great zeal and indefatigable diligence and perseverance in their Master's cause; their spirit was caught by many of the young prophets in Orange and Spotsylvania.

Lewis and Elijah Craig, John Waller, James Childs, John Burris, &c., animated by an ardent desire for the advancement of their Master's kingdom, sallied forth in every direction, spreading the tidings of peace and salvation wherever they went. Most of them illiterate, yet illumined by the wisdom from above, they would defend and maintain the cause of truth against the arguments of the most profound. Without visible sword or buckler, they moved on steadily to their purpose, undismayed by the terrific hosts of Satan backed by the strong arm of civil authority. Magistrates and mobs, priests and sheriffs, courts and prisons all vainly combined to divert them from their object. He that was for them was greater than all that were against them. They found that

> *"Prisons would palaces prove,*
> *If Jesus would dwell with them there."*

There was an Established religion. The Nebuchadnezzars of the age required all men to bow down to this golden image. These Hebrew children refused, and were cast into the burning fiery furnace of persecution; the Son of God walked with them there, to the utter dismay of their enemies. The decree finally went forth that none should be any more forced to worship the golden image.

The Establishment was overturned.

Their labors were not limited to their own counties. In Goochland, Messrs. Hariss and Read had baptized several; among whom was Reuben Ford, who had professed vital faith about seven years before, under the ministry of the renowned Whitefield and Davis. Mr. Ford was baptized in the year 1769, by James Read.

These plants were watered by the labors of the Spotsylvania preachers, particularly J. Waller, who, early in his visits to Goochland, baptized William Webber and Joseph Anthony, who, with Reuben Ford, had been exhorting, &c., previous to their being baptized. By the united labors of these several servants of God, the work of godliness progressed in Goochland and round about The conquests of Jesus differ from those of the kings of the earth; they aim to destroy their enemies; He turns enemies to friends; He arrests an infuriated Saul from the ranks of Satan, and makes him an inspired advocate for that cause which he once destroyed. So it fared with all these young preachers. They were no sooner captivated by the King of Zion than they immediately began to fight under His banner; their success was commensurate with their diligence; many believed and were baptized in Goochland; insomuch that they thought themselves ripe for an independent government, and were accordingly constituted as a church towards the last of the year 1771. It was called *Goochland church*, and contained about seventy-five members. This was the mother church of those parts, for from it have since been constituted several others. *Dover* and *Licking Hole* were both, shortly after, taken from Goochland church. William Webber became pastor of Dover, which office he held until his death, in 1808. Reuben Ford administered the Word and ordinances to Goochland and Licking Hole.

The spread of the Gospel is somewhat like the spread of fire. It does not in all cases advance regularly; but a spark being struck out, flies off and begins a new flame at a distance. In this manner did the Gospel take its rise in the counties of Middlesex, Essex, and the adjacent counties. One William Mullen, afterwards a useful preacher, had moved from Middlesex and settled in the county of Amelia. When the Gospel reached Amelia, Mr. Mullen embraced the truth. Coming afterwards, in 1769, on a visit to his relations in Middlesex and Essex, by arguments drawn from the Scripture, he convinced his brother John, and his brother-in-law,

James Greenwood, with several others, of the necessity of being born again. Of these, some found peace in believing before they ever heard the Gospel publicly preached. November, 1770, John Waller and John Burris came down and preached in Middlesex. They continued preaching at and near the same place for three days; great crowds came out; Waller baptized five. Persecution began to rage. Some said they were deceivers; others that they were good men. On the second day, a magistrate attempted to pull Waller off the stage, but the clergymen of the parish prevented it. The next day, a man threw a stone at Waller while he was preaching; the stone missed Waller and struck a friend of the man who threw it. James Greenwood and others now began to hold public meetings, by day and by night. Much good was done by them; many believed and only waited an opportunity to be baptized, there beings no ordained preacher nearer than Spotsylvania.

In the meantime the laborers had not been idle in that part of the vineyard south of James River. The two Murphys, viz., William and Joseph, aided by the indefatigable S. Hariss, had carried the Gospel into some of the counties above Pittsylvania, where Robert Stockton and some other preachers were raised. S. Hariss, J. Read, Jeremiah Walker, &c., had proclaimed the tidings of peace in Halifax, Charlotte, Lunenburg, Mecklenburg, Amelia and almost all the counties above Richmond, on the south side of the river. In these gatherings, there were many useful and several eminent ministers of the Gospel brought in, viz., John Williams, John King, James Shelbourne, Henry Lester, with some others. The Gospel was first carried hither, near as it was, into Culpeper and Spotsylvania, viz.: in consequence of a special message to the preachers from some of the inhabitants. They constituted the first church in 1769, with about forty members, which was called Nottoway, Mr. Walker soon moved and took pastoral charge of them. He had been preaching some time before this in North Carolina, his native State; he now removed to Virginia, and for several years acted a conspicuous part in the concerns Virginia Baptists.

CHAPTER THREE:
From the Commencement of Legal Persecution until the Abolition of the Established Church.

When the Baptists first appeared in North Carolina and Virginia they were viewed by men in power as beneath their notice; none, said they, but the weak and wicked join them; let them alone, they will soon fall out among themselves and come to nothing. In some places this maxim was adhered to, and persecution, in a legal shape, was never seen. But in many places, alarmed by the rapid increase of the Baptists, the men in power strained every penal law in the Virginia code to obtain ways and means to put down these disturbers of the peace, as they were now called.

It seems by no means certain that any law in force in Virginia authorized the imprisonment of any person for preaching. The law for the preservation of peace, however, was so interpreted as to answer this purpose; and, accordingly, whenever the preachers were apprehended, it was done by a peace warrant.

The first instance of actual imprisonment, we believe, that ever took place in Virginia, was in the county of Spotsylvania. On the 4th of June, 1768, John Waller, Lewis Craig, James Childs, &c., were seized by the sheriff and hauled before three magistrates, who stood in the meetinghouse yard, and who bound them in the penalty of one thousand pounds, to appear at court two days after. At court they were arraigned as disturbers of the peace; on their trial, they were vehemently accused by a certain lawyer, who said to the court, "May it please your worships, these men are great disturbers of the peace; they cannot meet a man upon the road, but they must ram a text of Scripture down his throat." Mr. Waller made his own and his brethren's defense so ingeniously that they were somewhat puzzled to know how to dispose of them. They offered to release them if they would promise to preach no more in the county for a year and a day. This they refused; and, therefore, were sent into close jail. As they were moving on, from the court-house to the prison, through the streets of Fredericksburg, they sung the hymn

"*Broad is the road that leads to death,*" &c.

This had an awful appearance. After four weeks' confinement, Lewis Craig was released from prison and immediately went down to Williamsburg to get a release for his companions. He waited on the deputy-governor, the Hon. John Blair, stated the case before him, and received the following letter, directed to the King's attorney in Spotsylvania:

Sir,—I lately received a letter, signed by a good number of worthy gentlemen, who are not here, complaining of the Baptists; the particulars of their misbehavior are not told, any further than their running into private houses and making dissensions. Mr. Craig and Mr. Benjamin Waller are now with me and deny the charge; they tell me they are willing to take the oaths as others have; I told them I had consulted the attorney-general, who is of opinion that the general court only have a right to grant licenses, and therefore I referred them to the court; but, on their application to the attorney-general, they brought me his letter, advising me to write to you. That their petition was a matter of right, and that you may not molest these conscientious people so long as they behave themselves in a manner becoming pious Christians and in obedience to the laws till the court, when they intend to apply for license, and when the gentlemen who complain may make their objections and be heard. The act of toleration (it being found by experience that persecuting dissenters increases their numbers) has given them a right to apply, in a proper manner, for licensed houses for the worship of God, according to their consciences; and I persuade myself that the gentlemen will quietly overlook their meetings till the court. I am told they administer the sacrament of the Lord's supper, near the manner we do, and differ from our church in nothing but in that of baptism, and in their renewing the ancient discipline; by which they have reformed some sinners and brought them to be truly penitent. Nay, if a man of theirs is idle and neglects to labor and provide for his family as he ought, he incurs their censures, which have

When the letter came to the attorney he would have nothing to
say in the affair. Waller and the others continued in jail forty-three
days, and were discharged without any conditions. While in prison
they constantly preached through the grates. The mobs outside
used every exertion to prevent the people from hearing, but to little purpose. Many heard, indeed, upon whom the Word was in
power and demonstration.

After their discharge, which was a kind of triumph, Waller,
Craig and their compeers in the ministry resumed their labors with
redoubled vigor, gathering fortitude from their late sufferings,
thanking God that they were counted worthy to suffer for Christ
and His Gospel. Day and night, and indeed almost every day and
night, they held meetings in their own and the adjacent neighborhoods. The spread of the Gospel and Baptist principles was equal
to all their exertions; insomuch that in very few sections of Virginia did the Baptist cause appear more formidable to its enemies
and more consoling to its friends than in Spotsylvania; and we
may add, so it is at this day.

We have already observed the spread of the Gospel in the county of Goochland, and that certain promising young preachers were
thrust into the work. Animated as they were with strong desires
for the welfare of souls, they could not restrain themselves within
the limits of one county. In December, 1770, Messrs. William
Webber and Joseph Anthony, two zealous young preachers,
passed James River into Chesterfield, having been previously invited by some of the inhabitants. They, however, met with rigid
treatment; the magistrates, finding that many were turning to
righteousness, (to *madness*, as they would have it) and that these
young laborers were likely to do them much harm, Issued warrants, and had them apprehended and cast into prison. The court

requiring them to bind themselves to do what they could not in conscience comply with, they continued in jail until the March following. While in prison they did much execution by preaching through the grates; many people attended their ministry and many professed faith by virtue of the labors of these the Lord's persecuted servants. This was the beginning of God's work in the county of Chesterfield; no county ever extended its opposition and persecution to the Baptists farther than this; and yet in few counties have Baptist principles prevailed more extensively than in Chesterfield.

When Webber and Anthony were let go they returned to Goochland to their own company, and resumed their great work. Mr. Webber, however, enjoyed his liberty only a few months; he consented to travel with John Waller on a course of meetings to Middlesex. They arrived in the upper end of Middlesex on the 10th of August, 1771; they came, but soon found there was no chance to proceed in their work. While William Webber was preaching from these words, *"Show me thy faith without thy works, and I will show you my faith by my works,"*a magistrate pushed up, and drew back his club with a design to knock Webber down. Some person behind him caught the club and prevented the mischief. Having a warrant to apprehend all who preached, and being backed by two sheriffs, the parson and a posse, he seized William Webber, John Waller, James Greenwood and Robert Ware. On the same day Thomas Wafford, who had traveled from the upper country with the preachers, though no preacher himself, was severely beaten by one of the persecutors with a whip, the scar of which he will probably carry to his grave; he, with the four above-named preachers, were tried by James Montague. They first searched their saddle-bags to find treasonable papers; finding none, they proceeded to trial, taking them one by one into private rooms, proposing to them to give bond and security not to preach in the county again. Each of them expressly refused. Wafford was discharged, not being a preacher; the other four were ordered to prison, and, being conducted by two sheriffs, they were safely lodged in close jail that night about 9 o'clock. The prison swarmed with fleas. They borrowed a candle of the jailer, and having sung the praises of that Redeemer whose cross they bore and from whose hands they expected a crown in the end; having returned thanks that it was a prison and not hell that they were in; praying for themselves, their friends, their enemies and persecutors, they laid down to sleep. The next day being Sunday, many of their friends came to see them and were admitted into the prison. James Greenwood preached to them. They were well supplied by their friends with the necessaries and comforts for living, which, added to the sense of Divine goodness that they enjoyed, they had no unpleasant season. They gave notice that they would preach every Wednesday and Sunday. Many came to hear them, insomuch that their enemies began to be enraged, and would frequently beat a drum while they were preaching.

On Monday, the 24th, being court day, they were carried to the court-house to be tried. A guard attended them, as if they had been criminals. They were not allowed to speak for themselves, but peremptorily required to give bond and security for good behavior, and not to preach in the county again for one year. These terms they expressly refused, and were remanded to prison, and orders given that they should be fed on bread and water. Accordingly, the next day they had nothing else, and not enough of bread. So it continued for four days, until the brethren and friends found it out; after that, they were furnished so plentifully that they bestowed in bounty upon the poor inhabitants of the town. On September the 10th they were allowed the prison bounds, by which they were much relieved; yet they were frequently under the necessity of resorting to the jail to avoid the rage of persecutors. The Lord daily opened the hearts of the people; the rich sent many presents—things calculated to nourish them in their sufferings and to alleviate their sorrows. William Webber fell sick. This excited the sympathy of their friends in a higher degree; they paid him great attention. The persecutors found that the imprisonment of the preachers tended rather to the furtherance of the Gospel. They preached regularly in prison; crowds attended; the preaching seemed to have double weight when coming from the jail; many viewed it with superstitious reverence, so that their enemies became desirous to be rid of them. Accordingly, on the 26th day of September, after having been thirty days in close confinement and sixteen days in the bounds, they were liberated upon giving a bond for good behavior.

The rage of persecutors had in nowise abated; they seemed,

sometimes, to strive to treat the Baptists and their worship with as much rudeness and indecency as was possible. They often insulted the preachers in time of service, and would ride into the water and make sport when they administered baptism; they frequently fabricated and spread the most groundless reports, which were injurious to the characters of the Baptists. When any Baptists fell into any improper conduct, it was always exaggerated to the utmost extent. On one occasion, when Robert Ware was preaching, there came one Davis and one Kemp, two sons of Belial, and stood before him with a bottle, and drank, offering the bottle to him, cursing him. As soon as he closed his service they drew out a pack of cards and began to play on the stage where he had been standing, wishing him to reprove them that they might beat him.[1]

Notwithstanding these severe oppositions, the Word of the Lord grew and multiplied greatly. Young preachers were ordained and churches constituted, the first of which was *Lower King and Queen church*, constituted October 17, 1772, with seventeen members, and on the 11th of February following Robert Ware was consecrated as pastor. *Glebe Landing church* was also constituted at the same time, and James Greenwood ordained a lay-elder. *Exol* and *Piscataway* churches were constituted in no great while after this (the former in 1775 and the latter, March 13, 1774). These new churches, filled with young and inexperienced members, were visited frequently by J. Waller, accompanied sometimes by one, and sometimes another of the preachers of his own vicinity. His ministrations were, on the one hand, exceedingly salutary and comfortable to his friends; but on the other, highly displeasing to the enemies of the Baptists. They viewed Waller as the ring-leader of all the confusion and disturbance that had befallen them. Great congregations of people attended the Baptist meetings, while very few went to the parish churches. The zealots for the old order were greatly embarrassed. "*If,*" said they, "*We permit them to go on, our church must come to nothing, and yet if we punish them as far as we can stretch the law, it seems not to deter them; for they preach through prison windows in spite of our endeavors to pre-*

---

[1] It is worthy of note that these two men died soon after this exchange. And upon questioning, each accused the other of leading him into so deteriorating a crime.—*Author's note.*

vent it." Sometimes the rector of the parish would give notice that, on a certain day, he would prove the Baptists to be deceivers and their doctrines false. The attempt was often made, but they uniformly injured their own cause; their arguments were generally drawn from the extravagancies of the German Anabaptists. To this the Baptists in a word replied *that they disclaimed all connection with the Anabaptists, and felt themselves no more responsible for their irregularities than the Episcopalians could feel for the fooleries of the Papists; that the Bible was the criterion; by that they were willing to stand or fall.* Not infrequently their leading men would attend the Baptist meetings, and would enter into arguments with the preachers; they insisted that their church was the oldest and consequently the best; that their ministers were learned men, and consequently most competent to interpret Scripture; that the better sort and well-informed adhered to them, whilst none, or scarcely any except the lower order, followed the Baptists; that they were all in peace and friendship before the coming of the Baptists; but now their houses and neighborhood were filled with religious disputes; that the Baptists were false prophets who were to come in sheep's clothing.

To these arguments Waller and the other preached boldly and readily replied that if they were wolves in sheep's clothing, and their opponents were the true sheep, it was quite unaccountable that *they* were persecuted and cast into prison. It was well known that wolves would destroy sheep, but never, until then, that sheep would prey upon wolves; that their coming might, indeed, interrupt their peace; but certainly if it did it must be a false peace, bordering on destruction and to rouse them from such lethargy was like waking a man whose house was burning over him; that the effect of their coming were similar to those foretold by Christ as arising from the propagation of His word, name, *"that there should be five in one house, three against two, and two against three";* that if the higher ranks of society did not countenance them it was no more than what befell their Master and His inspired Apostles; that rich men in every generation, with some few exceptions were enemies to a pure Gospel; but that God had declared that He had chosen the poor of this world to be rich in faith; that it was true that most of their present ministers were unlearned, yet that they had evidences that they were called to the

ministry by the will of God; that this was the most essential qualification of a minister, the want of which all the learning of all the
schools could not supply.

The Baptist preachers would often retort their own inconsisten-
cies upon them: that while they professed to be Christians, they
indulged themselves in the violation of most of the Christian precepts; that their communion was often polluted by the admission
of known drunkards, gamesters, swearers and revellers; that even
their clergy, learned as they were, had never learned the most essential doctrine of revelation, the indispensable necessity of the
new birth or *being born again;* that their public discourses were
nothing more than moral addresses, such as a pagan philosopher,
unassisted by the Bible, could have composed.

Foiled in their arguments, and galled by the reproaches cast
upon them, which doubtless were often done with too much acri-
mony, they again resorted to the civil power. In August, 1772,
James Greenwood and William Loval were preaching not far from
the place where Bruington Meeting-House now stands, in the
county of King and Queen, when they were seized, by virtue of a
warrant, and immediately conveyed to prison. After the first day
and night they were allowed the bounds. Having continued in
prison sixteen days, *i.e.,* until court, they were discharged upon
giving bond merely for good behavior. At this season they received the most unbounded kindness from Mr. Harwood, the jailer, and his lady. They preached regularly while in prison, and to
much purpose.

On March 13, 1774, the day on which Piscataway church was
constituted, a warrant was Issued to apprehend all the Baptist
preachers that were at meeting. Accordingly John Waller, John
Shackleford, Robert Ware and Ivison Lewis were taken and carried before a magistrate. Ivison Lewis was dismissed, not having
preached in the county; the other three were sent to prison. It appears from Mr. Waller's journals, which we have before us, that
while in prison, God permitted them to pass through divers and
fiery trials; their minds, for a season, being greatly harassed by the
enemy of souls. They, however, from first to last of their imprisonment, preached twice a week, gave much godly advice to such
as came to visit them, read a great deal, and prayed almost without
ceasing. In their stated devotion, morning, noon, and night, they

were often joined by others. They continued in close confinement from the 13th to the 21st of March, which was court day. Being brought to trial, they were required to give bond and security for their good behavior for twelve months, or go back to prison. Ware and Shackleford gave bond and went home; Waller being always doubtful of the propriety of giving any bond whatever, determined to go back to jail.

The trials of this man of God were now greater than ever. Deserted by his brethren, scoffed and persecuted by his enemies, locked up with a set of drunken, profane wretches, he had no alternative but to commit himself to the hands of Omnipotence, and wait his deliverance After remaining in prison fourteen days, he gained his own consent to give bond, and go home.

We have thus stated a few instances of the suffering of God's ministers, in those times: time and space would fail to enumerate them all; many of them, however, will be rehearsed, in treating upon the churches, and in the biography of some of the sufferers. The trial and imprisonment of all the rest differ only in small matters from those already described. From the beginning, the Baptists were unremitting in their exertions to obtain liberty of conscience; they contended that they could not be imprisoned by any existing law; that they were entitled to the same privileges that were enjoyed by the dissenters in England. Their judges, however, decided otherwise, and as there was no regular appeal, the propriety of that decision has not been legally ascertained. The prevailing opinion in the present day is that their imprisonment was unlawful. When they could not succeed in this, they resorted to the general court, for the purpose of obtaining licensed places for preaching, etc., agreeably to the Toleration law in England.

It was in making these attempts that they were so fortunate as to interest in their behalf the celebrated Patrick Henry. Being always the friend of liberty, he only needed to be informed of their oppression, when, without hesitation, he stepped forward to their relief. From that day until the day of their complete emancipation from the shackles of tyranny, the Baptists found in Patrick Henry an unwavering friend. May his name descend to posterity with unsullied honor! After some difficulty they obtained their object, and certain places were licensed accordingly. But to a people, prompted as the Baptists were with unwearied zeal for the propagation of the Gospel, a few licensed places in each county was but a small acquisition. They thirsted for the liberty of preaching the Gospel to every creature. In the meantime everything tended to favor their wishes. Their persecution, so far from impeding, really promoted their cause. Their preachers had now become numerous, and some of them were men of considerable talents. Many of the leading men favored them, (some from one motive, and some from another)—their congregations were large, and when any of their men of talents preached they were crowded. The patient manner in which they suffered persecution raised their reputation for piety and goodness in the estimation of a large majority of the people. Their numbers annually increased in a surprising degree. Every month new places were found by the preachers whereon to plant the Redeemer's standard. In these places, although but few might become Baptists, yet the majority would be favorable. Many that had expressed great hostility to them, upon forming a closer acquaintance with them professed to be undeceived. We have already seen that the first *Separate* Baptist church north of James River was formed in 1767, and the second in 1769; so that at the commencement of the year 1770; there were but two *Separate* churches in all Virginia north of James River; and, we may add, there were not more than about four on the south side. In 1774, by referring to the history of the General Association, we find that there were thirty on the south and twenty-four on the north side that sent letters, etc., to the Association, besides a probability of several that did not associate. This must be considered a very rapid increase for so short a time. The Baptist interest increased in a much greater proportion.

So favorable did their prospects appear that towards the close of the year 1774 they began to entertain serious hopes, not only of obtaining liberty of conscience, but of actually overturning the Church Establishment, from whence all their oppression had arisen. Petitions for this purpose were accordingly drawn and circulated with great industry. Vast numbers readily, and indeed eagerly, subscribed to them. The great success and rapid increase of the Baptists in Virginia must be ascribed primarily to the power of God working with them; yet it cannot be denied but that there were subordinate and cooperating causes, one of which, and the main one, was the loose and immoral deportment of the Established clergy, by which the people were left almost destitute of even the shadow of true religion. 'Tis true, they had some outward forms of worship, but the essential principles of Christianity were not only not understood among them, but by many never heard of. Some of the cardinal precepts of morality were disregarded, and actions plainly forbidden by the New Testament were often proclaimed by the clergy as harmless and innocent, or at worst, foibles of but little account. Having no discipline, every man followed the bent of his own inclination. It was not uncommon for the rectors of parishes to be men of the loosest morals. The Baptist preachers were, in almost every respect, the reverse of the Established clergy. The Baptist preachers were without learning, without patronage, generally very poor, very plain in their dress, unrefined in their manners, and awkward in their address, all of which, by their enterprising zeal and unwearied perseverance, they either turned to advantage or prevented their ill-effects. On the other hand, most of the ministers of the Establishment were men of classical and scientific education, patronized by men in power connected with great families, supported by competent salaries, and put into office by the strong arm of the civil power. Thus pampered and secure, the men of this order were rolling on the bed of luxury when the others began their extraordinary career. Their learning, riches, power, etc., seemed only to hasten their overthrow by producing an unguarded heedlessness which is so often the prelude to calamity and downfall.

We are not to understand that this important ecclesiastical revolution was effected wholly by the Baptists. They were certainly the most active; but they were also joined by other dissenters. Nor was the dissenting interest all united, by any means at that time, equal to the accomplishment of such a revolution. We must turn our eyes to the political state of the country to find adequate causes for such a change.

The British yoke now galled to the quick; and the Virginians, as having the most tender necks, were among the first to wince. Republican principles had gained much ground, and were fast advancing to superiority. The leading men on that side viewed the Established clergy and the Established religion as inseparable appendages of monarchy—one of the pillars by which it was supported. The dissenters, at least the Baptists, were republicans from interest as well as principle; if was known that their influence was great among common people; and the common people of every country are, more or less, republicans. To resist British oppressions effectually, it was necessary to soothe the minds of the people by every species of policy. The dissenters were too powerful to be slighted, and they were too watchful to be cheated by an ineffectual sacrifice. There had been a time when they would have been satisfied to have paid their tithes if they could have had liberty of conscience; but now the crisis was such that nothing less than a total overthrow of all ecclesiastical distinctions would satisfy their sanguine hopes. Having started the decaying edifice, every dissenter put to his shoulder to push it into irretrievable ruin. The revolutionary party found that the sacrifice must be made, and they made it.

It is said, however, and probably not without truth, that many of the Episcopalians who voted for abolishing the Establishment did it upon an expectation that it would be succeeded by a general assessment. And considering that most of the men of wealth were on that side, they supposed that their funds would be lessened very little. This, it appeared in the sequel, was a vain expectation. The people having once shaken off their fetters, would not again permit themselves to be bound. Moreover, the war now rising to its height, they were in too much need of funds to permit any of their resources to be devoted to any other purpose during that period; and we shall see that when it was attempted, a few years after the expiration of the war, the people set their faces against it. Having thus mentioned the Establishment, it will be proper to treat more fully respecting the origin and nature of those laws by which it arose and fell.

Our ancestors, being chiefly emigrants from England, brought with them all that religious intolerance which had so long prevailed in the mother country. Thus we see that the first care of our early legislatures was to provide for the Church of England, as established by the act of Parliament. By the first act of 1623, it is provided that in every plantation or settlement there shall be a house or room set apart for the worship of God. But it soon appears that this worship was only to be according to the canons of the Church of England, to which a strict uniformity was enjoined. A person absenting himself from divine service on a Sunday without a reasonable excuse, forfeited a pound of tobacco; and he that absented himself a month, forfeited fifty pounds. Any minister who was absent from his church above two months in a year forfeited half his salary; and he who absented himself four months, forfeited the whole. Whoever disparaged a minister whereby the minds of his parishioners might be alienated, was compelled to pay 500 pounds of tobacco and ask the minister's pardon publicly in the congregation. No man was permitted to dispose of any of his tobacco till the minister was satisfied, under penalty of forfeiting double his part of the minister's salary.

The first allowance made to the ministers was ten pounds of tobacco and a bushel of corn for each tithable; and every laboring person, of what quality or condition soever, was bound to contribute. In the year 1631 the Assembly granted to ministers, besides the former allowance of ten pounds of tobacco and a bushel of corn, the twentieth calf, the twentieth kid and the twentieth pig. This was the first introduction of tithes, properly called, in Virginia. But it did not continue long, for in 1733 the law was repealed.

To preserve the purity of doctrine and unity of the church, it was enacted in 1643 that all ministers should be conformable to the orders and constitution of the Church of England, and that no other persons be permitted to preach publicly or privately. It was further provided that the governor and council should take care that all *non-conformists* departed the colony with all conveniency.

The statute of England of the 3rd of James I. against Popish recusants was also adopted in the year 1643. This statute declared that no Popish recusant should exercise the office of secret counselor, register, commissioner (a term then used for justices of the peace), surveyor, or sheriff or any other public office. Nor should any person be admitted into any of those offices before he had taken the oaths of allegiance and supremacy. The same act of Assembly by which the statute of 3rd James I. was adopted, further declared that if any person should assume the exercise of any of those offices and refuse to take the said oaths, he should be dismissed, and moreover forfeit 1,000 pounds of tobacco. No Popish priest thereafter arriving in the colony was permitted to remain more than five days, if wind and weather permitted his departure.

During the existence of the Commonwealth of England, the church government of Virginia experienced an important change.

Instead of enjoining obedience to the doctrine and discipline of the Church of England, no injunction in favor of any particular sect appears. Everything relating to the affairs of the church was left at the entire disposal of the vestry, who being elected by the people, it may, in effect, be said that the people regulated their own church government.

The above law passed at the March session, 1657-'58. But only two years afterwards (at the March session, 1659-'60) when the Quakers first made their appearance in Virginia, the utmost degree of persecution was exercised towards them. No master of a vessel was permitted to bring in a Quaker under the penalty of £100 sterling; all Quakers were imprisoned without bail or mainprize till they found sufficient security to depart the colony; for returning, they were directed to be proceeded against as contemners of the laws and magistracy, and punished accordingly; and if they should come in a third time they were to be prosecuted as felons. All persons were prohibited, under the penalty of £100 sterling, from entertaining them or permitting their assemblies in or near their houses; and no person was permitted to dispose of or publish any books or pamphlets containing the tenets of their religion. An awful memento of the danger of giving to the civil authority power over the consciences of the people! This severe law against the Quakers passed during the Commonwealth, when the people were unrestricted in matters of religion; but it happened in this case, as it generally has, where the civil power undertakes to interfere at all, that the ruling party in the State will tolerate no religion of the church but their own.

A levy of fifteen pounds of tobacco per the poll was laid, in the year 1655, upon all tithables, the surplus of which, after paying the minister's salary, was to be handed out in purchasing a glebe and stock for the minister. This law was re-enacted in the revisal of 1657. After the restoration of Charles II., which happened on the first of May, 1660, a temporary provision was again made favoring the Established Church.

In the year 1661 the supremacy of the Church of England was again fully established. The first nine acts of the session held in March, 1661-'62, are devoted to that subject. A church was to be built in each parish, and vestries appointed. Glebes were directed to be procured for the ministers, and convenient houses built thereon; in addition to which their salaries were fixed at £80 per annum, at least, besides their perquisites. No minister was permitted to preach unless he had received ordination from some bishop in England. If any person without such ordination attempted to preach, publicly or privately, the Governor and Council might suspend and silence him; and, if he persisted, they were empowered to send him out of the country. In those parishes where there was not a minister to officiate every Sunday, a reader was to be appointed, whose duty it was to read divine service every intervening Sunday. The liturgy, according to the canons of the Church of England, was to be read every Sunday by the minister or reader; and the administration of the sacraments was to be duly observed. No other Catechism than that inserted in the Book of Common Prayer could be taught by the minister; nor could a reader attempt to expound that or the Scriptures. Ministers were compelled to preach every Sunday; one Sunday in a month, at the chapel, if any, and the others at the parish church; and twice a year he was compelled to administer the sacrament of the Lord's supper. Every person was compelled to attend church every Sunday, under the penalty of fifty pounds of tobacco. But Quakers and non-conformists were liable to the penalties of the statute 23rd Elizabeth, which was £20 sterling for every month's absence, and, moreover, for twelve months' absence, to give security for their good behavior. Quakers were further liable to a fine of two hundred pounds of tobacco for each one found at one of their meetings; and in case of the insolvency of any one of them, those who were able were to pay for the insolvents.

Various other laws passed between the above period and the commencement of the American Revolution by which the established religion of the Church of England was protected by the State. The salary of the minister was first settled at 16,000 pounds of tobacco, in the year 1696, to be levied by the vestry on the tithables of that parish, and so continued to the Revolution. Any minister admitted into a parish was entitled to all the spiritual and temporal rights thereof; and might maintain an action against any person who attempted to disturb him in his possession.

The same acts provided for the purchase of glebes for the ministers.

Though the Toleration Act is not believed to have bean strictly obligatory in Virginia, yet, as was frequently the case at that period, it was acted under in many instances. That it was doubtful whether acts of Parliament respecting religion were in force in Virginia, appears by the act of October, 1776, chapter 2, section 1. Even this act of toleration is a most flagrant violation of religious freedom.

At the October session, 1776, the first law passed suspending the payment of the salaries formerly allowed to the ministers of the Church of England. The preamble to this act is worthy of consideration, and was probably drawn by Mr. Jefferson, who was then a member. A number of memorials from different religious societies, dissenters from the Church of England, were presented to this Assembly, praying to be exempted from the payment of parochial dues to the Church of England, and for the abolition of the Established Church. In opposition to these there was a memorial from the clergymen of the Church of England praying that the Establishment might be continued.

These memorials formed the basis of the act of that session above mentioned. This act for "exempting the different societies of dissenters from contributing to the support and maintenance of the church as by law established, and its ministers," was preceded by set of resolutions recognizing the same principles which were afterwards engrafted into the act itself. It does not appear by what majority this act passed, as the ayes and noes were not taken on it. At the May session, 1777, the payment of the salaries allowed to the clergy of the Church of England was further suspended; and at the October session, 1779, so much of every act as related to the salaries formerly given to the clergy of the Church of England was repealed.

The question as to the propriety of a general assessment had long been much agitated, and a great variety of opinions existed respecting it. By the fifth section of the act of October, 1776, which first suspended the payment of the salaries allowed to the clergy of the Church of England, this question as to a general assessment is expressly left undecided.

In 1784, the subject of a general assessment was again revived. A bill, which had for its object the compelling of every person to contribute to some religious teacher, was introduced into the House of Delegates, under the title of "A bill establishing provision for the teachers of the Christian religion;" but on its third reading it was postponed till the fourth Thursday in November then next—ayes, 45; noes, 38. The following resolution was immediately afterwards adopted:

Resolved, That the engrossed bill establishing a provision for the teachers of the Christian religion, together with the names of the ayes and noes on the question of postponing the third reading of the said bill to the fourth Thursday in November next, be published in handbills, and twelve copies thereof delivered to each member of the General Assembly, to be distributed in their respective counties; and that the people thereof be requested to signify their opinion respecting the adoption of such a bill to the next session of Assembly.

The above resolution drew forth a number of able and animated memorials from religious societies of different denominations against the general assessment. Among a great variety of compositions, possessing different degrees of merit, a paper drawn up by Colonel James Madison (now President of the United States), entitled "A Memorial and Remonstrance," will ever hold a most distinguished place. For elegance of style, strength of reasoning, and purity of principle, it has, perhaps, seldom been equaled; certainly never surpassed by anything in the English language.

The sentiments of the people appearing to be decidedly against a general assessment, the question was given up forever.

At the same session, however (October, 1784), in which the bill providing for a general assessment failed, an act passed for "incorporating the Protestant Episcopal Church." This bill passed the House of Delegates by a small majority only, being ayes, 47; noes, 38; but in 1786 it was repealed. By the repealing law, the property belonging to all religious societies was secured to those societies respectively, who were authorized to appoint from time to time, according to the rules of their sect, trustees for the managing and applying such property to the religious uses of the society. And all laws which prevented any religious society from regulating its own discipline were repealed.

Under the old ecclesiastical establishment no person could celebrate the rites of matrimony but a minister of the Church of England, and, according to the ceremony prescribed in the Book of Common Prayer. Cases, however, frequently occurred, especially during the war, where the marriage ceremony was performed by others. This gave rise to an act of October, 1780, which declared all former marriages celebrated by dissenting ministers good and valid in law; and authorized the county courts to license dissenting ministers of the Gospel, not exceeding four to each sect, to celebrate the rites of matrimony within their counties only. It was not until the year 1784 that the dissenters were put on the same footing as all other persons with respect to celebrating the rites of matrimony. By this act the marriage ceremony might be performed by any minister licensed to preach, according to the rules of the sect of which he professed to be a member. The same act has been incorporated in the late revisal of our laws.

The Legislature of 1798 repealed all laws vesting property in the hands of any religious sect; by which the Episcopalians were deprived of the glebes, etc.; by which all religious sects were put into a state of perfect equality as it respected the favors of government.[1]

---

[1] Most of the above history of the laws of Virginia respecting religion was furnished by William W. Hening, Esq.—*Author's note.*

CHAPTER FOUR:
From the Abolition of the Established Church to the Present Times, Being the End of the General History of the Separate Baptists.

The war, though very propitious to the liberty of the Baptists, had an opposite effect upon the life of religion among them. As if persecution was more favorable to vital piety than unrestrained liberty, they seem to have abated in their zeal upon being un-shackled from their manacles. This may be ascribed to several causes: both preachers and people were so much engrossed with anxious thoughts and schemes for effecting the revolution, as well as with alternate hopes and fears for the event, it was not probable that religion should not lose some portion of its influence upon the minds of professors thus divided. The downfall of Jeremiah Walker and some other preachers of less note, together with the contentions arising from Waller's defection, contributed not a lit-tle towards dampening the zeal of the Baptists. Having lost some of their champions in israel, they could not, with the same bold-ness, face their enemies. Perhaps we may add that many did not rightly estimate the true source of liberty, nor ascribe its attain-ment to the proper arm—in consequence of which God sent them liberty, and with it leanness of soul. This chill to their religious affections might have subsided with the war, or perhaps sooner, if there had not been subsequent occurrences which tended to keep them down. The opening of free trade by peace served as a power-ful bait to entrap professors [of Christianity] who were in any great degree inclined to the pursuit of wealth. Nothing is more common than for the *increase* of riches to produce a *decrease* of piety. Speculators seldom make warm Christians. Kentucky and the Western country took off many of the preachers who had once been exceedingly successful in the ministry. From whatever cause, certain it is that they suffered a very wintry season. With some few exceptions the declension was general throughout the state. The love of many waxed cold. Some of the watchmen fell, others stumbled, and many slumbered at their posts. Iniquity greatly abounded. Associations were but thinly attended, and the business was badly conducted. God has left many promises that He will not always chide, nor be angry with His people; that He will turn again the captivity of Zion, etc. The long and great declension induced many to fear that the times of refreshing would never come, but that God had wholly forsaken them.

Their enemies likewise often reproached them, saying: "Where is the promise of His coming? We believed, and said, they would come to nothing, and our prediction is fast fulfilling." But *let God be true and every man a liar*. The set time to favor Zion at length arrived, and as the declension had been general, so also was the revival. It may be considered as having begun in 1783, on James River. It spread as fire among stubble, continuing for several years in different parts. Very few churches were without the blessing. How great the change! When religion was down, nothing but lamentations mixed with groans and tears could be heard from its zealous advocates. "Oh! that it were with us as in days past when the candle of the Lord shone upon us." "*How is the gold become dim; how is the most fine gold changed!*"

This cry was reversed so soon as Heaven smiled. "*We are as men that dream. This surely is too great to be real. Our mouths are filled with laughter, and our tongues with singing,*" On the part of the many who were convicted in the congregations, you could hear earnest cries for mercy, with many tears and lamentations. From lips that had previously been employed in blasphemy, you would hear, "*What shall we do to be saved? God be merciful to me a sinner!*" In a time of revival there are but few who go to meetings that are not more or less affected. Some, indeed, are much exasperated, and call it hypocrisy, delusion, enthusiasm, etc. Yet, even of these it does not unfrequently happen that some will become deeply convicted and finally profess that faith which they once despised.

The manner of conducting the general revival was somewhat extraordinary. It was not unusual to have a large proportion of a congregation prostrate on the floor; and, in some instances, they have lost the use of their limbs. No distinct articulation could be heard unless from those immediately by. Screams, cries, groans, songs, shouts, and hosannas, notes of grief and notes of joy, all heard at the same time, made a heavenly confusion, a sort of indescribable concert. Even the wicked and unenlightened were astonished and said, *the Lord hath done great things for this people*. At associations and great meetings, where there were several ministers, many of them would exercise their gifts at the same time in different parts of the congregation; some in exhortation; some in praying for the distressed; and some in argument with opposers. At first many of the preachers did not approve of this kind of work. They thought it extravagant. Others fanned it as fire from heaven. It is not unworthy of notice that in those congregations where the preachers encouraged these exercises to much extent, the work was more extensive and greater numbers were added. It must also be admitted that in many of these congregations no little confusion and disorder arose after the revival had subsided. Some have accounted for this by an old maxim; *"Where much good is done much evil will also be done. Where God sows many good seed the enemy will sow many tares."* Be that as it may, certain it is that many ministers who labored earnestly to get Christians into their churches were afterwards much perplexed to get out hypocrites. Perhaps the best conclusion is to avoid either extreme. A stiff formality or an inordinate confusion ought each to be shunned. A scriptural and rational animation is from God, and ought to be indulged and encouraged. Yet vigilance ought to be used to keep off actual fanaticism as being the effect of natural and unenlightened emotions.

It has already been said that this revival commenced in the year 1785. It continued spreading until about 1791 or 1792. Thousands were converted and baptized, besides many who joined the Methodists and Presbyterians. The Protestant Episcopalians, although much dejected by the loss of the Establishment, had nevertheless continued their public worship, and were attended by respectable congregations. But after this revival their society fell fast into dissolution. This revival among the Baptists did not produce as many young preachers as might have been expected. Mr. Leland, in his *Virginia Chronicle,* from which many of the foregoing remarks have been taken, makes the following observation:

In the late great additions that have been made to the

From this revival great changes took place among the Baptists, some for the better and others for the worse. Their preachers became much more correct in their manner of preaching. A great many odd tones, disgusting whoops and awkward gestures were disused. In their matter, also, they had more of sound sense and strong reasoning. Their zeal was less mixed with enthusiasm, and their piety became more rational. They were much more numerous, and of course, in the eyes of the world, more respectable. Besides, they were joined by persons of much greater weight in civil society; their congregations became more numerous than those of any other Christian sect, and in short, they might be considered, from this period, as taking the lead in matters of religion in many places of the State. This could not but influence their manners and spirit more or less. Accordingly a great deal of that simplicity and plainness, that rigid scrupulosity about little matters which so happily tends to keep us at a distance from greater follies, was laid aside.

Their mode of preaching, also, was somewhat changed. At their first entrance into the State, though not incoherent in their method and language, they were quite correct in their views upon all subjects of primary importance. No preachers ever dealt out to their hearers the nature of experimental religion more clearly and more warmly. As their respectability increased, the preachers and their hearers found a relish for stronger meat, which, to a proper extent, was very suitable; but it too often happened, in indulging this, that party spirit and even vanity had too much influence. To dive deeply into the mysteries of the Gospel; to tell or to make a plausible guess about what happened before the world was made or what will happen before it shall end, looked more wise and excited more applause than to travel on in the old track. Some of the preachers, likewise, falling unhappily into the Arminian scheme, stirred up no small disputation, and thereby imperceptibly drove their opponents to the borders, if not within the lines of Antinomianism.[1]

Practical piety was, in many places, too little urged. These things were followed by a relaxation in discipline in many of the churches, and a consequent state of disorder. It must not be understood that these irregularities went to very great lengths, or that they generally prevailed; this was by no means the case. They had not become as the church at Laodicea or Sardis; but rather as the church at Ephesus; they had in a degree left their first love. Wherever these evils prevailed disagreeable consequences sooner or later sprung from them. The Baptists' name fell into disrepute, their principles were reprobated as leading to licentiousness; their meetings were deserted by the people, who, thus misled, turned in many places to other societies.

It is a fact quite obvious to every religious character who has traveled through Virginia and made observations, that there are few instances in which the Baptists have not flourished to a considerable extent, except in places where their cause has been badly supported or completely betrayed by the disorders of professors.

Since the great revival just described, there have been several partial ones, which will be taken notice of in their proper places.

---

[1] Anarchy, against any law at all.

CHAPTER FIVE:

Containing a History of the General Association of the Separate Baptists, from Their First Session, until the Division in 1783

An Association is a council or assembly, composed of delegates or representatives from each church within the bounds designated for that purpose, the object of which is to take into consideration the welfare of the churches, and to assist them by their counsel in the preservation of order and discipline among themselves. Each church sends by their delegates a letter directed to the Association. These letters inform the Association whom they have deputed as delegates; what is the state and standing of the church; their number, deaths, removals, additions, and exclusions, etc.[1] The Baptist churches are independent, and consequently the business of Associations is not authoritative; they may advise, and indeed urge their advice, but cannot compel.

The business of Associations is commonly drawn from the letters, being inserted by the churches, by way of query. This, however, is not the only mode of introducing it. The debates are generally short, and the whole business is commonly completed in two days. In Virginia most, if not all the Associations, include Sunday as one of the days for their being together.

Nothing is attended to on this day except preaching and the different parts of public worship. Vast crowds in most places attend Associations for the purpose of hearing the preaching. For, in addition to the ministrations of Sunday, the congregations who assemble on the other days are entertained at some convenient place by preachers sent out by the Association for that purpose. Therefore, besides the good derived from the immediate business of an Association, the indirect advantages are very great. From a con-

---

[1] In a time of revival, it is quite animating to hear the letters read.—*Author's note.*

viction of this truth, the *Dover Association,* in one of her circular letters, inserts the following remarks:

The indirect advantages of Associations can only be known by experience. Those who have been accustomed to attend them have seen and felt the blessings conveyed through them. We conceive it is no inconsiderable advantage that an opportunity should be offered for brethren to see each other. "As iron sharpeneth iron, so a man sharpeneth the countenance of his friend." A second advantage is that they communicate to each other the transactions of the different parts of the country from whence they came. They tell how richly the grace of God is communicated; how profusely His blessings are poured out, and how wisely ordered are all His providences. "As cold water to a thirsty soul, so is good news from a far country." Thirdly, they may be beneficial to the church and neighborhood in and about which they may be held, seeing they have it in their power to hear those gifts and talents displayed that are best calculated to instruct, and most likely to profit. Fourthly, advantages may arise to almost every part of the district by the visits of the ministers as they pass to and from the Association.

There are fifteen Associations wholly within the State of Virginia, besides four others, of which a part only are within this State, the other part being in some adjacent State. Of the fifteen, six lie north of James River—viz., Ketocton, Culpeper, Albemarle, Goshen, Dover, and Accomac; six south of James River—Portsmouth, Middle District, Meherrin, Appomattox, Roanoke, and Strawberry; and three west of the Alleghany Mountains—New River, Greenbrier, and Union. The four of which only a part lies in Virginia are: Mayo, on the borders of Virginia and North Carolina; Mountain, on the borders of Virginia, North Carolina and Tennessee; Holston, on the borders of Virginia and Tennessee; and Redstone, on the borders of Virginia, Pennsylvania, and Ohio. A particular account of each of these will be given in their proper order. In the mean time we must begin with the Original Separate Baptist Association.

Having related how through their evangelical labors the Separates had disseminated the principles of the Baptists—or, rather, the doctrines of the New Testament—through various parts of the State of Virginia and North Carolina, we shall now inquire after what manner they were employed in their deliberative assemblies. We have already noticed that through the counsel of Mr. Stearns an Association was formed and organized January, 1760,[1] and who met again in July of the same year. Including both these meetings, the list of their churches stood thus:

Sandy Creek—Elder Shubal Stearns.
Deep River—Nathaniel Powel (a brother).
Abbot's Creek—Elder Daniel Marshall.
Little River—Joseph Breed (a brother).
Neus River—Ezekiel Hunter.
Black River—John Newton.
Dan River, Pittsylvania County, Va.—Elder Samuel Hariss.
Lunenburg County, Va.—William Murphy.

We are not to look for regularity and method among a people whose only study was the prosperity of vital godliness. No church had been regularly constituted in Virginia at the time of either of these Associations. It would seem, however, that those two mentioned in the list were sufficiently numerous to exercise the privileges of a church, and were therefore admitted into the Association. The chief business of these Associations was to receive petitions and to appoint preachers to travel into new places where the Gospel was likely to flourish.

> *We continued together* (says the manuscript of James Read, who was present) *three or four days. Great crowds of people attended, mostly through curiosity. The great power of God was among us. The preaching every day seemed to be attended with God's blessing. We carried on our Association with sweet decorum and fellowship to the end. Then we took leave of one another with many solemn charges from our reverend old father Shubal Stearns, to stand fast unto the end.*

At their next Association multitudes, both of friends and strangers, came, many from a great distance. The Rev. John Gano,

---

[1] The account of this Association is taken from Bacchus' *History of the Baptists of New England,* Volume 3, page 274.—*Author's note.*

from New England, was there. He was sent, it seems, to inquire into the state of these *New Light Baptists.* He was received by Stearns with great affection. But the young and illiterate preachers were afraid of him, and kept at a distance. They even refused to invite him into their Association. All this he bore patiently, sitting by while they transacted their business. He preached also every day. His preaching was in the Spirit of the Gospel. Their hearts were opened, so that before he left them they were greatly attached to him. So superior were Mr. Gano's talents for preaching that some of the young and unlearned preachers said they felt as if they never could undertake to preach again. This Association was also conducted in love, peace, and harmony. When Mr. Gano returned to his own country, being asked what he thought of these Baptists, replied, that *"doubtless the power of God was among them; that although they were rather immethodical, they certainly had the root of the matter at heart."*

At their third Association it seems they were gratified with the most pleasing accounts of the great spread of the Gospel. Very many requests were also sent from various quarters for preachers to be sent them. They had a very happy Association.

The Associations continued thus happy and thus increasing, insomuch, that at their fifth or sixth session, it appears they received delegates from some churches as high up as the mountains, and from thence to the ocean. In 1767, some of the Spotsylvania preachers attended the Association, and obtained the attendance of a presbytery, to constitute their first church. The sessions were all held in the vicinity of Stearns and the older preachers. The younger ones, from Virginia and both the Carolinas, attended constantly, and derived much knowledge and consolation from the conversation of the more experienced. From such accounts as can be had, it appears that all these Associations were conducted with peace and harmony, and were productive of extensive usefulness.

After the disagreement between the *Regulars* and *Separates,* which took place in Spotsylvania, attempts were made, on both sides, to effect a reconciliation. Among the *Separates,* the objections raised by a few popular characters prevailed. They, it seems, thought the *Regulars* were not sufficiently particular in small matters, such as dress, etc. They also expressed fears that the confession of faith adopted by the *Regulars* might in time bind them too much, as there were some objectionable parts. A majority of the *Regulars* were favorable to a union. Some, however, wished that the confession of faith should be adopted by the *Separates* by way of condition.

In 1769 an Association was held by the *Separates*, in North Carolina, to which the Ketocton or Regular Baptist Association, sent as messengers the Rev. Messrs. Garrett, Major, and Saunders with a letter, of which the following is an extract:

> *Beloved in our Lord Jesus Christ:*
>
> *The bearers of this letter can acquaint you with the design of writing it. Their errand is peace, and their business is a reconciliation between us, if there is any difference subsisting. If we are all **Christians**, all **Baptists**—all **New Lights**— why are we divided? Must the little appellative names, **Regular** and **Separate**, break the golden bond of charity, and set the sons and daughters of Zion at variance? "Behold how good and how pleasant it is for brethren to dwell together in unity"; but how bad and how bitter it is for them to live asunder in discord. To indulge ourselves in prejudice is surely a disorder, and to quarrel about nothing is irregularity with a witness. O! Our dear brethren! Endeavor to prevent this calamity for the future.*

This excellent letter was presented to the Association, and, after a lengthy debate, the proposal for a union was rejected by a small majority.

The Separate Baptist Association met again in 1770 at Grassy Creek meetinghouse, in North Carolina. The churches had now become numerous, there being a considerable number in each of the three States. It had been usual with them to do nothing in Associations but by unanimity. If in any measure proposed there was a single dissenting vote they labored first by arguments to come to unanimous agreement; when arguments failed, they resorted to frequent prayer, in which all joined. When both these failed, they sometimes appointed the next day for fasting and prayer, and to strive to bring all to be of one mind. At this session they split in their first business. Nothing could be done on the first day. They appointed the next for fasting and prayer. They met and labored the whole day until an hour by sun in the afternoon, and could do nothing, not even appoint a Moderator. The third day was appointed for the same purpose, and to be observed in the same way. They met early and continued together until 3 o'clock in the afternoon without having accomplished anything. A proposal was then made that the Association should be divided into three districts, that is, one in each State. To this there was a unanimous consent at once.

Whereupon they appointed the first session for the Association in Virginia to be held at Thompson's meetinghouse, in Louisa County, the last Saturday in September, 1771; For North Carolina, at Haw-River meetinghouse; and For South Carolina, at Seleuda.

The Association then dismissed, without transacting any other business.[1] It was, however, privately agreed upon among the Virginia delegates to hold an occasional session at E. Craig's meetinghouse, in Orange County, the second Saturday in May, 1771. This was designed more particularly for the purpose of forming regulations, etc.

They did accordingly meet in May, and as this was the first session of the Virginia Separate Baptist Association, it will not be unacceptable to our readers to insert the proceedings in full.

MINUTES OF THE
FIRST SEPARATE BAPTIST ASSOCIATION

At an occasional Association, held at Craig's meetinghouse, in Orange County, second Saturday in May, 1771. By a private poll Samuel Hariss was chosen moderator, and John Waller, Jr., clerk. The letters from the several churches were read. The state of each was as follows:

---

[1] The above relation is taken from a manuscript of Elijah Craig, who was present.—*Author's note.*

Names of Churches	Names of Delegates	Added by Baptism since October	Added by Experience or Letters	Removed by death	Removed by excommunication	Under Censure	Removed	Restored	Now under care
Fall's Creek church, Pittsylvania.	Samuel Hariss, Jacob Metciff	32	1						62
Bedford church (a new church)	William Lovell								29
Amherst church (a new church)	Thomas Hargitt, James Meneese								26
Buckingham church	Rane Chastain, Jr., William Johnston	16							52
Amelia church	Jeremiah Walker, David Ellington, John Williams	66	2	1	4	10	3	5	260
Louisa church	James Childs, David Thompson, Andrew Tribble	17		1	9	1	2	1	100
Lower church (Spotsylvania)	John Waller, John Burris, Reuben Ford, William Webber	103	3	2	3	3	57	2	253
Middle church (Spottsylvania)	Lewis Craig, Joseph Bledsoe, William Card, John Craig	31	10		1	3	1	1	105

Upper church (Spottsylva-nia	Elijah Craig, George Twiman, Bartlet Ben-net, George Eves		2	1	4		3		120
Culpepper church	John Mon-row, Thomas Peyton	1							21
Carter's Run church (Fauquier)	Joseph Hotsclaw, James Weth-ers	76			2	1			148
Shenandoah church (Frederick)	William Mar-shall, Reuben Pickett	78	1			2			159
Black Water church (Bedford)	Neither dele-gate nor letter								
Dan River church (Pittsylvania)	Neither dele-gate nor letter								
TOTAL:		420	19	5	23	20	66	9	1335

Adjourned till Monday morning, eight o'clock.

May 13, 1771, Monday morning—Met together all except our brethren David Ellington, James Childs, and Thomas Peyton, who disappeared. We all agreed to proceed to business, as follows:

1. It is unanimously agreed that the Association has no power or authority to impose anything upon the churches; but that we act as an advisory council.

2. We believe we have a right to withdraw ourselves from any church that may neglect to correspond with us and justify their conduct.

3. *With regard to the constitution of churches.*—Any number of members that live at a distance too far to assemble with ease, with the body of the church, at their monthly meeting, having first obtained leave from their church, have a right to petition any or-dained minister of the same faith and order, with what helps he chooses, being approved of by the members, to look into their sta-

bility; and if found ripe, to constitute them a church, describing their boundary and allowing the privilege to any member who lives near to the said limits to join which of the churches he pleases.

4. *With regard to ordination, etc.*—Every ordained minister of the same faith, etc., being legally called upon by any church, may administer the sacraments among them, and with the help of their church, ordain their elders or deacons if found qualified; and in case they have made choice of a minister whom they desire to be examined and ordained, they may petition neighboring ministers to proceed in the said work, and on special occasions any of them failing to come, one ordained minister with an ordained elder or elders may proceed in the ordination.

5. We advise any church, in distraction or distress, to send for helps from one or more sister churches to assist them in such a case.

6. It is agreed that if any delegate sent from any church should transgress, in any instance, unknown to his church, the offended party, his fellow-delegate and the moderator, may bar him from sitting.

7. All matters brought before the Association for their advice to be determined by a majority of voices, except what from the clearness of Scripture light forces conviction on all; then there is no necessity for putting it to the decision of votes.

8. It is agreed that an itinerant minister may be ordained without applying to the Association, by a presbytery of ministers (and we advise that as many as conveniently can, may be called for that purpose), upon their examination and a recommendation of his doctrine and manner of life from the church he is a member of.

9. It is agreed that a circular letter be sent by the Association to each church, informing them something of the heads of their business, etc.

Adjourned till tomorrow morning 7 o'clock.

Tuesday Morning.—Came together and proceeded as follows: The delegates' names being called over, our brethren David Ellington, David Thompson, Andrew Tribble, and Bartlet Bennet, failed to appear.

Present—David Thompson and Andrew Tribble

It is agreed that every church, with respect to covenanting, is left to use their own liberty.

We advise every church to insert all their queries in their letters to the Association. Present—Brother Bartlet Bennet.

The church of Shenandoah and Fauquier having requested help with respect to the ordination of elders, baptizing, etc., brother Samuel Hariss agrees (God willing) to go and answer the said request.

A query from the church in Orange, viz.: Whether we have a right to dismiss a member from under the care of our order?

Answered in the negative.[1]

A query from Amelia church, viz.: Whether church dealing ought not to be transacted privately, the members only being present?

Answered in the negative.

A query from Amelia church, viz.: What are the terms of communion fixed in the Word of God?

Answered. Fellowship in the same faith and order.

A query from Amelia church, viz.: Whether any member, who shall refuse to acknowledge himself obliged by the Scriptures to observe the Sabbath, should not be avoided as heretical till he retract his sentiments?

Answered. It is agreed to be referred to the next Association.

A query from Lower Spotsylvania church, viz.; Whether it is lawful and expedient for our ministers to obtain license from the civil law, for only one or more meeting-places, and so be restricted from general license given them by King Jesus—Mark 16th chapter, 15th and 16th verses, etc.?

Answered. It is agreed to be referred to the next Association.

Adjourned until tomorrow morning 7 o'clock.

Wednesday Morning,—Met and proceeded as follows: The church of Christ, on Black Water, in Bedford, having sent neither letter nor delegate to this Association, at the request of the Association, Brother Samuel Hariss and Brother William Lovell are agreed to visit them and invite them to appear by their delegate at the next Association.

The church of Christ, on Dan River, in Pittsylvania, having sent

---

[1] This means a dismissal from the Baptist Society altogether, and not a dismissal from one Baptist church to join another.—*Author's note.*

neither letter nor delegate to this Association, and hearing that said church is in distress, Brother Walker and Brother Burris are agreed, by and with the consent of the Association, to offer them their help, the second Friday, being the 12th of July, 1771; and they are requested to make a report at the next Association.

Our Brother Hariss, who was one of our delegates sent last fall to visit our sister churches in the South government in distress, made report full to our satisfaction.

We advise that a committee of three persons be appointed to settle all expenses that may fall upon the Association.

The committee being sent out, returned and made their report that there was a balance due from us, etc., to the amount of £4 15s.,[1] which was received.

The Association letter to the several churches being read, was approved of.

Brother Samuel Hariss was chosen as our delegate to hold up our correspondence with the North and South Carolina Associations.

Then adjourned till the last Saturday in September at Thompson's meetinghouse, in Louisa,

Samuel Hariss, Moderator.
John Waller, Jr., Clerk.

The Association, of which the above are the minutes, was held nearly forty years past. From them may be gathered a pretty correct view of the mode of government used by the Baptists of that day. It will be seen that the government of the present time varies from it very little.

It is worthy of note that one of the constitutional articles disclaims all power over the churches. Yet, the next declares a right in the Association to withdraw from delinquent churches in certain cases. Nothing less can be meant by this article than that the Association, in behalf of all orderly churches in her correspondence, would discountenance all disorderly ones. It is then a question whether a church, discountenanced by the Association, can any longer be considered a part of the Baptist Society. Would it not be deemed disorderly for any other church to continue their

---

[1] Four pounds, 15 shillings. The American dollar system was not yet in place at this time.

fellowship towards one that could not meet in the same Association? Churches may not only become disorderly in practice, but heterodox in sentiment. In Virginia, perhaps, we have been more fortunate; but in Kentucky, and in England, the majority of some of the Baptist churches have become Arians or Socinians. To give an Association power to deal with, and finally to put such out of their connection, must be proper, and indeed, must be what is designed by the above article. By no other means could a general union be preserved. By the article which disclaims all power, we must understand all power over the internal government of the churches. It is also worthy of note that while one of the articles declares that churches may be constituted, and preachers ordained without any application to the Association, it is recorded in the same minutes that at the request of a certain church a minister is appointed by the Association to assist in the ordination of eiders, etc. From which it would seem that any Association is a suitable medium through which such matters can be advantageously arranged.

The next session, they assembled at Thompson's meetinghouse, the last Saturday in September, according to the appointment made at Grassy Creek the year before. From thence they adjourned to Lewis Craig's meetinghouse, at which they held their next session, the second Saturday in May, 1772.

Their next session was held at Waller's meetinghouse, the last Saturday in September, 1773. Of the proceedings of these three sessions we can obtain no certain account.[1]

The next Association was held at Dover meetinghouse, in Goochland County, commencing May 8, 1773. Samuel Hariss was appointed moderator, and John Waller, Jr., clerk. Letters and delegates from thirty-four churches were received. These churches contained 3,195 members, of which 526 had been baptized subsequent to the last Association. The largest church was Carter's Run, in Fauquier, under the care of the Rev. John Picket, which contained 278 members. The largest number baptized in any one church was fifty-five, in Reedy Bottom Church, in Halifax, under

---

[1] The time and place were discovered from the letters of correspondence found among Mr. John Williams's (for of elder John Williams, see Appendix: Papers) —*Author's note.*

the care of Reuben Picket. There were sixty-one delegates, including among them almost every distinguished preacher in the State.

The following queries and solutions are recorded in the minutes of this Association, viz.:

1. Is the laying on of hands upon baptized members, merely as such, a Gospel ordinance or not?

Answer. The churches are left at their liberty to act as they may think best.

2. Ought persons in general, who are possessed of ministerial gifts, to be ordained merely as ministers, or ought they to be ordained to a particular charge?

Answer. A majority in favor of the latter.

3. Is it lawful to receive a member into fellowship who is married to his wife's sister?

Answer. No.

4. Is it agreeable to Scripture for an unmarried man to take the pastoral care of a church?

Answer. Yes.

An appointment of four ministers was made at this session to visit the Kehukee Regular Association and churches, in order to know their standing and make report. Samuel Hariss, E. Craig, John Waller, and David Thompson were appointed.

A motion was made by E. Craig to divide the Association into two districts, viz., one north and one south of James River. The motion was inserted in the minutes and referred to the next Association.

They held their next session at Meherrin meetinghouse, Lunenburg County, in the fall of the same year, 1773.

Not being able to obtain the minutes of this session, we do not know what business was done, except that they agreed to divide the Association according to the plan proposed in the last Association.

The Southern District agreed to meet at Hall's meetinghouse, Halifax County, second Saturday in May, 1774. The Northern, at Pickett's meetinghouse, Fauquier County, the fourth Saturday in May, 1774. This, it will be found in the sequel, was only a temporary division.

The Southern District met, according to appointment, at Hall's meetinghouse. Samuel Hariss was chosen moderator, and John

Williams clerk. Letters and delegates from twenty-seven churches were received. It appears that the churches in this district contained at that time 2,033 members, of whom 259 had been baptized since the last Association. The most numerous church was Banister, under the care of Nathaniel Hall, containing two hundred and ten members. The greatest number baptized in any one church was forty-two, in Meherrin, in Lunenburg County, under the ministry of John Williams.

For three or four years there had been severe persecutions against the Baptists in many parts of Virginia. Letters were received at this Association from preachers confined in prison, particularly from David Tinsley, then in Chesterfield jail. The hearts of their brethren were affected at their sufferings, in consequence of which it was agreed to raise contributions for their aid. The following resolution was also entered into:

> *Agreed to set apart the second and third Saturdays in June as public fast days, in behalf of our poor blind persecutors, and for the releasement of our brethren.*

At this Association, for the first time, the following query was introduced, which afterwards produced some weighty consequences:

Query. Ought all the ministerial gifts recorded in the 4th chapter of Ephesians, 11th, 12th and 13th verses, be in use in the present time?

Answer. A great majority suppose all the ministerial gifts recorded in said Scripture are, and ought to be, in use in the churches. Although we pay a due regard to the distinction between ordinary and extraordinary gifts.

They appointed their next session to be at Walker's meeting-house, in Amelia County, the second Saturday in October, 1774.

The Northern District also met in Fauquier, according to their appointment, on the fourth Saturday in May, 1774.

Samuel Hariss and John Williams having attended this Association as corresponding delegates from the Southern District; the former was appointed moderator, and John Waller clerk.

Letters were received from twenty-four churches, stating their numbers in all to be 1,921, of whom 158 had been baptized since the last Association. The largest church, viz., Lower Spotsylvania, now called Waller's, contained 188 members, being under the charge of John Waller. The greatest number baptized in any one church was twenty-eight. This was the church called the White-House, probably under the ministry of John Koontz.

A query. Whether the doctrine of the non-eternity of hell-torments ought to be deemed heretical, and what should be done with a member who held it?

Answered. The doctrine is heretical, and all persons holding it ought to be purged out of the churches.

To this Association was also sent the query mentioned above, viz.: Whether the ministerial gifts mentioned in Ephesians 4th chapter, and 11th, 12th, and 13th verses, *are now in use?* After two days' debate, a majority decided that it ought to be put off until the next Association.

The question respecting a confession of faith was agitated at this session, and decided that each church might exercise her own discretion in adopting the confession of faith or not.

The Southern District met in an annual Association, according to appointment, at Walker's meetinghouse, in Amelia County, second Saturday in October, 1774.

Letters from thirty churches were received, stating their number in all to be 2,083, whom 416 had been baptized subsequent to the spring Association. The greatest number baptized in any one church was seventy- two, in Banister church. Halifax County, under the pastoral care of Nathaniel Hall; this was also the largest church, containing 229 members. Samuel Hariss was appointed moderator, and John Williams clerk.

A letter was received from the Philadelphia Association, with a copy of their minutes. Likewise the minutes of the Charleston Association were received; all of which were read.

At this Association, the query respecting the proper interpretation of Ephesians 4:11-13 was again debated, and by a unanimous vote, three excepted, it was resolved that the said offices are now in use in Christ's church, and the said three submitted to the majority. It was further resolved that the said offices be immediately established by the appointment of certain persons to fill them, provided any possessed of such gifts could be found among them.—They then proceeded to the choice of an apostle, by private poll, and the lot fell, by unanimous consent, upon Elder Samuel Hariss. For the discipline of this high officer, the following rule is entered on the minutes, viz.: "If our messenger or apostle shall transgress in any manner, he shall be liable to dealing [with] in any church where the transgression is committed, and the said church is instructed to call helps from two or three neighboring churches, and, if by them found a transgressor, a general council of the churches shall be called to restore or excommunicate him." They then proceeded to ordain him, according to the following method:

The day being set apart as a fast day, we immediately proceeded to ordain him, and the hands of every ordained minister was laid on him. Public prayer was made by John Waller, E. Craig, and John Williams. John Waller gave a public charge, and the whole Association gave him the right hand of fellowship.

His work was to pervade the churches; to do, or at least to see to, the work of ordination, and to set in order things that were wanting, and to make report to the next Association.

The discussion of this subject caused no little warmth on both sides. Jeremiah Walker first agitated it, and was supported by most of the preachers of popular talents, not without suspicion of vanity and ambition. The opposition was headed by Reuben Ford, followed by a numerous party in the Northern District. Walker wrote a piece upon the subject, entitled *Free Thoughts, etc.,* in which, as also in his arguments, both in Associations and private companies, he very ingeniously maintained that *all the offices mentioned in the above texts were still in use*. Mr. Ford also wrote a *pamphlet in* answer to Mr. Walker, in which he rebutted his arguments with considerable ability. Both these were read before the Association. The majority favoring Mr. Walker's system, an experiment was made.

At an Association held for the Northern District this fall, John Waller and E. Craig were appointed apostles for the north side of the river.

It is sufficient to inform our readers that this scheme did not succeed. Either the spirit of free government ran too high among the churches to submit to such an officer or the thing was wrong in itself, and, not being from God, soon fell. These apostles made their report to the next Association, rather in discouraging terms, and no others ever were appointed.

The judicious reader will quickly discover that this is only the old plan of bishops, etc., under a new name.

In the last decision it was agreed that the office of apostles, like that of prophets, was the effect of miraculous inspiration and did not belong to ordinary times.

Both the Associations of this fall appointed their next session to be held at Manakin town, or Dover meetinghouse, the fourth Saturday in May, 1775.

May 27, 1775.—Both Associations met by their delegates, at Dover meetinghouse. Letters from sixty churches were received, viz.: Twenty-nine from the north and 31 from the south side of James River. Samuel Hariss was chosen moderator, and John Waller and John Williams clerks. Only about 300, for both districts, are numbered as having been baptized since the last Association. This number, compared with what had been for years previously, proves that cold times were now not only appearing, but actually arrived. The events which occurred at this and the succeeding session prove it more certainly.

The following query first occupied their attention:

"Is salvation by Christ made possible for every individual of the human race?" The debate on this query took up the whole of Monday. Every thinking man in the Association felt himself seriously interested. Most of them spoke to it, more or less. The weight of talents and influence seems to have been on the Arminian side. Samuel Hariss, Jeremiah Walker, John Waller, and many other distinguished preachers stood forward and zealously, as well as ably, supported the argument in favor of universal provision.

Talents and ingenuity were not wanting on the other side. William Murphy, John Williams, and E. Craig stood foremost in favor of a Calvinistic solution. These supported by truth, or at least by the more generally received opinion among Baptists, obtained after a long and animated debate a small majority. This decision was on Monday afternoon immediately before an adjournment. That evening the Arminian party holding a consultation, determined to bring on the subject again the next day, and to have a determination whether their opinions upon this point should be a matter of bar to fellowship and communion. On Tuesday when they met, the business became very distressing. The Arminian party, having the moderator with them, withdrew out of doors. The other side also withdrew, and chose John Williams as moderator. Everything was then done by message, sometimes in writing and sometimes verbally.

After some time spent in this way, the following proposal was made by the Arminian party:

Dear Brethren,—A steady union with you makes us willing to be more explicit in our answer to your terms of reconciliation proposed. We do not deny the former part of your proposal respecting particular election of grace, still retaining our liberty with regard to construction. And as to the latter part, respecting merit in the creature, we are free to profess there is none.

Signed by order.
Samuel Hariss, Moderator

To which the other party replied as follows:

Dear Brethren,—Inasmuch as a continuation of your Christian fellowship seems nearly as dear to us as our lives, and seeing our difficulties concerning your principles with respect to merit in the creature, particular election, and final perseverance of the saints are in a hopeful measure removing, we do willingly retain you in fellowship, not raising the least bar. But do heartily wish and pray that God, in His kind providence, in His own time will bring it about when israel shall all be of one mind, speaking the same things.

Signed by order,
John Williams, Moderator

These terms being acceded to on both sides, they again met in the meetinghouse and resumed their business. Their union was as happy as their discord had been distressing.

It was determined that the two Associations should again unite at their next session, and that that should be at Du Puy's meetinghouse, Powhatan (then Cumberland) County, the second Saturday in August, 1775.

It seems that one great object in uniting the two districts at this time was to strive together for the abolition of the hierarchy or church establishment in Virginia. The discontents in America, arising from British oppression, were now drawing to a crisis; most of the colonies had determined to resist, and some went for independence. This was a favorable season for the Baptists. Having been much ground under the British laws, or at least by the interpretation of them in Virginia, they were to a man favorable to any revolution by which they could obtain freedom of religion. They had known from experience that mere toleration was not a sufficient check, having been imprisoned at a time when that law was considered by many as being in force.

It was therefore resolved at this session to circulate petitions to the Virginia Convention or General Assembly throughout the State in order to obtain signatures. The prayer of these was that the church establishment should be abolished, and religion left to stand upon its own merits, and that all religious societies should be protected in the peaceable enjoyment of their own religious principles and modes of worship. They appointed Jeremiah Walker, John Williams, and George Roberts to wait on the Legislature with these petitions. They also determined to petition the Assembly for leave to preach to the army, which was granted.

Jeremiah Walker and John Williams, being appointed by this Association, went and preached to the soldiers when encamped in the lower parts of Virginia. Not meeting with much encouragement, they declined it after a short time.

They appointed the next Association to be held at Thompson's meetinghouse, Louisa County, on the second Saturday in August, 1776.

They met accordingly, and letters from seventy-four churches were received, bringing mournful tidings of coldness and declension. This declension is accounted for by some of the letters as arising from too much concern in political matters, being about the commencement of the revolution. Others ascribe it to their dissensions about principles, etc. Both, doubtless, had their weight. After they met, John Waller was appointed to preach, and took his text 1 Corinthians 13th and 14nth. He had fully embraced the whole Arminian system, and was determined to preach it at every risk. Being called to account before the Association, he and all his adherents withdrew from the Baptists and immediately set up for independence. The result may be seen in his biography. This was an exceedingly sorrowful time. Waller was held high in estimation among the Baptists. Serious consequences might reasonably be expected. The Association, however, took such measures as were within their power to prevent unpleasant effects.

It appears that it was agreed at this Association to divide into four districts—probably such a division as afterwards took place in 1783, viz., two south and two north of James River. But as this division was not permanent, we shall pursue the narrative by attending to the whole under one view, as if no such division had taken place.

The first session for that district, which included Halifax. etc., was held at Fall's Creek meetinghouse, Halifax County, first Saturday in November, 1776.

Their next session was at Williams's Sandy Creek meetinghouse, the last Saturday in April, 1777. Of these sessions we could obtain no regular account

By some means it happened that the districts were again united about this time. Being the height of the war, the Associations were but thinly attended and little business done.

Third Saturday in May, 1778, a General Association was held at Anderson's meetinghouse, in Buckingham County. Letters from thirty-two churches were received. William Webber, moderator; John Williams, clerk.

A committee was appointed to inquire whether any grievances existed in the civil laws that were oppressive to the Baptists. In their report they represent the marriage law as being partial and oppressive. Upon which it was agreed to present to the General Assembly a memorial praying for a law affording equal privileges to all ordained ministers of every denomination.

They appointed their next Association at Du Puy's meetinghouse, Powhatan County, second Saturday in October, 1778. They met according to appointment, and chose Samuel Hariss moderator, and John Williams clerk. Letters from thirty-two churches were read.

A committee of seven members were appointed to take into consideration the civil grievances of the Baptists and make report.

1st. They reported on Monday that should a general assessment take place, that it would be injurious to the dissenters in general.

2nd. That the clergy of the former Established Church suppose themselves to have the exclusive right of officiating in marriages, which has subjected dissenters to great inconveniences.

3rd. They therefore recommend that two persons be appointed to wait on the next General Assembly and lay these grievances before them.

Jeremiah Walker and Elijah Craig (and in case of the failure of either, John Williams) were appointed to attend the General Assembly.

Some rules for the government of Associations were formed at this session. In consequence of the warm dissensions that had taken place at some of the Associations a few years before this, combined with the ravages of war, the Associations were not so fully attended as they had been. From 60 and 70 churches, which usually corresponded, they had fallen to about 30 or 40. It seems that some had contracted unfavorable opinions of Associations, and wished them to be laid aside. This subject, being agitated at this session, produced the following entry:

Resolved, That a society of churches combined to seek the mutual good of the whole is desirable; that it also promotes acquaintance among brethren, and affords opportunity to consult respecting the best modes of counteracting national grievances. But Associations are not to interfere with the internal concerns of churches, except where their advice is requested by any church, in the way of query.

The next Association appointed the second Saturday in May, at Dover meetinghouse.

On the second Saturday in May, 1779, the Association met at Dover meetinghouse, Goochland County, of which session we have no account.

On the second Saturday in October, 1779, the Association met at Nottoway meetinghouse, Amelia County. Samuel Hariss, moderator; Jeremiah Walker clerk.

The report by Jeremiah Walker, as delegate to the General Assembly, was highly gratifying, upon which the following entry was unanimously agreed to be made:

> *On consideration of the bill establishing religious freedom, agreed: That the said bill, in our opinion, puts religious freedom upon its proper basis; prescribes the just lim-*

its of the power of the State, with regard to religion; and properly guards against partiality towards any religious denomination; we, therefore, heartily approve of the same, and wish it to pass into a law.

Ordered, That this our approbation of the said bill, be transmitted to the public printers, to be inserted in the Gazettes.

It seems that many of the Baptist preachers, presuming upon a future sanction, had gone on to marry such people as applied for marriage. It was determined that a memorial should be sent from this Association requesting that all such marriages should be sanctioned by a law for that purpose. The law passed accordingly.

For a set of preachers to proceed to solemnize the rites of matrimony without any law to authorize them might at first view appear incorrect, and, indeed, censurable; but we are informed that they were advised to this measure by Mr. Patrick Henry as being the most certain method of obtaining the law. It succeeded. It is, however, still questionable *whether this was not doing evil that good might come.*

The next Association was held at Waller's meetinghouse, Spotsylvania County, the second Saturday in May, 1780. No account could be obtained of the proceedings of this session. The next was appointed to be at Sandy Creek meetinghouse, Charlotte County, second Saturday in October, 1780.

They met at the time and place appointed. Samuel Hariss, moderator; John Williams, clerk. Letters from only twenty-nine churches were received.

From the minutes it appears that some jealousy was still entertained respecting the power of Associations. In consequence of which an entry is made disavowing any authority over the churches.

A letter was received from a committee of the Regular Baptists, requesting that a similar committee should be appointed by this Association to consider national grievances in conjunction. This was done accordingly, and Reuben Ford, John Williams, and Elijah Craig were appointed.

The third Thursday in November following was appointed a day of fasting and prayer, in consequence of the alarming and distressing times.

The next Association was appointed at Anderson's meeting-house, Buckingham County, second Saturday in May, 1781. They met according to appointment. About this time the British, under Lord Cornwallis, were marching through Virginia from the South, and were now at no great distance from the place of the Association. On this account there were but sixteen churches that corresponded. They chose William Webber moderator, and J. Williams clerk. After making some few arrangements and appointing the next Association at Dover meetinghouse, Goochland County, the second Saturday in October, 1782, they adjourned.

They met at Dover meetinghouse agreeably to appointment. Letters from thirty-two corresponding churches were read. William Webber, moderator; John Williams, clerk.

Jeremiah Walker was appointed a delegate to attend the next General Assembly, with a memorial and petitions against ecclesiastical oppression. Robert Stockton attended the Association as a delegate from the Strawberry Association.

The large number of churches and the great distance which many of their delegates had to travel rendered a General Association in Virginia extremely inconvenient, so that they would, probably long before this date, have divided into districts if they had not been held together by apprehensions of oppression from civil government.

They could not make headway against their powerful and numerous opponents with any hope of success unless they were united among themselves. In order to be all of one mind it was necessary that they should all assemble around one council board. For these reasons the General Association was kept up as long as it was. Finding it, however, considerably wearisome to collect so many from such distant parts, and having already secured their most important civil rights, they determined to hold only one more General Association, and then, dividing into districts, to form some plan to keep a standing sentinel for political purposes. In order to mature this plan for dividing into districts they agreed to have two spring Associations, one on the south side and one on the north side of James River. It was expected that the churches on each side would send delegates to the Associations in their respective districts.

They then proceeded to appoint the Association at Du Puy's

meetinghouse, Powhatan County, second Saturday in October, 1783. The one on the south side was appointed at Nottoway meetinghouse, in Nottoway County, the second Saturday in May, 1783; the one on the north side, at Noel's meetinghouse, in Essex County, the first Saturday in May, 1783.

The first Wednesday in November was appointed a day of fasting and prayer, on account of the prospects of famine, and to avert the judgments of God on account of the increasing wickedness of the land.

On the second Saturday in October, 1783, they met in General Association, according to appointment, and for the last time. Thirty-seven delegates, including most of the active preachers in Virginia, were present. William Webber, moderator; John Williams, clerk.

The following business was transacted in this Association:

Resolved, That our General or Annual Association cease, and that a General Committee be instituted, composed of not more than four delegates from each District Association, to meet annually, to consider matters that may be for the good of the whole society, and that the present Association be divided into four districts—Upper and Lower Districts—on each side of James River.

A motion was made by John Williams, that as they were now about to divide into sections, they ought to adopt some confession of faith, by way of affording a standard of principles to subsequent times. They then agreed to adopt the Philadelphia Confession of Faith, upon the following explanations: "To prevent its usurping a tyrannical power over the consciences of any: We do not mean that every person is to be bound to the strict observance of everything therein contained, nor do we mean to make it in any respect superior or equal to the Scriptures in matters of faith or practice; although we think it the best human composition of the kind now extant, yet it shall be liable to alterations whenever the General Committee, in behalf of the Associations, shall see fit."

Reuben Ford and John Waller were appointed delegates to wait on the General Assembly with a memorial; then dissolved.

CHAPTER SIX:

Containing a History of the General Committee from Their First Session until Their Dissolution in 1799

Circumstanced as the Baptists were at this period, it would have been the height of folly to have dissolved the General Association without substituting some other assembly capable of consulting and devising measures for the benefit of the whole connection. In most respects a meeting composed of representatives from the different Associations was preferable to the General Association. Being a small number, they could act more promptly; they would have fewer local matters, and could, therefore, devote their attention more intently to those of general concern; and lastly, there being three other Associations now in the State, besides the one called the General Association, these could unite in a General Committee and contribute their aid in measures interesting to all.

The General Committee accordingly met for the first time on Saturday, October 9, 1784. Delegates from four Associations assembled. William Webber was appointed moderator, and Reuben Ford clerk.

Of the plan of government the following are the only articles proper to be noticed:

1. The General Committee shall be composed of delegates sent from all the District Associations that desire to correspond with each other.

2. No Association shall be represented in the committee by more than four delegates.

3. The committee thus composed shall consider all the political grievances of the whole Baptist Society in Virginia, and all references from the District Associations respecting matters which concern the Baptist Society at large.

4. No petition, memorial or remonstrance shall be presented to the General Assembly from any Association in connection with the General Committee; all things of that kind shall originate with the General Committee.

Under this constitution they proceeded to business.

The law for the solemnization of marriage and the vestry law were considered political grievances. They also resolved to oppose the law for a general assessment and that for the incorporation of religious societies, which were now in agitation.

A memorial to the General Assembly praying for a repeal of the vestry law and for an alteration in the marriage law was drawn and committed to the hands of the Rev. Reuben Ford to be presented to the next Assembly.

Saturday, August 18, 1785.—The General Committee met a second time at Du Puy's meetinghouse, Powhatan County. Delegates from four Associations were present. William Webber was chosen moderator, and Reuben Ford clerk.

Reuben Ford reported that, according to the directions given him, he presented a memorial and petition to the honorable General Assembly; that they met with favorable reception; that certain amendments were made to the marriage law which he thought satisfactory. To this report the General Committee concurred.

They were further informed that at the last session of the General Assembly a bill for a general assessment was introduced and had almost passed into a law; but when at that stage in which it is called an engrossed bill, a motion was made and carried that it should be referred to the next Assembly in order to give the people opportunity to consider it.

The General Committee, as guardians of the rights of the Virginia Baptists, of course took up the subject and came to the following resolution:

Resolved, That it be recommended to those counties which have not yet prepared petitions to be presented to the General Assembly against the engrossed bill for a general assessment for the support of the teachers of the Christian religion, to proceed thereon as soon as possible; that it is believed to be repugnant to the spirit of the Gospel for the Legislature thus to proceed in matters of religion; that no human laws ought to be established for this purpose; but that every person ought to be left entirely free in respect to matters of religion; that the holy Author of our religion needs no such compulsive measures for the promotion of His cause; that the Gospel wants not the feeble arm of man for its support; that it has made, and will again through divine power, make its way against all opposition; and that should the Legislature assume the right of taxing the people for the support of the Gospel, it will be destructive to religious liberty.

Therefore, This committee agrees unanimously that it will be expedient to appoint a delegate to wait on the General Assembly with a remonstrance and petition against such assessment.

Accordingly, the Rev. Reuben Ford was appointed.

It was then consulted, whether it would not be desirable to establish among the Baptists some uniform mode for the solemnization of marriage. Upon which it was resolved to adopt and recommend the form laid down in the Common Prayer-Book, leaving out a few exceptionable parts; and that it be printed together with the catechism entitled *Milk for Babes.*[1]

Saturday, August 5, 1786.—The next meeting of the General Committee was held at Anderson's meetinghouse, Buckingham County. Delegates from five Associations assembled.

Reuben Ford, who was appointed to wait upon the Assembly with a memorial and petition against the bill for a general assessment, reported that he waited on the House of Assembly according to appointment; that the law for assessment did not pass, but on the contrary, an act passed explaining the nature of religious liberty.

This law, so much admired for the lucid manner in which it treats of and explains religious liberty, was drawn by the venerable Thomas Jefferson. It may be found in the 29th page of the Revised Code of the Virginia laws.

The committee concurred in the report and declared themselves well pleased with the law above mentioned.

Here let us remark that the inhibition of the general assessment may, in a considerable degree, be ascribed to the opposition made to it by the Baptists, for it is stated by those who were conversant with the proceedings of those times, that the reference made to the people, after the bill was engrossed, was done with a design to give the different religious societies an opportunity of expressing their wishes. The Baptists, we believe, were the only sect who

---

[1] It is much to be deplored that this, or some other form of religious instruction for children, has not been in more common use among the Baptists.—*Author's note.*

plainly remonstrated. Of some others, it is said, that the laity and ministry were at variance upon the subject, so as to paralyze their exertions either for or against the bill. These remarks, by the by, apply only to religious societies acting as such. Individuals of all sects and parties joined in the opposition.

The General Committee then went into the consideration of a law for the incorporation of the Episcopal society, and thereby vesting certain property in them. Upon this subject they wrote:

> *Resolved, That petitions ought to be drawn and circulated in the different counties and presented to the next General Assembly, praying for a repeal of the incorporating act, and that the public property which is by that act vested in the Protestant Episcopal Church be sold and the money applied to public use, and that Reuben Ford and John Leland attend the next Assembly as agents in behalf of the General Committee.*

The schism which took place among the Regular and Separate Baptists soon after their rise in Virginia had never been, as yet, entirely removed, although a very friendly intercourse had been occasionally kept up among them.

The time was now at hand when all differences and party spirit was about to be forever wiped off. The Ketocton or Regular Baptist Association sent delegates to this General Committee, and they were received upon equal footing with those from the other Associations. This gave rise to the following recommendation:

> *It is recommended to the different Associations to appoint delegates to attend the next General Committee for the purpose of forming an union with the Regular Baptists.*

Friday, August 10, 1787—The fourth session of the General Committee was held at Dover meetinghouse, in Goochland County. Delegates from six Associations assembled.[1]

The Rev. Messrs. Ford and Leland, who were appointed to wait on the General Assembly, reported that according to their instructions they presented a memorial praying for a repeal of the incor-

---

[1] There were only six associations at this time in the State, so that all were represented.—*Author's note.*

porating act; that the memorial was received by the honorable house, and that that part of the said act which respected the incorporation of the Protestant Episcopal Church as a religious society, and marking out the rules of their procedure, was repealed; but that that part which respected the glebes, etc., remained as it was.

Whereupon the question was put whether the General Committee viewed the glebes, etc., as public property. By a majority of one they decided that they were. They did not, however, at this time send any memorial to the General Assembly.

Agreeably to appointment the subject of the union of Regular and Separate Baptists was taken up, and a happy and effectual reconciliation was accomplished.

The objections on the part of the Separates related chiefly to matters of trivial importance, and had been for some time removed as to being a bar of communion. On the other hand, the Regulars complained that the Separates were not sufficiently explicit in their principles, having never published or sanctioned any confession of faith; and that they kept within their communion many who were professed Arminians, etc. To these things it was answered by the Separates that a large majority of them believed as much in their confession of faith as they did themselves, although they did not entirely approve of the practice of religious societies binding themselves too strictly by confessions of faith, seeing there was danger of their finally usurping too high a place; that if there were some among them who leaned too much towards the Arminian system they were generally men of exemplary piety and great usefulness in the Redeemer's kingdom, and they conceived it better to bear with some diversity of opinion in doctrines than to break with men whose Christian deportment rendered them amiable in the estimation of all true lovers of genuine godliness. Indeed, that some of them had now become fathers in the Gospel, who previous to the bias which their minds had received had borne the brunt and heat of persecution, whose labors and sufferings God had blessed, and still blessed to the great advancement of His cause. To exclude such as these from their communion would be like tearing the limbs from the body.

These and such like arguments were agitated both in public and private, so that all minds were much mollified before the final and successful attempt for union.

The terms of the union were entered on the minutes in the following words, viz.:

The committee appointed to consider the terms of union with our Regular brethren reported that they conceive the manner in which the Regular Baptist confession of faith has been received by a former Association is the ground-work for such union.

After considerable debate as to the propriety of having any confession of faith at all, the report of the committee was received with the following explanation:

*To prevent the confession of faith from usurping a tyrannical power over the conscience of any, we do not mean that every person is bound to the strict observance of everything therein contained; yet that it holds forth the essential truths of the Gospel, and that the doctrine of salvation by Christ and free, unmerited grace alone ought to be believed by every Christian and maintained by every minister of the Gospel. Upon these terms we are united; and desire hereafter that the names **Regular** and **Separate** be buried in oblivion, and that, from henceforth, we shall be known by the name of the **United Baptist Churches of Christ in Virginia.***

This union has now (1809) continued upwards of twenty-two years without any interruption. The bonds of union are apparently much stronger than at first. It is quite pleasing sometimes to find that members and even ministers of intelligence among the Baptists have manifested a total unacquaintance with the terms *Regular* and *Separate*, when they have been occasionally mentioned in their company. From this it is plain that all party spirit is now laid aside, and that it was a union of hearts as well as parties.

It is worthy of remark that this conjunction of dissevered brethren took place at a time when a great revival of religion had already commenced, and not far from the time when it burst forth on the right hand and the left throughout the State. Some of our readers will impute this to a providential interference of God, disposing the hearts of His people to love and peace in order to prepare them for the day of His power. Others will say rather the work having already begun, a revival of true religion always tends to open the hearts of the friends of God and makes them stretch the robe of charity so as really to cover a multitude of faults. Whether to the one or the other, or to both these causes maybe ascribed the accommodating temper of the two parties, certain it is that nothing could be more salutary. The ointment poured upon Aaron's head was not more savory; the dew on Hermon was not more fructifying than is the union of brethren; it is there "even where love reigns," that the Lord commands His blessing—life eternal—life forevermore.

The next General Committee met at Williams's meetinghouse, Goochland County, Friday, the 7th of March, 1778. Delegates from four Associations attended.

The religious-political subjects which were taken up at this session were:

1. Whether the new Federal Constitution, which had now lately made its appearance in public, made sufficient provision for the secure enjoyment of religious liberty; on which, it was agreed unanimously that, in the opinion of the General Committee, it did not.

2. Whether a petition shall be offered to the next General Assembly, praying for the sale of the vacant glebes. After much deliberation on this subject, it was finally determined that petitions should be presented to the next General Assembly, asking the sale of the vacant glebes, as being public property; and accordingly four persons were chosen from the General Committee to present their memorial, viz.: Eli Clay, Reuben Ford, John Waller, and John Williams.[1]

3. Whether a petition should be offered to the General Assembly, praying that the yoke of slavery may be made more tolerable. Referred to the next session.

It appears from the minutes of this session that letters had been received from the Rev. Asa Hunt, of Massachusetts, and the Rev. Lemuel Powers, of New York State, proposing a correspondence between the General Committee and the Northern Associations, to which proposal the General Committee readily agreed, and ap-

---

[1] The memorial was presented, and similar memorials and petitions continued to be presented to the Legislature from the General Committee until 1799, when they gained their object.—*Author's note.*

pointed Mr. Leland to visit as many of them as he could conveniently. Letters of correspondence were also prepared. Hopes were entertained by some, about this time, of forming a general meeting, to be composed of delegates from all the States in the Union. Such a plan, however desirable, was never put into practice.

The first proposal for publishing "A History of the Rise and Progress of the Baptists in Virginia" was made at this session.

The next session of the General Committee was at Du Puy's meetinghouse, August the 11th, 1788. Delegates from five Associations attended.

The question whether a memorial should be sent to the General Assembly at their next session respecting the glebe lands was taken up; whereupon it was resolved that the business should be entrusted to the care of Elders Leland, Waller, and Clay, to be left discretionary with them to present a memorial or not, as they might think best. On examining the papers directed to the General Committee at this session, it was found that a letter was received from Rev. James Manning, president of Providence College, in Rhode island, recommending and encouraging the Baptists of Virginia to erect a seminary of learning. This subject was, of course, taken up, and they came to the following decision, viz.:

> Resolved, *That a committee of five persons on each side of James River be appointed to forward the business respecting a seminary of learning; accordingly Samuel Hariss, Eli Clay, Simeon Walton, and David Barrow were appointed on the south, and Robert Carter, John Waller, William Fristoe, John Leland, and Reuben Ford on the north side of said river.*

> Resolved, *That Samuel Hariss, John Williams, Simeon Walton, John Leland, Henry Toler, and Lewis Lunsford be appointed to collect materials for compiling and publishing a History of the Baptists in Virginia, and report to the next General Committee.*

The next General Committee met in Richmond, August 8th, 1789. Delegates from seven Associations met. Samuel Hariss, moderator; Reuben Ford, clerk. At this session letters and minutes of correspondence were received from various quarters. The usefulness of the General Committee in keeping up a correspondence and intercourse among the Baptists throughout the United States was inconceivable. From Georgia to Massachusetts they were known, and received occasionally from some, and statedly from others, letters, minutes and other indications of fellowship. So that, if a general union of men, embarked in the same heavenly cause, could be esteemed desirable, then ought we to esteem the General Committee as an institution founded in wisdom.

The committee for the promotion of a seminary of learning, appointed last year, was continued, with the alteration of a few persons.

Sundry persons were also added to those appointed last year for the collection of documents for printing "A History of the Rise and Progress of the Baptists in Virginia."

The propriety of hereditary slavery was also taken up at this session, and after some time employed in the consideration of the subject, the following resolution was offered by Mr. Leland and adopted:

> Resolved, *That slavery is a violent deprivation of the rights of nature and inconsistent with a republican government, and therefore recommend it to our brethren to make use of every legal measure to extirpate this horrid evil from the land; and pray Almighty God that our honorable Legislature may have it in their power to proclaim the great Jubilee, consistent with the principles of good policy.*

Those who had formerly gone under the name of *Regulars* sent a letter to this General Committee, remonstrating against some things licensed among that part of the Baptists formerly called *Separates*. To which an answer was sent by the General Committee, which proved satisfactory.

At this General Committee was Joshua Barnes, a preacher, who was born blind. As the God of nature would be merciful, whenever he deprives any of His creatures of one natural endowment He commonly doubles their capacity in something else. Mr. Barnes properly possessed the most singularly retentive memory as to anything he heard, especially what was read to him, of any other man living. He would preach a long sermon and quote an uncommon number of texts of Scripture to prove his points, of which he would always tell both chapter and verse. He was an excellent preacher and a very pious man. He was a native and resident of North Carolina, but traveled much in Virginia. He died in the year 1796.

The select committee appointed for compiling a History of the Baptists in Virginia reported that they had proceeded so far therein as to find a foundation laid for entering on the said work.

> *Resolved, therefore, That the Rev. John Leland and John Williams be recommended by the General Committee to engage in compiling the said History, and that the brethren hitherto engaged in collecting materials do furnish the said compilers as far as they can, and that the profits arising from the work be wholly to the compilers.*

The business respecting a seminary of learning was referred to the next General Committee.

The next General Committee met at Nuckol's meetinghouse, Goochland County, May 14, 1791. Delegates from seven Associations were enrolled.

The first business in which they engaged was to consider whether they had not departed from their former plan. This question produced a long debate. It was determined that they had deviated from their original plan; that the original design of the General Committee was only to consider religious-political grievances and to seek for redress.

> *Resolved, therefore, That that part of the third article which contains these words, "And all references from the District Associations respecting matters that may concern the whole body," be struck out.*

Considering that neither the Associations nor the General Committee ever pretended to anything more than the power of giving advice, this decision was certainly very injudicious. What possible mischief, it may be asked, could arise from receiving references from the Associations respecting matters of a general nature? It would seem to an impartial mind to be the surest road to uniformity and, consequently, to harmony and peace. This decision, or something else, proved fatal to the rising prosperity of the General Committee, for from that session it began to decline, and so continued until it was finally dissolved in the year 1799.

Having thus cramped themselves, they proceeded to the consideration of other matters. The memorial against the glebes, etc., was the only business before them.

This session of the General Committee was the fullest and the most respectable of any that had ever been held in Virginia, there being an assemblage of the greatest Baptist preachers residing within the State, besides two or three from Georgia, who in point of talents might be honorably compared with any in any part of the world. These were the Rev. Silas Mercer and the Rev. Jeremiah Walker, of the latter of whom much has already been said. These two men, although agreed upon the point of baptism, and therefore both Baptists, were much at variance upon the doctrines of free will and free grace; or as they are sometimes, by way of distinction, called Calvinism and Arminianism. Mr. Mercer was a decided Calvinist, and Mr. Walker as decided an Arminian; though it must be confessed that neither of them carried their system to such extremes as they have been carried by many. Mr. Mercer denied the doctrine of eternal reprobation, and Mr. Walker acknowledged that of imputed righteousness. In the General Committee each had a respectable party, though the Calvinistic side was much the largest. It is hard to say which of the two had the advantage in point of talents. They were both men of superlative original genius, and neither had the advantage of a classical education, to remedy the defect of which each of them had applied himself to reading, though at somewhat a late period of life, and it is not easy to determine which of the two was most advanced in the knowledge of books. As it respected address, either in or out of the pulpit, Walker had greatly the superiority. His manners in private companies were exceedingly engaging. Gentle, affable, polite, familiar yet dignified; he was, in a word, everything that could encourage the backward or soothe the irritable. His conversation was sensible and judiciously adapted to those with whom he was conversing. He was by no means urgent or positive in supporting his opinions, but would ply his competitor with strong arguments, as if they were pearls thrown before him, which he might gather up as his own or leave them; and it is probable few men could make gewgaws look more like jewels than Jeremiah Walker. His was a sweetened dose. In the pulpit, although Walker possessed but little oratorical fire (at least in his last days), yet he was singularly entertaining. When Walker preached there were few listless hearers.

Mercer, on the other hand, both in his countenance and manners, had considerably the appearance of sternness; and to feel quite free in his company it was necessary to be well acquainted with him. He seldom talked on any other subject except religion; and when in company with young preachers, or those who might question his doctrine or his opinions, his remarks chiefly turned on polemical points. He was indefatigable in striving to maintain his points, and for this purpose would hear any and all objections that could be raised, and would then labor assiduously to remove them. His arguments, however, neither in private nor public, were ever dressed with oratorical ornament. He did not aim at it. Indeed, he did not seem to wish it. He spoke and acted like one who felt himself surrounded by the impregnable bulwarks of truth, and therefore did not wish to parley. Regardless of the mountings of his armor, his whole attention was occupied in wielding it well, and in assuring himself and others that it was made of durable metal. He seemed to be afraid of marring the real splendor of his diamonds by a fictitious glistening. Having thus shortly portrayed these two men as they appeared to us when in Virginia in 1791, we will give some account of their measures to support their opinions while with us.

Mercer, being on the popular side, was chosen to preach on Sunday. Walker, with some difficulty, obtained leave to preach on Monday. Mercer went fully into the arguments tending to illustrate and prove his system. He was masterly, indeed. He spoke as one having authority.

His sermon left deep and durable impressions. Walker also defended his principles in an ingenious and masterly manner. Feeling himself measurably pressed down by the popular current, he could not display the same bold and commanding spirit as his competitor felt. He was, however, by no means deficient in close and forcible arguments. From the General Committee they both traveled and preached extensively through the State, creating wherever they went much conversation and agitation of mind among the people. Walker published a pamphlet entitled "The Fourfold Foundation of Calvinism Examined and Shaken." It was certainly no mean performance, and was thought to have made temporary impressions upon many strong Calvinists. Mercer also had books upon the contested points, but not of his own composition. The ultimate consequence of this investigation of principles was a decrease of Arminianism among the Baptists of Virginia, and a much greater uniformity in the doctrines of grace. Some were thought also, after these events, to have pushed the Calvinistic scheme to an Antinomian extreme.

Their next meeting was at Tomahawk meetinghouse, Chesterfield County, May 13, 1792. Delegates from nine Associations met.

It was now made a question whether the last General Committee had not cramped themselves by the amendment to the constitution, in the third article. In order to decide this point a committee was appointed to frame a solution, which, after some amendments, was in the following words, vtz.:

> *After maturely deliberating on a variety of circumstances, your committee suppose that the business of the General Committee is to consider all the political grievances of the whole Baptist Society in Virginia and all references from Associations, as also other circumstances which evidently relate to the external interest of the whole body of Baptists, and no other concerns whatever.*

This explanation of the power of the General Committee is certainly very obscure. It is still doubtful how far their power extended, seeing various constructions might be put upon the import of the words "external interest." But the most obvious impropriety exists in the proceedings of this and the last General Committee upon this subject. The General Committee for 1791 alters the constitution by which it exists; that of 1792 alters it again, and almost, if not altogether, brings it back *to status quo.* Now it may be asked, Can it be proper for any Assembly who derive their powers, not from themselves, but from some other source, to abridge or enlarge those powers without consulting those from whom they originated? The constitution having been either directly or indirectly sanctioned by all the Associations composing the General Committee, no alteration could rightly be made without their approval. If it were otherwise, it would be perfectly needless to have any constitution, as they would be no longer bound by any part offensive to themselves than the time it would take to alter it. Frequent changes in any institution invariably tend to lessen its stability.

The old question, respecting the glebes and churches, as it was generally called, of course was taken up, and fell into its usual channel. At this session several books, designed for publication, were offered to the General Committee in order to obtain their sanction. This was granted. This is one of many ways in which the meeting might be useful. To bring a book, designed for publication, immediately before a public assembly, in order to gain their approval, would be impracticable; but a general meeting might be useful, by appointing a standing committee for the purpose of examining anything intended for the press which directly concerns the honor and interests of the Baptists. This select committee might make a report stating the outlines of the book, according to which the general meeting could properly give or withhold their recommendation; this would probably, on the one hand, give currency to such tracts as possess merit; while, on the other hand, it might happily suppress such as would do injury to the cause of God and truth.

The General Committee continued to be held at the usual time of year, at the following places, viz.: 1793 Muddy Creek meetinghouse, Powhatan County; 1794 at Winn's meetinghouse, Hanover County; 1795 at Roundabout meetinghouse, Louisa County; 1796 at Du Puy's meetinghouse, Powhatan County; 1797 at Upper King and Queen meetinghouse, King and Queen County; 1798 at Buckingham Old Church, Buckingham County; 1799 at Waller's meetinghouse, Spotsylvania County, where they agreed to dissolve. During this period an unreasonable jealousy of their exercising too much power was often manifested, both by Associations and individuals. This, added to some other causes, produced a gradual declension in the attendance of members as well as a nerveless languor in the transaction of business. The remonstrance respecting glebes, &c., was the only business which excited no jealousies, and that was the only matter which was ever completed after the year 1792.

The business respecting a seminary of learning was, in 1793, committed to the hands of the Rev. John Williams and Mr. Thomas Read, of Charlotte, who reported the following plan: That fourteen trustees be appointed, all of whom shall be Baptists; that these at their first meeting appoint seven others of some other religious denomination; that the whole twenty-one then form a plan and make arrangements for executing it. This scheme was proceeded in so far as to appoint the whole of the trustees, who had one or two meetings, in which advances were made towards maturing the plan. But apprehensive that they should not be able to procure sufficient funds, with some other discouragements, they finally abandoned it. The compilation of a history of the Virginia Baptists having been committed wholly to the hands of Mr. Williams, after Mr. Leland's removal, he, after making no inconsiderable progress in collecting documents, in consequence of the decline of his health, found himself under the necessity of resigning his trust. This he did in a letter to the General Committee in 1794. The Committee received his resignation, and resolved to decline it for the present.

The last act of the General Committee was to recommend to the Associations to form a plan for a general meeting of correspondence to promote and preserve union and harmony among the churches. Of this meeting a short account may be found in the following chapter.

CHAPTER SEVEN:
The Origin and History of the General Meeting of Correspondence.

May, 1800, delegates met at Lyle's meetinghouse from several Associations for the double purpose of revising the Confession of Faith and as a convention to form a constitution for a general meeting. The business was committed to a select committee. On Monday morning the constitution, as prepared by the select committee, was reported and received. The great jealousy which had been expressed by the Associations respecting the General Committee, put the Convention so much upon their guard that in forming the constitution they almost gave themselves nothing to do. Their business, if it could properly be called the business of a meeting, was to collect and publish useful pieces, somewhat in the nature of a magazine, which was to be sold to defray its own expense. The advantages resulting from a general intercourse of the Associations in Virginia were so obvious that its friends were willing to have a meeting upon any terms which would accomplish that end. It must have been foreseen that unless they could be employed in something which might be thought beneficial, the meetings would be but thinly attended. But few could be found willing to travel long distances without having any other business, except that of seeing each other and communicating the good or evil tidings which everyone brought with him. Accordingly the meetings were attended by but few for several years.

Only three Associations, viz., Dover, Goshen, and Albemarle, adopted the constitution at first. When they met from year to year, nothing being prepared for the press, little else was done than to regulate the internal concerns of the meeting and appoint the time and place of the next. So dragged on the General Meeting of Correspondence, until May, 1807, when they met at Buckingham Old Church, in Buckingham County. Delegates from four Associations met (Appomattox having fallen in). Likewise the Roanoke sent a messenger to gain information, not having as yet determined. This meeting, finding from experience the improbability of ever carrying the first constitution into effect, resolved to form a new one;[1] such as they in their judgments, believed to be for the good of the cause, and not merely with a view to adapting it to the suspicious minds of a few leading characters, who were perhaps actuated by upright though mistaken motives. In order to give full time for the investigation of this new constitution, the next General Meeting was fixed on the fourth Saturday in October, 1808.

Accordingly, on the above date, the General Meeting assembled at Bethel meetinghouse, in Chesterfield County. Six Associations had adopted the new constitution and sent their delegates, viz., Dover, Goshen, Albemarle, Appomattox, Roanoke, and Meherrin.

The former moderator being absent by death, Robert B. Semple was chosen moderator, and Reuben Ford clerk. The General Meeting took up the following business: The propriety of offering an address to Mr. Thomas Jefferson, President of the United States, who, having served his country faithfully for many years, was now about to retire from public life. The address was unanimously voted and sent on; to which the President returned an immediate answer. (See Appendix.) It also appeared from some late publications that the Baptists in Virginia had been misrepresented as to their sentiments respecting human learning. It was determined at this meeting to rebut this calumny by publishing a few remarks on that subject in the form of a circular letter, which was accordingly done.

The Philadelphia Association, a short time before this, had published their centurial sermon, the author of which had written on that he had reserved 150 or 200 copies of that sermon for the disposal of the General Meeting, as a present to them. At this meeting harmony and peace reigned. The preaching and the public exercises generally appeared to have the divine smiles. It was an encouraging meeting.

The next General Meeting of Correspondence was held at Tarwallet meetinghouse, October 28, &c., 1809. Delegates from five Associations assembled.[2]

---

[1] By this constitution they could take up any matter, previously decided on, in any Association.—*Author's note.*

[2] The constitution of the General Meeting of Correspondence had now been

The same moderator and clerk were chosen as last year. Two subjects were brought forward at this meeting, which, if ever matured, must greatly conduce to the future happiness of the Baptists as a religious society: The religious education of children and the establishment of some seminary or public school to assist young preachers to acquire literary knowledge.

The first was disposed of by recommending to parents the use of catechisms, and especially one lately published for use of the Baptist Society; and the other, by appointing two persons to acquire information and digest a plan for such a seminary.

In the following and all the tables of the Association there are a few cases in which no positive information could be had, particularly respecting the time of the constitution of churches, and their number at constitution. In such cases our informants made their statements to the best of their recollection.

---

adopted by a majority of Associations in the State, but from some cause, several failed to meet.—*Author's note.*

TABLE OF THE DOVER ASSOCIATION

Name of churches	Year	Number at Constitu-	Present Number	By Whom Planted	Former Pastors	Current Pastors	Counties
Dover	1773	45	275	S. Hariss, James Read	W. Webber		Goochland
Goochland	1771	75	200	S. Hariss, J. Read. J. Waller	R. Ford	R. Ford	Goochland
Hopeful	1807	174	180	Reuben Ford	R. Ford	R. Ford	Hanover
Chickahominy	1776	50	240	J. Waller, S. Hariss, J. Read	J. Clay, R. Ford, W. Webber	B. Bowles	Hanover
Hungry	1791	40	100	S. Hariss, J. Read. J. Waller	No Pastor at first	B. Reynolds	Henrico
City of Richmond	1780	14	560	J. Morris	J. Morris	J. Courtney	Henrico
Board Swamp			90	E. Baker	Austin		Henrico
Four Mile			248	E. Baker	J. Lindsey	J. Lindsey	Henrico
Charles City	1776	20	217	E. Baker	J. Bradley	W. Clopton	Charles City
Black Creek	1777	12	200	J. Clay	W. Barnes, T. Courtney	J. Turner	New Kent and Hanover
James City	1778	30	96	J. Anthony, E. Baker	J. Goodall		James City
Williamsburg	1791	330	500	G. Pamphlet	G. Pamphlet		James City
Grafton	1777	22	497	E. Baker	J. Wright	J. Gayle	York and Warwick
Hampton	1791	90	305	J. Wright	J. Young	R. Hurst	Elizabeth City
Reeds	1773	16	267	S. Hariss, J. Read	J. Shackle-	J. Self	Caroline
Tuckahoe	1774		219	L. Craig	T. Noel	J. Sorrel	Caroline
Salem	1802	88	106	T. Noel	J. Courtney, W. Breeding		Caroline
Upper College	1775	12	250	J. Young			King William
Lower College	1792	100	310	J. Courtney	J. Mill	J. Mill	King William

Name of churches	Year	Number at Constitu-	Present Number	By Whom Planted	Former Pastors	Current Pastors	Counties
Upper King and	1774	25	257	L. Craig	Y. Pitts	T. Noel	King and Queen
Bruington	1790	150	300	J. Greenwood	R.B. Semple	R.B. Semple	King and Queen
Exol	1775	30	228	J. Waller	I. Lewis	I. Lewis	King and Queen
Lower King and	1772	17	147	J. Waller	R. Ware	W. Todd	King and Queen
Pocorone	1807	100	92	R. Ware	J. Healey	J. Healey	King and Queen
Upper Essex	1772	40	280	L. Craig	T. Noel	Various	Essex
Piscataway	1774	11	229	J. Waller	J. Greenwood	J. Greenwood	Essex
Glebe Landing	1772	20	284	J. Waller	W. Mullin	I. Lewis	Essex, Middlesex
Hermitage	1789	346	230	J.Waller	J. Mullin, J. Healey		Essex, Middlesex
Zoar	1808	100	99	J. Mullin	D. Corey		Middlesex
Gloucester, or Petts-worth	1790	88	283	I. Lewis	R. Hudgins, W. Lemon		Gloucester
Abingdon	1801	200	263	I. Lewis	R. Stacy	R. Stacy	Cloucester
Matthews	1775		430	I. Lewis	D. Tinsley, J. Gage	W. Fitchet	Mathews
Hanover	1789	93	256	J. Shackleford	J. Davis	J. David	King George
Nomini	1786	17	875	H. Toler, L. Lunsford	H. Toler	H. Toler	Westmoreland
Farnham	1790	80	60	J. Greenwood, W. Mullin	W. Mullin, B. Phillips		Richmond
Wicomico	1804	20	238	L. Lunsford	S. Straughn	S. Straughn	Northumberland
Morattico	1778	14	201	L. Lunsford	L. Lunsford, J. Creath	S. Straughn	Lancaster

CHAPTER EIGHT:
The History of the Proceedings of the Dover Association.

In our history of the General Association the reader will find that in 1783 they divided into four districts, of which two were on the south and two on the north side of James River, called the Lower and Upper Districts, &c., fixing their boundaries on the north side, from Manakin town, on James River, in a straight line by Fredericksburg to the Potomac. The two on the north side, it appears, agreed to meet together once a year, and to hold besides one separate session in each district.

The minutes for 1784 and 1785 have not been procured. In November, 1786, they met at Ground-Squirrel meetinghouse, in Hanover County. William Webber was chosen moderator, and Reuben Ford clerk.

The only business of general application transacted at this session was the solution of the following query: *How is ordination legally performed?*

Answer. "A presbytery of ministers are fully empowered to ordain any faithful man properly recommended, whom they shall judge able to teach others; and that ministers shall be subject to ministers with regard to their call to the ministry and the doctrines they preach. The church where the minister is a member shall take cognizance of his moral character."

This decision, though founded in reason and Scripture, gave umbrage to some, who indulged strong jealousies respecting ministerial influence, and who held that a call from a church was sufficient ordination. In consequence of this opposition, the subject was again introduced into the Dover Association in the year 1792, to our history of which the reader is referred.

October 12, 1787.—They met again at the Factory, in Westmoreland County. Letters from twenty-one churches were received. Many local matters were taken up and decided. The preaching at this Association was warm and heart-searching. Some who were there speak of it as a very precious season. Such is always the case when God is about to revive His work.

October 8, 1788.—The next and last session of the united districts was at Burris' meetinghouse, in Caroline County. Twenty-one churches corresponded. After attending to a great deal of local business, they agreed to finally divide.[1] To the Lower District they agreed to attach the name Dover, and Orange to the Upper.

May 16, 1789.—The Dover Association met at Upper King and Queen meetinghouse. Letters were received from twenty-one churches. This being the time of the great revival, almost throughout the district, the letters teemed with the most glorious intelligence. This Association was attended by preachers from various quarters of the State. Their labors, by day and by night, were abundantly blessed. The souls of saints were comforted, and many, very many, sinners were won over to Christ. It was a blessed time. At this Association, as well as at several before and after this, the perplexing question with regard to the marriage of slaves was introduced. The Association resolved that the state of the slaves of Virginia was of so singular and delicate a nature that no general rule could apply. They therefore advised the churches to adapt their proceedings to the nature of each case in the most prudent way.

October 16, 1789.—The Association met at Kilmarnock meetinghouse, in Lancaster County. Seventeen churches corresponded by letters, in which very refreshing news is communicated. The revival was still progressing. Many hundreds had been baptized in the course of the year. No business of importance was entered upon.

May 1, 1790.—They met at Hoar Swamp meetinghouse, Henrico County. Letters from nineteen churches were received. The revival, it appeared from the letters, had subsided in a considerable degree. The preaching and other religious exercises at this Association were exceedingly pleasant to the pious who were present.

A matter that had produced considerable confusion in some parts of the Association was now considered, viz., whether baptism "was valid when administered by an unordained person." To which the Association replied: "That in cases where the ordinance

---

[1] The Lower District held several meetings separate from the other, but they were thinly attended, and but little was done.—*Author's note.*

had been administered in a solemn and religious manner, that it might be considered as valid, and that persons so baptized might be admitted as members of the church upon hearing and approving their experience."

October 9, 1790.—They met at Diamond meetinghouse, in Essex County. Letters from twenty-nine churches were received, which speak of pleasant times. The only business of a permanent nature transacted at this Association was the decision of the following query: Is a minister in duty bound to serve a church that does not support him? It was answered in the negative.

The correctness of this decision has since been much questioned.

Is the union of pastor and church merely a contract between them as parties? If it is, then the decision is correct; but if assuming the pastoral care of a church partakes of the nature of a vow to God, as well as a contract with the church, then the minister is bound to discharge the duties of a pastor until he has satisfactory evidence that God has exempted him from such duties and designs him for some other place. The non-compensation of ministerial services is not sufficient proof that God does not will his further labors in such a place, seeing many ministers have been highly favored of God in places where they have received little or no compensation from their hearers. The best conclusion, therefore, is that although the church is censurable for withholding from the pastor his just right, yet the pastor is bound to God, and has His promise that he that trusts in Him shall want no good thing.

The circular letter on justification, by Mr. Toler, was much approved, and was ordered to be printed with the minutes. This is the first instance of the minutes of the Association being printed.

October 8, 1791.—Pursuant to appointment the Association met at Kingston meetinghouse, Mathews County.[1] Letters from twenty-seven churches were received. They give no pleasing accounts of revivals, but hold forth a state of peace and tranquility among the church.

October 13, 1792.—The Association met at Bruington meetinghouse, King and Queen County. Letters from twenty-five churches were received. By them it appeared that in Dover Dis-

---

[1] Now called the Matthew's meetinghouse.—*Author's note.*

trict the harvest was past and the summer ended. Coldness and languor were generally complained of. The great revival had now subsided and the axe of discipline was laid at the root of the tree. Many barren and fruitless trees were already cut down. In many of the churches the number excluded surpassed the number received. The Association, however, was full. Great crowds attended the preaching, and it was doubtless a happy season to God's children.

Among other business of less note, the subject of the ordination of elders, or church officers, was taken up at this Association. A question had been agitated for some years, whether ordination ought to be by the imposition of the hands of a presbytery or plurality of elders (the mode commonly practiced in Virginia), or whether a solemn call from a church was not sufficient.

On the part of the advocates of ordination without the imposition of hands, it was argued that churches were acknowledged to be independent, but if they could not obtain the full services of a minister, unless he had been previously examined and ordained by a presbytery, their independence was so far destroyed; that churches were better judges what gifts would suit them than presbyteries could be; that the imposition of hands mentioned in the Scriptures was with a view to miraculous and not common gifts; and lastly, that it had the appearance of being governed too much by forms.

To these arguments it was answered that the New Testament did surely sanction the practice of laying on of hands in some cases where no miraculous consequences did ensue; that although the imposition of hands was a form, yet it was a significant form used in all ages of the Christian Church for the purpose of consecrating or setting apart persons for holy offices; that baptism and the Lord's supper were also external forms, but being significant and sanctioned by the Word of inspiration, they were owned and blessed to the church; that it was true that churches were, and ought to be, independent, to a proper extent, but this independence did not authorize them to ordain officers contrary to revelation, unless they were independent of God also; that no minister or deacon was imposed upon them but by their own consent; that although a church might judge better than a presbytery what suited her, it was not reasonable that those who had not exercised a public gift should be so competent to judge of public gifts as those who had.

After the subject had been investigated for years at different times and in different ways, it was finally decided in this Association in favor of the imposition of hands. After this very little was ever said about it.

The purchase of lottery tickets was considered by this Association as a species of gaming, and not sufferable in members of churches.

October 12, 1793.—They met at Glebe Landing meetinghouse, in Middlesex. Most of the letters complained of cold times. *The only* business of a general nature which occupied their attention was the recommending that rules for family discipline and the instruction of youth should be formed. This, however, has never as yet gone fully into operation. It was at this session that a church in the city of Williamsburg, composed wholly of black people, or rather people of color, was admitted into the Association. They have continued ever since to send their delegates.

It was in this year that the pestilential fever prevailed to such a distressing extent in the city of Philadelphia. The Association, believing it to be a judgment of God, appointed a day of fasting and prayer to deprecate His wrath.

At this Association the preaching was uncommonly animating; the business was conducted with much harmony, and all parties, pleased with the interview, separated from each other in love and peace. The circular letter was written by Mr. Lunsford on the covenant of grace.

October 11, 1794.—They again met at Nomini meetinghouse, Westmoreland County, according to appointment. Nothing of a singular or general nature was transacted at this time. The letters said nothing of a revival, but of the contrary. The preaching, debates, conversation, &c., were all apparently calculated to do permanent good as well as to minister immediate gratification. It was a feast to the Lord's family. The circular letter was written on the "Nature of Associations," from which a quotation has been already made.

October 10, 1795.—The next session was at Four-Mile Creek meetinghouse, Henrico County. No business was transacted worthy of notice. From first to last of the meeting everything went on agreeably. The circular letter was written by Elder Reuben Ford on the duty of ministers, deacons, and churches. The writing of the circular letter on this subject arose from this circumstance: A very worthy and useful minister had undertaken to discharge some public office, by which he was much hindered from his ministerial duties. It was supposed that the reasonable demands of his family made it necessary, he having been neglected by the church. The letter was composed with a view to stimulate churches, ministers, and deacons to a regular performance of their duties to each other. The next Association was appointed at the Lower College meetinghouse, in King William County.

October 8, 1796.—Met agreeably to appointment. Nothing important was attended to. There were no angry disputations, no whisperings, no parties; but after friendly debates, there were most commonly unanimous decisions. The circular letter was composed on the religious education of children, which subject was also taken up upon the following query: How ought the religious education of children to be conducted?

Answer. By the use of catechisms; and we recommend for the present such as may be judged useful.

A committee was also appointed to compose a suitable one for the use of the members of the Association. The next Association was appointed at Bestland meetinghouse, in Essex County.

October 14, 1797.—Met agreeably to appointment. Elder John Leland, from New England, attended. His preaching and conversation at this Association were highly entertaining, as well as instructing, especially to young and inexperienced ministers. At this session nothing but business of a local nature called their attention. The circular letter for this Association was written by Elder Reuben Ford, without any appointed subject. The Association met in peace, continued in love, and parted with sorrow and hope.

October 13, 1798.—The next Association met at Mathews meetinghouse, Mathews County, according to appointment. The letters did not detail anything very interesting. The business was altogether local, except as to the following query: *What is the opinion of the Association concerning the washing the saints' feet?*

Answer. We do not consider the washing of feet an ordinance of the Gospel, but an act of entertainment, and being a servile act, appears to have been enjoined by Christ, to be observed by his disciples, as a token of humility, and may include any other act usually performed by servants.

The circular letter was written upon the subject of fasts. As usual, it was a time of love to God's people. The next Association was appointed at Hickory Neck meetinghouse, James City County.

October 12, 1799.—They met according to appointment. The letters of correspondence seemed now to afford more pleasing accounts. The day-star began to dawn. Great revivals were in embryo. The place of this meeting was inconvenient to a majority of the churches; in consequence of which there was not so full a representation of the churches as at some other Associations. It was also thought that the congregations were not so large as they usually were on such occasions. The business of the Association, which was entirely local, was, however, conducted harmoniously. The circular letter was written on the connection between pastors and churches. The next Association was appointed at Nuckol's meetinghouse, Goochland County.

October 11, 1800.—They met according to appointment. Good news and glad tidings now saluted the ears and hearts of the pious. Glorious revivals were spoken of in most of the letters. So pleasing was the information that the Association resolved to decline printing for the present the circular letter written by the directions of the last Association, and now to draw up an account of the revival, which was accordingly done. Nothing singular or general was transacted at this Association. It was a time of life, love, and peace. The next Association was appointed at Mattaponi meetinghouse, King and Queen County.

October 10, 1801.—They met according to appointment. From the letters it was learned that the revivals spoken of last year were still gloriously going on, and some new ones begun. At this Association the preaching and other religious employments seemed to have singular effects. The souls of Christians were enlivened, and although for many years the Association at all her meetings had experienced uninterrupted harmony and peace, it must be admitted that the religious enjoyment at this rather surpassed that of any other.

A good deal of local, but no general business occupied the attention of the Association. The circular letter was written upon the use and abuse of spirituous liquors. The reason for taking up this subject is obvious to any who know the state of civil society. The next Association was appointed at Nomini meetinghouse, Westmoreland County.

October 9, 1802.—They met according to appointment. By the letters it appeared that the revivals in some places were rather on the decline; in others new ones were commencing. Upon the whole the cause of godliness was progressing. At this Association an attempt was made to establish a uniformity among the churches, in holding their church meetings. Some churches admitted to their church meetings, even for discipline and government, all the members of the church, male and female, bond and free, young and old. Others admitted all male members, whether slaves or free. By experience this plan was found vastly inconvenient. The degraded state of the minds of slaves rendered them totally incompetent to the task of judging correctly respecting the business of the church, and in many Churches there was a majority of slaves; in consequence of which great confusion often arose. The Association at Mattaponi directed that the subject should be treated in a circular letter. The letter argued and advised that although all members were entitled to the privileges, yet that none but free male members should exercise any authority in the church. The Association, after some debate, sanctioned the plan by a large majority. Nomini meetinghouse stands in the Northern Neck, quite inconvenient for a majority of the churches. The Association was of course not so full as usual, but as usual it was an agreeable time. The next Association was appointed at Upper King and Queen meetinghouse, King and Queen County.

October 8, 1803.—Met according to appointment. By the letters we learn that in some churches times were very pleasing; but in others very much the reverse. A subject, long a matter of debate among the Baptists of Virginia, was debated and settled at this Association, viz., the propriety of preaching funeral sermons. A query had been introduced into the Association the year before, and it was made the subject of the circular letter. The sentiments of the letter were, that preaching funeral sermons and funeral ceremonies generally were matters of perfect indifference, and could have neither good nor evil in them; but that things of indifference could be turned by bad men to bad purposes, and it was equally obvious that good men, when it was in their power, could, and ought to direct them to good purposes; that the Gospel ought to be preached on all occasions when there was a hope of its doing good; that preaching over the dead was a kind of invitation to go to the house of mourning where the living might lay it to heart. These, with some other arguments of less weight, seemed to clear up most of the doubts. The letter was received with an almost unanimous vote.

In this Association an animated debate took place on the propriety of passing church censures upon members who will not contribute a reasonable proportion to the expenses of the church. The decision was that no censure ought to pass on that account. The subject was, however, resumed the ensuing year, and the decision was given in the following words:

> *We never doubted but that according to the Gospel it was the duty of every member of the church to contribute to the expense of the church according as the Lord had prospered him; but we supposed it might be productive of disagreeable consequences if the church undertook to judge of the ability of members and to censure or approve them.*

At this Association times were agreeable, so far as respected religious employment, but the happiness of many was somewhat lessened by a practice which had long prevailed, more or less, at Associations and great meetings, but which here arose to a very distressing height, viz., the selling of spirituous liquors by wicked and worthless persons, in consequence of which many who were so unprincipled and wicked as not to restrain themselves became intoxicated, and of course disorderly. Warned by these events, measures have been taken by the Association, since the above period, to prevent such abuses, and they have been as successful as could be expected in such a case. The next Association was appointed at Four-Mile Creek meetinghouse, Henrico County.

October 18, 1804—They met according to appointment. From the letters it appears that no revival existed in any church, but from some there were considerable expectations. Several matters of a general and important nature occupied the attention of the Association at this meeting, viz., "The Confession of Faith, *The History of the Baptists in Virginia*, the appointment of Union Meetings, and a Remonstrance against a law of Virginia respecting night meetings—all of which will be noticed in other places of this work. About this time, the Baptists in this Association received a grievous wound in the wretched apostasy of one Thomas Bridges, who had been a preacher of some celebrity, but was now convicted and sent to the penitentiary for horse-stealing. The friends of Zion mourned, not because the foundation of God was shaken, or could be shaken, but because the cause of truth was too plausibly, though fallaciously, reproached. To obviate the evil as much as possible, the circular letter was written upon the subject of religious apostasy. It was thought that good effects arose from it. The next Association was appointed at Bruington meeting-house, King and Queen County.

October 12, 1805.—They met according to appointment. By the letters of correspondence the Association was informed of great and good news from several parts. In most of the churches in the lower end of the district, between Rappahannock and James Rivers, there were previous revivals. In some, several hundred had been baptized. The preaching and other religious exercises at the Association were correspondent with this heavenly news. It was a time of feasting upon fat things. No business whatever of a singular and general nature was transacted, except that some attention was paid to the history noticed in the last. Elder Toler, according to appointment, produced a most excellent circular letter on the subject of brotherly love. The next Association was appointed at Grafton meetinghouse, York County.

October 11, 1806.—They met according to appointment. Information was received that a great and glorious work of God was going on in the Northern Neck. Most of the churches in this quarter participated more or less; but Nomini, under the care of Mr. Toler, was superlatively favored. The business which occupied the attention of this Association was altogether local. The Association was not so full as usual, being in an eccentric place; but those who did go said it was good for them that they were there. The circular letter was written on the place and object of good works. The next Association was appointed at Ware's meetinghouse, King and Queen County, which, on account of the pressure of business, was appointed to hold four days.

October 11, 1807.—They met according to appointment. No

new revivals are spoken of in any of the letters. In some places where revivals had been a few years past, they speak of distressing times; that the love of many was waxing cold. There must be a fanning time as well as a harvesting time. The Association, according to last year's appointment, continued four days. Some business of a general, and much of a local nature occupied their attention. The year 1806 was a year of great drought; and crops of corn were uncommonly scanty, insomuch that many poor people suffered for the necessaries of life. In the time of the drought most of the Baptist churches appointed and observed fast days. The crops of the year 1807 were uncommonly plentiful. The Association, taking this matter into consideration, determined to appoint a thanksgiving day.[1] The circular letter, appointed to be written upon the nature of sanctification, by Elder Toler, was read and approved by a majority; but supposing that the investigation of a subject, sufficiently settled on the main points and too intricate on subordinate ones to expect unanimity, would produce no good effect, it was determined not to print it. A short address on the propriety of appointing public days for special religious purposes was printed in the place thereof. For the space of eighteen years the Association fund had been gradually increasing, so that, on the settlement this year, it was found that there were in the hands of the treasurer £68 11s., 6d., which, with the present contribution, after paying all expenses, amounted to £78 9s., 8d. This being a respectable sum, and upon inquiry, finding that in case of the death of the present treasurer, the Association not being incorporated, they might find some difficulty in regaining the money, it was resolved that three trustees should be appointed to take the obligations of the treasurer, payable to them as trustees; thus having a definite number, an action at law might be maintained. It was also agreed to pay one hundred and fifty dollars for the encouragement of the history of the Virginia Baptists. The next Association was appointed at Salem meetinghouse, Caroline County.

October 8, 1808.—They met according to appointment. The letters generally spoke of languor and lukewarmness among the churches. There was no business proper to be noticed in this histo-

---

[1] This day was uniformly observed throughout the district, to the great satisfaction of almost all sorts of people.—*Author's note.*

ry transacted at this session. The public ministrations were pleasing, and the time of continuing together was spent in a happy and useful manner. The circular letter was written upon the "Duty of Christians to Obey the Civil Laws."

October 14, 1809.—The Association assembled at Mathews meetinghouse, in Mathews County. The uniform language of the letters was complaint of the lifeless state of religion in all the churches, yet it appeared that peace and harmony and brotherly love, with earnest longings for a revival, were generally felt. At this Association it was proposed to recommend to parents, &c., the use of a catechism that had been lately published for the religious instruction of children. This catechism, though too long deferred, had really been published in conformity to the resolution of the Association in their session of 1796. It, however, met with great opposition upon the principle that nothing of the kind was necessary; that the Bible was sufficient; that things of that kind had a dangerous tendency towards lessening the dignity of the Scriptures; that the most corrupt and absurd sentiments had been inculcated through catechisms.

The advocates of the recommendation replied to these objections that corrupt men could communicate corrupt sentiments through the most sacred channels; that the pulpit and the press, conversation, and even public prayer had been occasionally the vehicles of unsound doctrines; that it could be no indignity to the Scriptures to inculcate in the minds of children principles and duties completely sanctioned by the Scriptures; that such forms of instruction greatly assisted parents in the discharge of their duty, seeing there could be few parents capable of explaining the Bible suitably for the instruction of children; that the manners and morals of the children of Baptists lately grown up plainly evinced that religious education had been too much neglected; that the opponents to the measure had probably fallen into the same mistake that the disciples of Jesus Christ had who forbade little children to be brought to their Master, for which they received His rebuke. After a long and warm debate, the majority decided in favor of the recommendation.

The same subject was taken up a few weeks later by the General Meeting of Correspondence, and by a unanimous vote the catechism was recommended. It is devoutly to be wished that this may be the beginning of a reformation among the Baptists of Virginia as to this duty. For, considering their exemplary piety in other respects, they have certainly been too remiss in training up their children in the nurture and the admonition of the Lord. The circular letter was written upon "Christian Order." The next Association was appointed to be held in the city of Richmond.

CHAPTER NINE:
Historical Sketches of the Churches of the First Union Meeting District in Dover Association.

Having detailed the proceedings of the Dover Association at her different sessions, we shall now proceed to the history of the churches. We have mentioned, in our account of the session of 1804, that the Association established union meetings. This was done by laying off the district into three sections. These were called union meeting districts, and were numbered first, second, and third. The first included all the churches between York and James Rivers; the second, all between York and Rappahannock; and the third, all between Rappahannock and Potomac. In these districts it is expected that the preachers shall meet two or three times every year, agreeably to the appointment of the Association, and keep up preaching for two or three days. The meetings have accordingly been observed tolerably regularly ever since, and from them it has been thought that many advantages have resulted.

In treating of the churches, we shall be governed by this arrangement, and shall commence with those of the first district.

Dover

This church has already been mentioned in the general account of the rise of the Baptists in these parts. Since that time it has been a flourishing church, having had some very refreshing revivals. That which took place in 1799 and 1800 was a great one indeed.

From soon after their constitution until his death Elder William Webber was their pastor. He died in 1808. They have not secured the services of any minister as yet in the character of a pastor. Mr. Matthew Woodson was a member and a deacon of this church, and one of the best of men. In this church there have been several preachers raised up, viz., Joseph Anthony, concerning whom see biography.

Augustine Eastin, who removed to Kentucky, and who, though

a man of some talent, was never any credit to the cause of truth. He appears always to have been carried away with the opinions of others whom he wished to imitate. Sometimes he was a professed and positive Calvinist; then shifting about he becomes as warm an Arminian. Then to the right about again he is reconvinced that Calvinism is the only true way. Having moved to Kentucky he finds some professors of high standing in civil life who lean to the Arian scheme. Mr. Eastin soon becomes their champion, and even writes a pamphlet in defense of Arianism. This last change has made much noise among the Baptists in Kentucky. But, thanks to Divine protection, no Arian or Socinian Baptists are known in Virginia. Mr. Eastin's moral character has not been impeached. On this head both he and his coadjutors are men of high respectability.

Mr. Farro, an ordained preacher, still resides in this church. He is a respectable man.

Goochland

This is a mother church, as may be seen elsewhere. From about the year of their constitution (1771) to the present time they have been blessed with the pastoral care of the Rev. Mr. Ford. Nothing singular has happened since the period to which her history was brought down. They were revived in the year 1799, which, says Mr. Ford in his manuscript, "was as pleasant as rain to the thirsty ground, or bread to the hungry soul." About 120 were added to the church. It has sometimes happened among the churches that partial revivals have been granted in which there would be only those of a particular description brought in. A remarkable stir of this kind took place among the black people in this church in the year 1806. More than 100 of them were baptized.

The following churches have been constituted off from this church, viz.: Dover, in 1773; Chickahominy, in 1776; Licking-Hole, in 1776; Hungry, in 1791; and Hopeful, in 1807. Several preachers have also been raised and have resided in this church.

Mr. Ford is now about 68 years of age, and is a venerable man indeed. Few men ever deceived less by their physiognomy than Elder Ford. No man ever sees him, who does not view him with reverence at his first appearance, and no man ever was disappointed in him. Grave, without the least moroseness; cheerful, without a symptom of levity; modest, gentle and affectionate in his manners, yet firm in his purposes; he has everything out of the pulpit which might serve as a model of a Gospel minister; his life is truly spotless; hit talents are of the useful kind; in his doctrine he is somewhat tinctured with Arminianism.

Hopeful

This is quite a new church. The members live partly in Hanover and partly in Louisa. They are a pious, orderly and affectionate people. The church was raised almost wholly through the ministry of the venerable Mr. Ford, to whom they are uncommonly united. They were formerly a branch of the Goochland church.

Chickahominy

This church is composed of members living partly in Hanover and partly in Henrico. Their meetinghouse is in Hanover, a very short distance from the county line. Soon after their constitution they chose Mr. John Clay as their pastor. Under his care they did not prosper. He died in about four years. The church having been raised chiefly through the labors of Elders Ford and Webber, they again resorted to them for aid. They attended them jointly once a month for several years. In 1785 they had a pleasant refreshing; about sixty were added, and among them two young preachers, viz., John Penny, who afterwards moved to Kentucky, and Benjamin Bowles, their present pastor.

In 1800 they were again favored with the smiles of heaven, when about eighty were baptized.

Elder Bowles is a solid, experimental preacher. When he feels religion he is more transported than is usual, and on such occasions will not, cannot, cease to proclaim the Divine goodness to all around him. Such exhortations have done much good.

Hungry

This church was constituted from Chickahominy, and had at first Mr. Peter Cottrel for their pastor; he falling into disorder and being expelled, the church was left destitute. They then procured the stated attendance of Elders Courtney and Webber until about 1798, when Elder Bernard Reynolds settled among them, and was chosen pastor, in which office he has continued until this time.

Mr. Reynolds was once a preacher in the Methodist connection, but being fully convinced of the verity of Baptist principles, he united with them, and has since remained unwavering. His preaching is now sound and evangelical; he is respected in civil as well as in religious matters, having been appointed a magistrate for the county. Whether holding this, or any such office, is entirely compatible with that ministry, which should not be entangled with the affairs of this life, is a matter to be settled by each man's conscience. It is probably better left to laymen.

City of Richmond

Within the limits of the Dover Association is Richmond, the metropolis of Virginia; here, although the Baptists are not the most flourishing sect, they stand upon respectable ground. They have built by public subscription a large brick meetinghouse, and probably move on, both as it respects discipline and the conducting of public worship, with as much regularity as any people in the Union. Their pastor, Elder Courtney, took the care in the year 1788, and under his labors they have enjoyed peace and prosperity. He is now (1809) about sixty-six years of age.

This church arose from the labors of Joshua Morris, their first pastor. He, living in the Boar Swamp church, set up a meeting at one Franklin's, near the city of Richmond, where, baptizing a few and soon after moving to Richmond to live, a church was constituted under his care. After residing in Richmond some years he moved to Kentucky.

Within this church there are, besides Elder Courtney, several ordained and licensed preachers, viz.: George Williamson, who is first master armorer; Herman Sneade, a teacher; William Brame, who travels and preaches a great deal, and others not so permanently fixed.

Boar Swamp

This church is about fifteen miles below Richmond and about ten northeast of Four-Mile Creek. This was once a prosperous and flourishing church, but having had no pastor for many years they have rather declined.

Four Mile

The meetinghouse to this church is about nine or ten miles below Richmond. They have Elder John Lindsey for their minister.

He is old and infirm, but a pious and useful minister. They have some very respectable pious members.

Charles City

This church is in the county of the same name, and was raised by the labors of Elijah Baker and Joseph Anthony, who first began their service in this neighborhood about the year 1774. They at first sustained much opposition, but no personal violence. During the year 1775 several were baptized. In the year 1776 James Bradley, afterwards their pastor, was converted and baptized, and soon began to preach.

Soon after the church was constituted Mr. Bradley was chosen pastor, and continued to discharge the duties thereof until he died, on the 6th of September, 1803. Mr. Bradley at first preached by form, or, in other words, read his sermons to the people; but soon laid aside his notes and preached *ex tempore*. Although he was not a very successful nor popular preacher, there were few men who stood in higher estimation, in point of piety and uniformity of conduct, than Mr. Bradley. He was universally esteemed an honest and faithful servant of God.

Since his death, Mr. William Clopton, who had long been a leading member of the church, seeing the great need of a preacher, began to speak publicly, and finally was ordained to the ministry. The state of religion in this church is rather adverse, yet order and peace are preserved among the members, while the wicked will do wickedly. When the set time to favor Zion shall arrive, she will doubtless come again with rejoicing, bringing the sheaves of the spiritual harvest. In this church there used to be, and still are, a great number of blacks. For some cause they were forbidden to preach, upon which they set up a kind of independence, and went on, not only to preach, but to baptize. It all, however, ended in confusion.

Black Creek

This church has gone through as many revolutions as any in the Association. Her misfortunes arose, as is often the case, from the errors and misconduct of their preachers. Their first pastor was William Barnes, who being a remarkably weak, though a well-meaning preacher, the church languished under his care; he moved away about the year 1785. In 1788 Thomas Courtney moved from King William into the bounds of Black Creek, and the church being in much confusion, was reconstituted under Mr. Courtney's care. About 1791 they had a revival, when some very respectable members were added. Mr. Courtney moved, in 1795, to Richmond, and there died with the small-pox. After Mr. Courtney's death, the church fell into confusion again, and was constituted a third time. From the first origin of this church, R. Snead, a preacher of some talents, resided within her limits. This man was the cause of a great part of the confusion; he was really a double-minded man, who was unstable in all his ways; sometimes he would be a Quaker; sometimes a Pedo-Baptist; and again return with double violence to Baptist principles. He was alternately a Calvinist, an Arminian and a Universalist. When excommunicated for his principles (for his morals were correct), he would return after some time and make such apparently sincere concessions that it would seem uncharitable not to excuse him. He died in the church. John Turner, who has lately undertaken the care of the church, Herman Snead and John Goodman, preachers, were all sons of this church.

While Thomas Courtney resided among them, they enjoyed considerable prosperity. Mr. Courtney was brother to Elder Courtney, pastor of the Richmond church. Though not a very able, he was a lively and agreeable preacher; he was singular for his good humor and pleasant temper; he was a bad economist, and by that means was often embarrassed in his affairs. This excepted, Mr. Courtney might be considered a first-rate religious character. He died triumphing in redeeming love. Mr. Clopton, who has for many years represented this district in Congress, is a member of this church.

James City

This church, in the county of the same name, was also planted by the labors of Elijah Baker, who began his labors within its limits about the year 1772. Previous to this, Jeremiah Walker had preached among the people, and was much opposed by the parson of the parish and others; his preaching, however, was not effectual. Soon after, Mr. Baker visited this neighborhood, and several obtained hope in Christ and were baptized. Mr. John Goodall, who had been much approved as clerk of the church, obtained a hope but thought he would do without baptism, but going to see some of his neighbors baptized, he could no longer rest, but sent the next day for the ministers and was baptized. Soon after his baptism he began to preach, and was ordained to the care of the church a few years after it was constituted. He continued to exercise the pastoral functions until 1806, when he removed to Kentucky. This church is not at present in a flourishing state. The Methodists are numerous in this neighborhood. Elder Joshua Morris, a preacher of considerable gifts, who afterwards resided in the city of Richmond and then moved to Kentucky, was a native of this church. His father and uncle also occasionally preached.

Williamsburg

This church is composed almost, if not altogether, of people of color. Moses, a black man, first preached among them, and was often taken up and whipped for holding meetings. Afterwards, Gowan, who called himself Gowan Pamphlet, moved from Middlesex, where he had been preaching for some time. He became popular among the blacks, and began to baptize as well as to preach. It seems the Association had advised that no person of color should be allowed to preach, on the pain of excommunication; against this regulation many of the blacks were rebellious, and continued still to hold meetings. Some were excluded, and among this number was Gowan, just mentioned. Continuing still to preach, and many professing faith under his ministry, not being in connection with any church himself, he formed a kind of church of some who had been baptized, who, sitting with him, received such as offered themselves; Gowan baptized them, and was, moreover, appointed their pastor. Some of them knowing how to write, a church-book was kept. They increased to a large number, so that in the year 1791, when the Dover Association was held in Mathews County, they petitioned for admittance into the Association, stating their number to be about five hundred. The Association received them, so far as to appoint persons to visit them and set things in order. These making a favorable report, they were received, and have associated ever since. A few years since Gowan died.

Grafton

This church was planted by the labor of the indefatigable E. Baker. His first labor in the bounds of this church was about the year 1775; some were awakened. This encouraged him to continue to visit them, and in no great while he baptized several. Joshua Morris, a young preacher from James City, watered the plants. John Wright was baptized about 1776, and soon began to exhort and preach. In 1777 they were constituted, and Mr. Wright became their pastor. Mr. Wright was a blessed man of God. He was faithful to occupy his talents. No man could find him out of his place. He lived and died a pious Christian, and a faithful as well as useful minister of Christ. He was a poor man, and had a family to labor for, which prevented him from being as extensively useful as he would probably have been under more affluent circumstances; but his vineyard, though small, was well kept; his duty was his delight. In discipline he was tender, yet vigilant and impartial.

Once when much disorder had crept into the arm of the church, round about Hampton, through the misconduct of Chisman, the old man went down and began to winnow with so heavy a hand that some persons observed in company he would leave but few of the Doctor's disciples; yet, said a gentleman who knew him, he would turn out the last man tomorrow before he would countenance disorder. He died about 1795, much respected by all sorts of people.

Contrasted with this character lived in the same church Dr. Thomas Chisman, a practitioner of medicine, but who, professing grace, was baptized about 1781 or 1782. He soon commenced preaching, and soon also became popular. With the judicious he never ranked above mediocrity, and indeed, hardly ascended to that grade; but with many he was considered almost inimitable. Some of the externals of the orator he possessed in a great degree; his person and mien were dignified; his voice clear and sonorous; his gesture, though violent, was expressive, and his style by no means contemptible; his manner warm, and sometimes pathetic; but his mind a perfect chaos; darkness and confusion sat regents; he had no invention, no wit, a fallacious judgment, and but little information. But these defects were considerably remedied by an invincible boldness. Taking the most ingenious texts, he would push on, in the fullness of confidence, giving interpretations which were never dreamed of by the inspired author. These discourses were much admired by many, and gained for the Doctor a great name. All this, however, might have been swallowed, even by those who knew his weight, if the Doctor had possessed that part of the preacher without which all others are null, viz., a pious life. For seven or eight years he was thought by most of his acquaintances to be singularly zealous and pious. He emancipated his slaves, and in other respects made great apparent sacrifices; but his day ended in darkness. Yielding to temptations of the most diabolical sort, he became the greatest stumbling-block that that county ever witnessed. The effects were melancholy beyond description; he was quickly excluded, but continued his vicious pursuits for a considerable time. At length he was found by the hand of God, and surely few men ever felt the rod more severely. To appearance he was exceedingly penitent, and many pitied him, and regained some faith in his piety, but others thought differently. He had been baptized by Elder Leland while he resided in Virginia, and was uncommonly attached to him. Just before he died, which happened in the year 1797, he was informed that Mr. Leland had come into Virginia and had made appointments to come down to York. On hearing this he raised himself in bed and expressed great joy at the expectation of seeing him once more. But as if God had resolved that his expectations should perish, he died a few days before Mr. Leland got down. It is not for us to decide how God has disposed of him, but it is surely lawful to wish and to pray that none such may ever again be permitted to dishonor a Gospel church in so gross a manner.

Elder Matthew Wood, a pious and useful preacher, still resides in this church, but Elder Gayle, who moved from Mathews, was, in 1796, chosen pastor. They had in the year 1805, under the united labors of Elders Gayle and Wood, one of the most heavenly revivals; not less than about 330 or 340 were baptized. After the revival they had a winnowing season. Many that seemed to be somewhat proved to be nothing. Yet there is still a large and respectable church. Elder Robert Stacy, now pastor of Abingdon, was raised up and ordained in Grafton.

Hampton

This church, through the downfall of Chisman, never prospered much until 1805, when they had a revival, and about 200 were baptized; after which they chose Elder Richard Hurst to be their pastor, who had been raised up in the church, and under whose labors chiefly the revival had been conducted. He is a lively and warm preacher. Before the revival Elder Gayle had attended them statedly.

CHAPTER TEN:
Historical Sketch of the Churches in the Second Union Meeting District in Dover Association.

Reed's

This church lies in the lower end of Caroline, having some members in the upper end of King William. The first laborers within the limits of this church were Hariss and Read. John Young soon after this became a convert and a preacher, and was ordained pastor to the church at her first constitution. The church, however, rather languished until 1788, when sixty or seventy were added.

About 1798 Mr. Young moved to Albemarle, where he has been useful, and is still living. After Mr. Young's removal the church chose for their pastor Elder John Self, who had long been an assistant elder in this church. Nothing remarkable has occurred since Mr. Self took the care. This church has generally had more than one ordained preacher. Elder Hipkins Pitman was for many years a resident member. At present Elder Richard Broaddus is a member, and labors jointly with Elder Self. Samuel Brame, a young preacher of the most conspicuous talents, was raised in this church. He afterwards removed to Halifax and died. His mother, Mrs. Brame, is now living, and a member of this church, and was in her early days a stated hearer and communicant of the famous Mr. Samuel Davies. She frequently heard Mr. Whitefield in his travels through America, and sometimes had him at her house. 'Tis pleasant to hear this mother in israel tell the interesting anecdotes which she treasured up respecting these great men of God. Mrs. Brame is truly one of the daughters of Sarah.

Considering the date at which the Baptists began to preach within the limits of this church, it might reasonably be expected that persecution more or less attended them. Nor will this expectation be disappointed. Mr. Young was committed to jail for preaching, and there kept for four months, until he appealed to the general court, and by a writ of *habeas corpus* was carried to Williamsburg. Elder H. Pitman was once taken up and threatened to be whipped, but was discharged without any further injury.

Tuckahoe

The first Baptist preacher that ever ministered within the bounds of this church was John Corbley. After Mr. Corbley had preached, the clergyman of the parish, who had come to hear him, attacked him by way of argument. After the argument had been continued for some time, and as might be expected, they came to no conclusion, the parson appointed the next Sunday to preach against the Baptists. His text was, "Will ye also go away?" His discourse made not much impression, and indeed from his subsequent conduct there were grounds to suspect that he was shaken in his own mind. For afterwards when Waller and Craig were put into prison at Fredericksburg this gentleman went to the prison and entered into a friendly conversation upon the subject of religion, and before he left them offered to be their security if they chose to give bond. It does not appear that anything effectual was done by the preaching of Mr. Corbley.

In the year 1771 Lewis Craig came and preached in the bounds of this church. God owned and blessed his labors. Many were awakened and some converted. After him came John Waller, and preached with considerable success. Mr. Craig continued to visit this place and to cultivate the seed sown. Believers were added from time to time. Satan took the alarm and stirred up opposition to Mr. Craig. A warrant was Issued, and Mr. Craig was carried before a magistrate, to whom he gave bond not to preach in the county within a certain number of days; but feeling himself hampered by this measure he thought it best to incur the penalty, and accordingly preached some little time after at one Reuben Catlett's plantation, and was taken up by virtue of a warrant and committed to prison, where he stayed three months. When Mr. Craig went to jail he found Edward Herndon and B. Choning there, who, being nothing more than exhorters, were soon turned out. In the year 1773, James Ware and James Pittman were imprisoned sixteen days for having preaching in their houses. They offered to give bond for good behavior generally, but not for permitting preaching in their houses in particular. This at first was refused them, but afterwards was acceded to and they were discharged. Of these James Pittman is still living, and a member of Tuckahoe church.

The last violence offered to any within the bounds of this church happened in the year 1775, when Younger Pitts, a preacher, and a man by the name of Picket were taken up and carried by force some distance, as if with a view to bring them before a magistrate, but after some abuse, &c., they set them at liberty.

Tuckahoe church, though small at first, became a flourishing church under the care of Elder John Shackleford, who about two years after its constitution moved from Spotsylvania and took the pastoral care. It was not until 1788 that they had a revival. It was a memorable time indeed, not in this church only, but almost throughout the State of Virginia. In the course of this divine season Mr. Shackleford baptized about 300. Mr. Shackleford's narrow circumstances, with some other causes, induced him to move to Kentucky in the year 1792. He was an excellent Gospel preacher and an affectionate man. Since his removal to Kentucky he has been very useful in the ministry. Sometime after Mr. Shackleford left the church they were fortunate enough to secure the services of Elder John Sorrel, under whose pastorship they have been happy and peaceable.

Salem

This church was taken off from Upper King and Queen. Until the year 1787 there were scarcely any Baptists within the precincts of this church. In this and the succeeding year was the great revival in neighboring churches, viz., Upper King and Queen and Tuckahoe. They met here as upon half-way ground The meetings were exceedingly powerful, and great numbers were baptized; most of them were united to the Upper King and Queen church, and fell under the care of Elder Noel; they remained as an arm of that church until 1802, when they were constituted. They have had uniform peace and love among themselves. Elders Andrew and Richard Broaddus were raised here.

Upper College

This church is so called from many of their members living on and about the lands appropriated for the use of the College of William and Mary. The Gospel was first brought into these parts by

Elder John Young and others. Their first pastor was Elder John Courtney; under his care the church prospered. When he moved to Richmond they made choice of Elder William Breeding; he was a pious and zealous preacher, and under his care they had in the years 1788 and 1789 a great revival; great numbers were baptized; but Mr. B., exerting himself beyond his strength, broke a blood vessel, and died not long after with the puking of blood. Elders Courtney, Toler, Breeding, Abraham, Whitlock, and Brame are sons of this church.

Lower College

This church was for a long time an arm of Upper College. About the time of their constitution they were attended by Elders Thomas Courtney and Robert B. Semple jointly. After Mr. Courtney removed to Richmond, R.B. Semple attended them until the year 1796, when they made choice of their present pastor, Elder John Mill. In 1800 they were favored with divine showers, and many were added. Elder Mill has been for several years in bad health, too much so to preach often. Of late he has much recovered. He was previous to his baptism in the Methodist connection; he is now a sound, steady, pious Baptist preacher. His labors in the church previous to his ill-health were greatly blessed, and it is hoped God has raised him up again for a good purpose. William Hargrove is an ordained preacher in this church, and is useful in supplying other churches as well as his own in the inability of their pastor.

Upper King and Queen

This church, in the county of the same name, was first constituted under the care of Younger Pitts, but he becoming disorderly was silenced. The church languished, and by the advice of experienced ministers dissolved their constitution, intending to join the Upper College, but being required by that church to relinquish their monthly meeting, and not wishing to do so, they again the next month resumed their constitution and chose Elder Theodrick Noel for their pastor. This happened in the year 1780. Under the ministry of Elder Noel the church flourished, and gradually increased until the year 1788: In this year God descended in mighty power. A greater work of grace has probably never been known in

Virginia within the limits of one church. It continued with little abatement during the year 1789. It was usual to baptize every monthly meeting, and for many months there were seldom, if ever, less than twenty baptized, but more frequently forty, fifty and sixty. Many respectable private persons and three or four preachers were among these. Since this blessed and memorable season there have been but few additions. In 1802 Salem was taken off from this church.

Bruington

This is a large and prosperous church indeed. Unless the compiler feels a blinding partiality for these people, they have from their beginning, and do still experience a larger portion of religious harmony and happiness than ordinarily falls to the lot of churches. But lest this fine gold should at some future day become dim, we will curtail our remarks.

Exol

This is a church of long standing, for though not the first, yet she was among the first in those parts. Mr. Ivison Lewis is still their pastor, and has been ever since their first constitution. This church, though blessed with a faithful and amiable pastor, has sustained great injury in past days through disorderly preachers. Some of them, becoming popular, drew many astray through their bad examples. The church for several years has enjoyed peace and harmony, and some degree of prosperity. Elder John Clark is an ordained and useful minister in this church.

Exol was an orderly and thriving church until 1788, when they had a considerable revival, in which about two hundred and fifty were baptized. It was after this revival that the bars of discipline were measurably broken down. Few churches have raised more preachers than this; some good and valuable, others the reverse. Mr. Lewis, their pastor, is in the highest estimation as a good man and a zealous, active, heart-searching preacher, he aims chiefly at persuading sinners to repent, and many, through him, have been persuaded.

Lower King and Queen

This is a mother church, spoken of in our General History. The church did not advance in any considerable degree under the care of Elder Ware, yet there were some very respectable and valuable characters added. After his death, which happened about the year 1804, Mr. William Todd was called to the pastoral care. Few churches are more united to a pastor than this church is to Mr. Todd. In the years 1805 and 1806 they were visited by sovereign mercy. Her cords were lengthened and her stakes were strengthened. In 1807 the lower arm of this church was constituted and called Pocorone. They have two meetinghouses, some distance from each other, in both of which business is transacted.

Pocorone

This church was taken from the last-named church, and is orderly and happy, feeding upon the bread of life sent them from God by Elder James Healy.

Upper Essex

This is a mother church. Lewis Craig and others, as early as 1768 or 1769, preached in these parts. Their labors were not in vain; a few were baptized from time to time, until in the year 1772 a church was organized and lay elders ordained. Not having any pastor, Mr. Craig continued to visit them, and was much beloved.

When he could not attend as often as they wished, they invited Elder Joseph Bledsoe to take the care of them. He, however, living in Spotsylvania could not, or did not, perform the duties of pastor. This ended rather in confusion. In August, 1773, Elder Noel was baptized, and soon began to blow the Gospel trumpet. Being ordained, he discharged the duty of pastor without being regularly inaugurated. Few men have been more successful in the ministry than Mr. Noel. It is probable that he has baptized as many persons as any other preacher now living in Virginia. Among them have been a number of preachers, some of whom rank high in the ministry as men of talents and usefulness. He is now, and has been for many years, pastor of the Upper King and Queen church.

The first person that Mr. Noel baptized after he was ordained was a young woman. Her brother promised to dip any person who should dip her. In fulfillment of his word, he made the attempt, but could not get Mr. Noel under the water. Being pursued by some of the wicked, who resented this treatment of the preacher, he was obliged to make the best of his way off. He died a few weeks after, having first sent for Mr. Noel to ask pardon. Mr. Noel's talents as a preacher seemed to be singularly calculated for a revival; hence, from this or some other cause, since the revival has declined, his popularity as a preacher is considerably lessened; his friends, however, hope to see him blaze forth again in his last days. Upper Essex church has been, in one sense, a little like the burning bush: they have had, from the first, much of the fire of contention among themselves, and yet they are a respectable church. They have no pastor, but procure the stated services of neighboring preachers. They have some very worthy private members.

Piscataway

This church is under the care of the Rev. James Greenwood, as may be seen by the table. From its constitution Mr. Greenwood has been the faithful minister of this people. The church, under his care, has prospered without intermission. In 1788 and 1804 there were precious revivals, in each of which years a respectable number was added to the church; but it is worthy of note that even in the coldest and dullest seasons the church still gradually gained strength, enjoying uniform serenity and peace. Elder Greenwood has been for a time in a very low state of health; but friends of piety begin to hope that he will recover, and that God will add a few more years to so useful a life; for if it were said that of all religious characters he is the most spotless, all who know him, himself excepted, would pronounce it a well-merited eulogy. He is now (1809) about sixty years of age, and has been truly a laborer in the Lord's vineyard nearly or quite forty years. From Piscataway was constituted, in 1790, Bruington, under the care of Robert B. Semple.

Glebe Landing

This is a mother church, for the account of whose origin see General History. William Mullen was their pastor for many years, and a faithful one he was. During his continuance among them order and peace prevailed. They were revived by divine grace in the year 1788, when about one hundred were added. The church was happy, and gradually increased until the year 1792, when God called hence their faithful and diligent pastor. No church probably ever felt the loss of so valuable a preacher less than they did that of Mr. Mullen, for they immediately procured the stated monthly services of Elder Lewis, who has attended them ever since.

As to discipline, they had several old and experienced members who were fully competent to the task of setting things in order. Of these Richard Street was first appointed moderator. He dying in some short time, they appointed John Sadler, who lived many years, and during his life discharged the duties of his office with as much diligence, judgment, and success as any minister in Virginia could have done. These may be called the precious sons of Zion. They have entered into their rest, and their works will follow them.

Mr. Mullen as a preacher could not be said to rank high. His talents in the pulpit were not conspicuous, yet he might be called a solid and sound experimental preacher. He was a judicious disciplinarian, and in preserving order he succeeded better than common. He died in full hope and assurance of a resurrection to a better life.

Hermitage

This is a church of long standing, having been constituted from Glebe Landing under the care of John Mullen. During his life they enjoyed peace and prosperity in a moderate degree; but about the year 1793 or 1794 they lost their pastor. Soon after his death John Healey was ordained to the pastoral care, having long exercised a public gift among them. In 1802 he also died. Since his death the church has had no pastor, but are favored with the monthly services of Elder Lewis. They have also two gifted members, viz., James Healey, ordained, and Samuel Jesse, licensed. These are old Baptists, but young preachers thrust into the vineyard at the eleventh hour. Being faithful, they will doubtless receive their penny. Mr. Healey attends Pocorone church in the nature of a pastor, though not regularly installed. Mr. John Mullen was among the first who professed vital faith in those parts in which he resided. From the time of his profession to the day of his death he had the reputation of being a spotless Christian. He was indeed a good man, though not an able preacher. His life was good preaching to all who knew him. As he lived so he died, beloved of God and approved of men.

Zoar

This church was stricken off from Hermitage, under the charge of Elder David Corey, but in the midst of their flattering prospects the Great Shepherd and Bishop has in the mysteries of His providence thought proper to snatch from them their beloved pastor; he died February, 1809, lamented, deeply lamented, by every good man that knew him. Captain Corey was a native of New England, but came to Virginia and professed religion at an early period of life. It was not, however, until he had been baptized fifteen or sixteen years that he began to preach. He labored only five or six years in the ministry; during that time he did much good round about in his neighborhood. He had followed seafaring for a livelihood for many years, but in consequence of its interference with his ministry he had in a great measure laid it aside and commenced farming.

Pettsworth or Gloucester

The Gospel first made its way into this neighborhood through the ministry of Elder Lewis. Mr. Robert Hudgin, a native of Mathews, had moved into this part of Gloucester, but in some of his visits to Mathews, having heard Mr. Lewis preach, he invited him to come into his neighborhood, which he did in the year 1775. His labors were productive of great good. Several joined the society, and finally a church was constituted, under the care of Robert Hudgin, who began to preach soon after he was baptized. This church continued to prosper moderately until Mr. Hudgin's death. They were then left without any person to go in and out before them. They at length did what it would hardly have been supposed would have been done by Virginians; they chose for their pastor William Lemon, a man of color. He, though not white as to his natural complexion, had been washed in the laver of regeneration; he had been purified and made white in a better sense. As a preacher, though weak, he was lively and affecting. He also died after several years. Since then they have been destitute of stated ministerial aid. Mr. William Leigh exercises a public gift, and, it is said, is useful. The Methodists are numerous in these parts.

Abingdon

This church in the lower end of Gloucester was taken off from Pettsworth. The members chiefly live in that part which has sometimes been called Guinea. When Mr. Lewis first preached in this neighborhood he met with violent opposition from individuals; but treating them with levity and meekness he soon made many of them as friendly as they had been hostile. This church is under the care of Robert Stacy, a sound, good preacher. They appear to be happy under his ministry.

Mathews.

As early as the year 1771 one Johnston, a Baptist, preached within the bounds of this church. His preaching left no durable impression. In 1772 or 1773 Rev. Ivison Lewis, who was not yet baptized, went down on a visit to his relations, who lived in this county, and having lately obtained a hope of salvation, he was zealous to inculcate the necessity of vital religion wherever he went. His conversation made such impressions upon the minds of those with whom he conversed that it was rumored about in the neighborhood that a new preacher had come among them. This drew out a large company of people to the house where Mr. Lewis stayed to hear him preach, without any previous appointment. Mr. Lewis, having never attempted to preach in regular form, felt much alarmed; but, relying upon supernatural aid, he went on to address the people. God unstopped their ears and opened their hearts. They received his doctrine as from God. Mr. Lewis, not long after, became a Baptist and a preacher, and continued to visit Mathews with much success. A number of respectable characters professed faith and were baptized. Mr. Lewis, though he lived about forty miles off, visited this place once a month for several years. In the year 1782 the church induced David Tinsley to settle among them. His labors were not as beneficial as was hoped. In the course of two or three years, viz., 1785, he moved off to Georgia, where, turning an Arminian, he joined the General Baptists, headed by Jeremiah Walker. Tinsley was a good preacher, and had been, in the early part of his ministry, considerably successful as an itinerant.

After Mr. Tinsley's removal Mathews church had no preacher until John Gayle, a gifted member, was ordained. Under his ministry and the ministry of visiting preachers they had a great revival in the year 1787; several hundreds were baptized. By many judicious professors this revival was thought not to have been prudently conducted, as it respected some of the leading visiting ministers. Persons were baptized upon too slight reasons, as many thought. This circumstance, added to the slackness of their discipline, produced a good deal of unhappiness after the revival subsided. Nor, indeed, have they since ever completely regained that regularity and order so necessary to the full enjoyment of religious society. In many respects, however, this is a commendable church, having some who have not defiled their garments. They long tried to secure a preacher of talents to reside among them, but did not succeed entirely. For a few years Mr. Jacob Creath, a preacher of popular talents, dwelt among them. He, however, married in Lancaster, and removed thither, and then went to Kentucky, where he still lives. A few years past they made choice of Mr. William Fitchell, a gifted man and one of their own members, as a pastor. No persecution further than reproaches and slander has ever disgraced the people in this neighborhood.

CHAPTER ELEVEN:
Historical Sketches of the Churches in the Third Union Meeting District

Hanover

This church was taken off from Tuckahoe and Nomini. Jesse Davis, some years after their constitution, was inducted into the church as pastor. Before Mr. Davis became pastor a Mr. Sthretchley used to preach and read sermons for them; but this not being satisfactory to the church, Mr. Sthretchley took umbrage and joined the Methodists, and afterwards positively professed himself a deist.

Under Mr. Davis's ministry Hanover has been a respectable and orderly church. Mr. Toler once attended them statedly.

Nomini

Mr. Lunsford was the first who preached in these parts. He had baptized a few scattered members previous to the year 1783. In this year Elder Toler, who is now the pastor of this church, was invited by an old lady, who had been baptized by Mr. Lunsford, to preach in the neighborhood of the present meetinghouse; he went, and but few people attended; these were distant and reserved; none but a very poor man invited him to his house. Yet how unsearchable are the ways of God! This meeting was the beginning of great events, as it respects this neighborhood. Mrs. Pearce, wife of Captain Joseph Pearce, attended, having been in a low state of health for some time; the Word reached her. When Mr. Toler attended again, Mrs. Pearce sent for him to Mr. Templeman's, her son-in-law, and had the preaching at his house, he being from home on a journey. His preaching made deep impressions upon her mind. When Mr. Templeman returned, he was sorely displeased at the liberty which had been taken with his house, and talked of leaving it, as being contaminated. Before Mr. Toler came again, Mrs. Pearce died a great penitent, enjoining it on her husband to open his house for preaching. To this Captain Pearce consented, and had Mr. Toler's next meeting appointed at his house. Light dawned. The prejudices of the people wore off. Several persons of different classes were converted and baptized. Among them was Mr. Templeman, mentioned above, and his wife, Captain Pearce, and some of his children (and in a few years *all* of them), and some other people. This, says Mr. Toler, was a gracious glorious, pleasant time. Those who had been baptized by Mr. Toler, together with a few others who had been baptized previous to his coming, were formed into a church April 29, 1786, having in all seventeen members. Elder Toler was chosen to attend them as pastor, and in a year or two moved here to live.

On the same day after the constitution of the church five others were baptized, and at the end of this year the number was seventy-three. In 1787 it increased to 119; in 1788 to 222; in 1789 to 300; in 1790 to 331; in 1791 to 348; in 1793 to 354; in 1793 to 357; in 1794 to 367; and in 1795 to 408. From this date for ten years there were but few additions. Order and discipline were preserved, but professors seemed to lack life and spirit in religion. By deaths and removals the church was much reduced in number. The preachers continued their meetings, and afterwards found that even in this lifeless season their labors were not lost. This was a trying time to the feelings of these public servants, especially to Mr. Toler, their pastor. So much was he worn down by discouragements that he had strong thoughts of moving off. When every hope of another revival was almost given up, quite unexpectedly, in the early part of the summer of 1806, the work of God again appeared. In a short time it spread to an extent beyond the former revival. In three months ninety were baptized. At various times thirty, forty, fifty, and sixty were baptized at one time, so that from first to last in this revival there have been added between five and six hundred, mounting the church from its low standing up to eight hundred and seventy-five—the most numerous church in Virginia. This was a pure revival. Very little extravagance of any kind was ever seen. The convictions appeared to be deep and powerful, and the conversions clear and rational. It was a harvest indescribably glorious.

Mr. Toler, the pastor of the church, became a Baptist at a very early period of life. He soon commenced public speaking. Appearing to be promising, he was assisted by a friend to acquire a more extensive education, having had rather limited opportunities previously; accordingly he read under the tutorage of Dr. Samuel

Jones in Pennsylvania. His progress was considerable. After Mr. Toler left school he became a correct and handsome speaker. As a speaker he was sound and experimental, affectionate in his address, and when animated himself, very animating to his hearers. Few preachers having families have been more indefatigable in propagating the Gospel than Mr. Toler. He has been in the service now between thirty and forty years.

Mr. Templeman, mentioned above, began to preach soon after he was baptized, and was ordained in 1792. Having been long accustomed to public life as an active magistrate, as a merchant, and as one who is often called on to transact the affairs of others, Mr. Templeman has divided his attention between these employments and his ministry. It is hardly probable that many, if any, can be found in Virginia who have succeeded so completely in giving satisfaction in so many various occupations. There are but few that ever heard him who do not think him a good preacher; and it happens, unfortunately in some respects, that himself is one of those few, for it is exceedingly difficult to get him to preach where there are any others. As a man of business, both as it respects integrity and cleverness, he is universally esteemed by all who know him. In 1807 he was chosen moderator to the Association, and acquitted himself with general approval. His absence prevented his continuance in that office. Besides these there are other preachers and public speakers in this church. Of these Mr. Hazard has been ordained.

Besides those remaining in this extensive church they have lost some distinguished members. Captain Pearce, mentioned above, from the time of his profession until his death, was a pious and steady member, as well as an excellent deacon. His house was a house of preaching as well as prayer.

Mrs. Steptoe, a lady of the first rank, both as to family and fortune, was long a member of this society. She was an ornament to religion. She took her seat in the church about 1786. In her will she left an annuity of £10 to Mr. Toler so long as he should remain pastor of Nomini church.

Robert Carter, Esq., once a member of the Virginia Executive Council, and on that account commonly called "Counselor" Carter, was baptized by Mr. Lunsford shortly after he began to preach in these parts. He was one of the richest men in the State of

Virginia, having, as some say, 600 or 800 negroes, besides immense bodies of land, &c. After being baptized some years he became conscientious about the lawfulness of hereditary slavery. In a letter to Mr. Rippon, of London, he says: "The toleration of slavery indicates great depravity of mind." In conformity to this sentiment he gradually emancipated all that he possessed.

This was a noble and disinterested sacrifice. For fourteen or fifteen years he continued an orderly Baptist; but being a man naturally of an unstable disposition, and falling in with certain Arminian writings, he fully embraced their doctrines. Had he stopped here he might still have continued in the Baptist society, though not so happily as before. But, alas, there are so many wrong roads in religious pursuits, that when a man once gets wrong, it is impossible to foresee where he will stop. From Arminian errors Mr. Carter fell into the chimerical whims of Swedenborg. When he first heard of the books of Swedenborg he made very light of them; but upon reading them, having a mind naturally fond of specious novelty, he fully embraced the whole of that absurd system, and was of course excluded from the Baptists. He was now as zealous for the New Jerusalem church as he had been formerly for the Baptists. He moved to Baltimore in order to find a preacher and a society of his own sentiments, and expended large sums of money to have Swedenborg's writings republished. He continued orderly in his moral conduct, and died a few years since, after having lived to a considerable age. Mr. Toler's amiable character may be gathered from his labors described above.

Farnham

This church was raised under the united labors of James Greenwood and William Mullen. About 1776 Mr. Greenwood was invited by a Mrs. Sucket, who lived in Richmond County, on the Rappahannock, to preach her house. Before he went he was apprehensive of considerable opposition, but was agreeably disappointed. The people were attentive. Being encouraged, he and Mr. William Mullen continued to visit them, preaching at private houses, until a stage and seats were fixed. They were sometimes threatened to be treated roughly, but these threats never were executed. Their labors proved effectual, and several were baptized and a church constituted. Mr. Mullen continued to visit them statedly for twelve or thirteen years and the church prospered. After him they chose Mr. Philips for their pastor, who had been raised among them. Mr. P. not being a man of popular talents, the church rather declined until a little time before his death, which happened in the spring of 1806. Truly could it be said of Mr. P. that his last days were his best days. For two or three years times were much better and the church looked up. He baptized a considerable number within about two years before he died. He is one of the very few concerning whom there is any good ground to suppose that his death was brought on by the ordinance of baptism. Having several persons to baptize on a cold, damp day, and having also to preach out of doors on a stage, where he was much exposed to the wind, he observed to some friends that he had rather wear out than rust out, and went on with his service. In a few days he was taken with pleurisy. In his illness he appeared to have and to enjoy the divine presence in a glorious manner so long as he was in his senses; and even in his delirium his conversation, though incoherent, was almost wholly upon religion. Just before he died he said with a strong voice, "Come, let us go," and immediately fell asleep. If any shall say, 'Here is an instance of baptism killing a person,' we reply, 'So it may be; yet it proves that God blesses the ordinance either by preventing any evil even where it might reasonably be looked for, or that, permitting the evil, He makes it terminate in the greatest good.' Since Mr. P.'s death they have had no pastor, but have had preaching from neighboring ministers and from some licensed preachers in their own church.

Wicomico

This church was taken off in the year 1804 from Morattico and constituted under the care of Elder Samuel Straughan. Few churches enjoy more harmony and brotherly love than this. They seek not their own things, but the things of Jesus Christ. As it is a new church there has nothing extraordinary occurred worthy of notice, except that soon after their constitution they had a comfortable revival, which swelled their number from twenty to two hundred and forty.

Mr. Straughan was baptized about the year 1803, and after some time began to preach. His gifts are of the most useful sort. He is "an eloquent man and mighty in the Scriptures." As he is still young we will only add our devout wishes that he may go on in the way he has begun, and that he may abound more and more.

Morattico

This has been a church of as high standing as any in the Dover Association. Mr. Lunsford was the most successful Baptist preacher in these parts. Soon after he first visited them, his ;abors were blessed, and the church was constituted, including all the members within the four or five lowest counties in the Northern Neck. It appears, from their church book, that in no great while after they were organized as a church, they were respectable both for numbers and for men of weight. Mr. Lunsford was their pastor from the time of their constitution until his death. Never was a minister more beloved by a people, and never, probably, was there one that deserved it more. He has not been dead more than sixteen years, and yet he is seldom mentioned by any of the members of the church without some lamentation.

When Mr. Lunsford died, they were left destitute. Mr. Toler attended them statedly, for some time, but being nearly forty miles from them, he could not perform those duties which were requisite. In the year 1799, Mr. Jacob Creath married, and settled within the bounds of this church. Mr. Creath being a man of talents, the church soon called upon him to take the pastoral care, which he accepted. Under his ministry, they seemed rather to rise; but in a few years, Mr. Creath became dissatisfied with his circumstance, and in order to better them, moved to Kentucky in 1803. The church was again left destitute. Mr. Toler and others visited them occasionally until about 1808, when they procured the stated services of Elder Samuel Straughn, a preacher who had care of the Wicomico church, and who had been baptized by Mr. Creath, just before he moved. The church, from the time of Mr. Lunsford's death, had by deaths, removals, &c. gradually declined; but few were baptized. But within three or four years past, all the churches in the Northern Neck, belonging to the Dover Association, have somewhat revived. Morattico, among the rest, has gained some ground, though by no means the same as some others. The remains of a respectable congregation of Presbyterians are still in this neighborhood. This congregation once had the celebrated Mr. Waddell for their minister. Since his removal, they have declined, until but few remain. Their meetinghouse is occupied by the Baptists chiefly.

Table of the Goshen Association

Year	Original Number	Present Number	By Whom Planted	Former Pastors	Current Pastors	Counties
1769	30	285	S. Hariss, James Read	J. Waller	A. Waller	Spotsylvania
1791	43	35	J. Waller	H. Pendleton	H. Pendleton	Spotsylvania
1767	25	21	S. Hariss, James Read	L. Craig	E. Abel	Spotsylvania
1789	40	46	J. Waller	H. Goodloe	H. Goodloe	Spotsylvania
1788	25	198	T. Mastin	T. Mastin	A Waller	Spotsylvania
1778	25	130	Joseph Bledsoe, L. Craig, A. Dudley	J. Bledsoe, A. Bledsoe	E. Ely	Spotsylvania
1774	45	175	J. Waller	N. Holloway	A. Waller	Spotsylvania
1804	15	51	A. Broadus	A. Broadus	A. Broadus	Spotsylvania
1805	25	45	J. Leland	Nat. Saunders	A. Waller	Spotsylvania
1782		97	J. Waller	W. Waller, J. Waller		Spotsylvania and Caroline
1800	66	108	A. Broadus	A. Broadus	A. Broadus	Caroline
1773	71	205	S. Hariss, J. Read	J. Waller	A. Broadus	Caroline
		130	J. Waller, J. Leland	J.W.H. Goodloe, J Poindexter	E. Purrington	Goochland and Lousia
1776	35	500	J. Waller, R. Ford	R. Ford, H. French	L. Page	Goochland
1770	16	85	S. Hariss, J. Read	D. Thompson, J. Leland, G. Morris	W. Waller	Louisa
1791	50	226	J. Waller	J. Poindexter	J. Poindexter	Louisa
1777	60	64	J. Waller	W. Dawson	H. Goodloe	Louisa
1791	65	75	J. Waller	J and A. Waller	W. Cook	Louisa
1774	20	180	E. Craig, A. Bledsoe	A. Bledsoe		Orange

Name of churches
Wallers
Mine Road
Craigs
Piney Branch
Massaponax
Wilderness
Guineas
Fredericksburg
Zoar
County Line
Bethel
Burrus's
Williams's
Licking Hole
Thomson's or Goldmine
Roundabout
Scarrot's
Little River
N. Fork, Pamunkey

CHAPTER TWELVE:

History of the Proceedings of the Orange and Goshen Associations

The proceedings of the two districts north of James River, from the division of the General Association in 1783, to the subdivision in 1788, have already been given.

After the separation from the Dover the Orange Association met for the first time at Crooked Run meetinghouse, in Culpeper County, May 8, 1789. Letters from twenty-two churches were received, affording the most pleasing intelligence of the spread of the Gospel and of the increase of the churches.

October 9, 1789.—They met at Pamunkey meetinghouse, in Orange County.

June 1790.—Mr. Iceland, as moderator, called an extraordinary session of the Association at Thompson's meetinghouse, Louisa County.

October 8, 1790.—They met at Carter's Run meetinghouse, in Fauquier County.

October 13, 1791.—They met at Rapidan meetinghouse, Culpeper County (now Madison).[1]

There was no business transacted at any of these sessions which will not be noticed in some more convenient place, except the division of Orange District into three others, by which the name Orange was dropped. The entry for the division is in the following words:

We have agreed to divide our Association into three District Associations, as follows: Beginning at Fredericksburg; thence up the Rappahannock River to Barret's Ford; thence along the Carolina road to the Three-Notched road; thence down the same to the Burnt Ordinary; thence down the Byrd

---

[1] Messrs. Waller And Leland acted alternately as clerk and moderator until Mr. Iceland removed to New England in 1790, when Mr. John Poindexter wan Appointed clerk, and continued until the division of the Association.—*Author's note.*

Creek to James River, to compose one Association to be known by the name of 'Goshen Association.'

Secondly. Beginning at Barret's Ford; thence up the Rapidan to the head of the same, leaving Blue Run church to her choice which of the two upper Associations she chooses to join. All the churches of the south side of the said boundaries to compose a second Association, which is to be known by the name of the 'Albemarle Association.'

Thirdly. All churches on the north side of said boundaries to compose a third Association, to be known by the name of the 'Culpeper Association.'

Of these three districts we must treat separately, beginning with the Goshen.

This Association contains all the churches in the counties of Spotsylvania and Louisa, together with a part of those in Caroline, Hanover, Goochland and Orange.

They held their first meeting at Roundabout meetinghouse, Louisa County, Friday, 17th October, 1792. Letters were received from fifteen churches, eleven of which sent an account of their members in full fellowship, amounting to 1,434, in which also it was stated that there had been 170 baptized in the course of the preceding year. In no church is any revival mentioned, except at the Roundabout, where Elder John Poindexter had the pastoral care. In that church there had been 109 baptized in the course of one year.

No business of a general nature was transacted; and, indeed, very little of any sort. The next Association was appointed at Burris's meetinghouse, in Caroline County.

October 15, 1793.—They met according to appointment. Letters were received from sixteen churches. Two only speak of a revival, viz., Salem and Roundabout; the rest complain of great coldness and languor. The Rev. John Waller, the oldest minister in the Association, and among the oldest in Virginia, applied to the Association for, and received a letter of recommendation, having resolved to move to South Carolina.

It was agreed to print the present minutes. The next Association was appointed at Thompson's meetinghouse, Louisa County.

October 17, 1794.—They met according to appointment. They

were visited by John Waller, a father in this Association. Letters from seventeen churches were read. Several churches speak of hopeful appearances; but none of revivals. Since the last Association it appears that in all the churches there were 126 baptized. No business of a general nature was transacted. The next Association was appointed at Bledsoe's meetinghouse, Orange County, beginning on the third Saturday in October.[1]

Saturday, October 17, 1795.—They met according to appointment. Letters from seventeen churches were read. A complaint of coldness is universal in all the churches. The Association recommended a day of fasting and prayer to be observed throughout the churches to avert the dangers apprehended from the treaty of amity and commerce between Great Britain and America. This measure, doubtless, arose from the violent party heat which at that time agitated the minds of Americans generally, and which it seems frequently made its way into the pulpit and religious assemblies. If the Association stepped out of her province by interference in political measures, she seems to have done it in a safe way. Fasting and prayer will seldom do us much injury, although we may be put to it from strange causes.

The following query was introduced: "Has a minister a right to baptize persons and join them to a church at a remote distance?" which was answered in the negative. From this query and solution it seems great disturbance arose. George Morris, an ordained minister, had been in the habit of violating this rule. When the subject was debated in the Association, Mr. Morris became so exasperated that he abruptly left his seat and went home. Continuing still to profess the same principles, and publicly to censure the Association for their decision, and thereby to create no little confusion, the moderator, by the advice of friends, thought proper to call a conference, *i.e.,* a kind of occasional Association. The conference accordingly met at Waller's meetinghouse on the first Saturday in January, 1796. Thirteen churches were represented, and Morris was present. The moderator, by the instruction of the conference, asked Morris such questions as tended to effect a reconciliation if it was possible; but Morris continued refractory. Whereupon he

---

[1] Upon trial it was found more convenient for the Association to commence their session on Saturdays and adjourn on Mondays.—*Author's note.*

was censured by the conference, and cited to appear at the next Association to answer for his conduct. At the next Association no reconciliation could be effected, and a committee was appointed to deal with Morris before his churches. The committee reported that they had settled the existing differences to the mutual satisfaction of all parties. This, however, was but the beginning of trouble arising from Morris. The next Association was appointed at Waller's meetinghouse, Spotsylvania County.

October 15, 1796.—They met according to adjournment. Only twelve churches were represented. Three, under the care of George Morris, adhered to him in his contest with the Association, and at this session wrote to the Association remonstrating in favor of Morris. A committee was appointed by the Association to visit and admonish these churches. Their return is in these words:

> *The committee are happy to inform the churches that they have settled the existing differences to the satisfaction of Elder Morris and his churches.*

For the credit of religion it is devoutly to be wished that this reconciliation had been permanent; but the sequel will show that Morris was not for peace.

It had been the rule hitherto for the Association to appoint quarterly meetings, from year to year, in the different parts of the district. At this session a yearly meeting to last two days was agreed on in lieu of quarterly meetings; the ministers to attend them were nominated by the Association, and responsible for failure. It is pleasing to find from the record of this Association that in the midst of distress the Lord remembered mercy to some of the churches. Two churches speak of a comfortable revival. The next Association was appointed at Burris's meetinghouse, Caroline County.

October 31, 1797.—They met according to appointment. Letters were received from seventeen churches; most of whom complain of coldness. Some precious exceptions, however, are made. The churches at Waller's, Burris's and Williams's meetinghouses speak the language of praise. At this Association was Elder John Leland from New England; his preaching was not in words only, but in power and in the Holy Ghost. No business worthy of historical attention was transacted. It was an agreeable time. The next

Association was appointed at Foster's Creek meetinghouse, Louisa County. -

October 30, 1798.—They met according to appointment. Letters from sixteen churches were received. With scarcely an exception, they all expressed sad complaints of a declension in religion. No important matter was taken up except the revisal of the confession of faith. The next Association was appointed at Wilderness meetinghouse, Spotsylvania County.

October 19, 1799.—Letters from eighteen churches were received. It appears to have been a comfortable season. The following is an extract from the general observations made in the record book:— "Nothing of the pleasing kind appears on the face of the letters except a spirit of general love and union." It was at this session that Elder H. French, and his church at Licking Hole, were received as a part of this Association. No business of a general nature, not mentioned elsewhere, occupied their attention at this session. The next Association was appointed at County Line meetinghouse, Caroline County, to commence on the third Friday in October.

October 16, 1801.—Letters from twenty-one churches were received, all of whom either say that they are in a state of languor, or that the revival is in a state of declension. Winter and summer do not more regularly succeed each other in the natural world than revivals and declensions in the religious. A good God makes them both subserve His purpose. The next Association was appointed at Roundabout meetinghouse, to commence the second Saturday in October.

During this year a mournful scene took place. George Morris (of whose turbulent deportment towards the Association mention has already been made), a preacher of some talents, who had the pastoral and partial care of three churches, was by common report charged with crimes of the deepest dye. Such was his influence with the church of which he was a member that, notwithstanding the reports were well authenticated, they paid no attention to them until urged to it by a committee appointed by the Association. Morris contrived to keep back many of the charges, and finally to obtain from the church a favorable decision as to such as were exhibited. The moderator of the Association, who was one of the committee, finding the matter thus smothered to the disgrace of religion, called the Association together. They met in conference, in Waller's meetinghouse, on the fourth Saturday in February. Twenty churches sent deputies. After a fair and full investigation of the business before the conference, it was decided that Morris was guilty of the crimes laid to his charge, and that the church had manifested a criminal partiality in retaining him in her fellowship. The church was excluded from the Association and a committee appointed by the conference to visit them for the purpose of pronouncing the sentence of exclusion, as also to invite a minority of the church, who differed from the other part, to form a church among themselves.

The new church, under the name of Goldmine, was accordingly constituted, and in a little time was joined by several of the majority. But what was more consoling, they were blessed with the outpouring of the Holy Spirit. A precious revival ensued. Many were added by baptism. Morris and his party, as being the majority, retained the old meetinghouse and kept up preaching. But to them none were disposed to unite themselves. After a vain attempt for two or three years to stand upon independent ground, being forsaken by their most respectable members, Morris proposed that he and his party should again coalesce with the Goldmine church by making concessions. To this the Goldmine church replied that they were at all times ready to hear what any individuals of them had to say, but could not receive them as a body, seeing this would recognize in them a character which they had hitherto discountenanced. Another reason, it was said, existed for not receiving them into their body, viz.: There were among them many persons under the imputation of gross immoralities. So the matter rests. Morris and some of the most obstinate of his party continue out of communion. The churches called Salem and Bethesda, of whom Morris had the ministerial care, adhered to him in his contest. These churches were also expelled from the Association and a new one, formed out of the minority, received. In these proceedings some, who were by no means favorable to Morris, were of opinion that the Association were in some of her measures rather precipitate; not using towards the churches deluded by Morris a sufficient degree of lenity. Such opinions were probably induced by a partial view of the subject, especially through the want of sufficient acquaintance with the intriguing temper of Morris. The following is a short comment made on his character by the secretary and sanctioned by the Association:

> *Like Diotrephes, he loved and sought the pre-eminence. Jealousy and discontent apparently were his inseparable concomitants. In a word, he was not unlike Jude's wandering stars, always unsteady, until they shoot in some eccentric direction, and disappear forever.*

Having given a succinct account of this schism, from first to last, it is proper to return to the common proceedings of the Association.

October 15, 1802.—The Association met according to appointment. Letters were received from eighteen churches. The comment made by the secretary as to the state of religion is in the following words:

> *It appears as if poor Zion will shake to her centre, and her watchmen proclaim 'the glory is departed from israel.' Yet the mighty God of Jacob is still the same, and His everlasting arms are underneath the mourning sons of Zion. Several of our churches seem to enjoy gentle breezes of divine grace....*

In Bethel church, one of the constituents of this Association, a rule had been formed, by a large majority, compelling each person, under the penalty of the displeasure of the church, to contribute towards her expenses according to what he was worth. This rule gave great umbrage not only to a minority in the church, but to other churches likewise. At this Association a query was introduced in the following words:

"Does the Association approve of a church that raises money by assessing her members?" which received the following solution:

> *We do not approve the method of raising money by assessments, upon the principle of its not being sanctioned by New Testament examples, and the general principles of the Baptists, and because of the unhappy consequences which may result from such a practice.*

Would not the solution to this query have been better thus: The

New Testament certainly requires of every member of a church to contribute to the expenses of religion according to what he hath, but says nothing as to how this must be carried into effect, leaving the mode of collecting discretionary? We are therefore persuaded that the above mode is lawful; but all things that are lawful are not expedient. We are of the opinion that at this time this mode is not expedient, because of the prejudices of many who have not rightly considered the subject.

This was an agreeable session. The next Association was appointed at Licking Hole meetinghouse.

October 15, 1803.—Letters from sixteen churches were read. The comment made by the secretary was, "that the letters breathe the spirit of universal love and harmony, but complain of coldness." Of the Association he says: "Much peace and love prevailed among the members of this Association during the whole session."

It was at this session they first took up the business of composing a history of the Baptists in the Goshen District, and accordingly made an order requesting the churches to send accounts to the next Association. This plan was afterwards relinquished in favor of the present work. The next Association was appointed at Bethel meetinghouse, Caroline County.

October 20, 1801.—Letters from eighteen churches were read. In a few churches revivals are mentioned. All the churches seem to enjoy peace. The next Association was appointed at Waller's meetinghouse.

October 19, 1805.—Letters were received from eighteen churches. Two or three churches speak of revivals. From the foregoing Association 216 had been baptized. The next Association was appointed at Goldmine meetinghouse, Louisa County.

October 18, 1806.—Letters from eighteen churches were received. No revival, yet times were rather promising than otherwise. The subject of encouraging missionaries was taken up in this session. The Association expressed her approbation of encouraging missionaries to travel and preach the Gospel among the indian tribes, provided any practicable plan could be invented.

During the foregoing year, and for many years, the churches had been much imposed upon by certain impostors, who went under the appellation of Baptist preachers. In order to detect such characters the Association entered into the following resolution;

*In order to detect impostors traveling through the church-
es under the name of licensed or ordained Baptist preachers,
this Association resolves to adopt the following method, viz.:
Every stranger coming under the name of a Baptist preacher
shall produce to the church where he may preach, or have
opportunities to preach, a copy of the minutes of the Association where he professes himself a member, showing his
name in the list of delegates, the minutes to be dated within
one year.*

The Association authorized the secretary to publish this resolution in some public paper printed in the city of Richmond, recommending and requesting at the same time the adoption of a similar rule by all our sister Associations in the State. Nothing could
be more salutary than a regulation of this sort. The society had
been much disgraced by some of these miscreants, who had been
fostered by inexperienced, well-meaning Baptists. The next Association was appointed at Guinea's Bridge meetinghouse.

Several excellent circular letters were written for this Association by Messrs. A. Broaddus, A. Waller, and John Poindexter, alternately; but being chiefly on doctrines of divinity often treated
of in religious books, they have not been noticed.

CHAPTER THIRTEEN:
Historical Sketches of the Churches in the Goshen Association

Waller's

This is a mother church indeed. Their corresponding letter to the Association in 1791 says: "We have lately constituted two new churches, which make fifteen that have been taken off from our church." She was first called Lower Spotsylvania, in contradistinction to Upper Spotsylvania, now called Craig's. Elder John Waller was chosen pastor January 2, 1770, which was a few months after the church was constituted; he continued to fill that office until 1793, when he moved to South Carolina. When Mr. J. Waller declared himself independent, this church adhered to him, and was, of course, excluded from the Association. When he was reinstated, so was the church. It is worthy of remark, that although Mr. Waller was an Arminian, and on that account broke with the Association, and carried with him this church, yet the church was far from being unanimously Arminian.

Some of Mr. Waller's nearest relatives stood firm to the Gospel plan. At one time, previous to Mr. Waller's reinstatement into the Association, there were few, if any, less than 1,500 members in this church. Although she has had various ebbs and flows, and knows well the difference between declensions and revivals, yet few, if any, have experienced more uninterrupted prosperity. Of so much importance to the good standing of a church is an exemplary preacher, who understands the art of combining the hearts of all in one great object, it seemed providential that, when their former pastor, who had grown old and thought proper to change his place of residence, their present pastor was ripe, both in talents and experience, to fill his place; and, it would seem, had obtained his uncle's mantle and a double portion of his spirit; for under his care the church has flourished more than under that of their first pastor. They have one of the best built and most comfortable meetinghouses in Virginia. For, however the Baptists may excel in matters of greater magnitude, they cannot be admired for the elegance or convenience of their houses of worship.

In 1787, the set time to favor this part of Zion arrived, and under the ministry of Elder Hariss, who was now on a visit to them, this revival burst forth on every hand, nor did the war cease until many of the sons and daughters of the enemy of God fell as victims to invincible grace. About two hundred were baptized. In 1790, as if to encourage their young and ardent pastor, God granted a heavenly move among the people, and Mr. Waller baptized fifty-four. Few years have elapsed in which there were not some baptized.

Mine Road

This is a small church taken off from Waller's in 1791. Mr. Henry Pendleton was ordained to the care of the church at the time of the constitution. From first to last this church has rather dragged on heavily, having had no revival, or none to any extent. Their present number is now less than at their first constitution.

They have, however, some useful members, among whom is Mr. Henry Pendleton, Sr., father of the preacher, and himself a preacher in another sense. He preaches by a pious walk and godly conversation. He is now a venerable old man, of about four-score years of age.

Henry Pendleton, their first pastor, was, until a few years before his death, considered a very pious and rational man. He had fallen into the Arminian system, to which he adhered in all its branches; but, being viewed as a pious man, was held in estimation. Strange to tell, in 1800, he put an end to his own existence by shooting himself. His conduct for some length of time previous to this fatal extent indicated some degree of melancholy insanity. To this state of mind charity requires us to ascribe an act so unpardonable, if perpetrated by one not in a state of insanity. Elder Philip Pendleton is their present pastor.

Craig's

This church, formerly called Upper Spotsylvania, is the oldest constitution between James and Rappahannock Rivers; it was not until November, 1770, about three years after their constitution, that they received Lewis Craig as pastor. Under his care, and previously, this was a flourishing church. In 1776 the Word of God grew mightily among them, and one hundred were added. But in 1781, to the great mortification of the remaining members, Mr. Craig, with most of the church, moved to Kentucky. Soon after this event, the mother church was obliged to relinquish her constitution. In 1788, being reinforced by some new recruits, they resumed their constitution. They have not flourished of late, as much as some other churches; yet their number, though small, contains some worthy characters, on whose shoulders the government of the church seems chiefly to rest.

For a season they had Elder Ephraim Abel for their pastor, but he also moved away. At present Elder Edward Elly attends them occasionally.

Piney Branch

This church was taken off from Waller's. Their meetinghouse is about twelve or fourteen miles from Fredericksburg. They have had from first to last as their pastor Elder Henry Goodloe. Nothing remarkable has occurred in this church. Their course has been smooth and even, having had neither revivals nor declensions worthy of note. They began with the number of forty, and they continue nearly at the same stand.

Elder Jeremiah Chandler has lately become a minister here, and has been useful in the ministry. The church appears of late rather to be on the increase.

Massaponax

This church is in the vicinity of Fredericksburg. Messrs. Dudley, Shackleford, and Mason had preached with some success in this neighborhood previous to the year 1785, when Mr. Mastin moved among them. Some who were seals to the ministry of the first-named preachers were baptized by Mr. Mastin. These, together with a considerable number who professed faith under the ministry of Mastin, were constituted in the year 1788. Mr. Mastin was a confirmed Arminian, having been ordained to the ministry by Mr. J. Waller in the time of his independence.

Most of those who had been proselyted by his ministry received the stamp of his principles, whilst a respectable part of the church, who had been illumined through the ministry of others, were of Calvinistic sentiments. This diversity of opinion was a source of great unhappiness among them. The Arminian party was most numerous, and was not only unsound in principle, but negligent in discipline. It seems, indeed, that Mr. Mastin, in receiving and baptizing members, was too remiss, which, together with the slackness of his discipline after they were received, proved a source of much confusion and disorder. There were a few who were much chagrined at these things. They took opportunities to remonstrate against them with the pastor, as also against his legal doctrines. He was displeased. In 1801, Elder Hipkins Pitman, who was a supporter of Calvinism, moved into the bounds of this church. His ministry being acceptable to that part of the church who coincided with him, Mr. Mastin grew jealous and almost declined preaching among them. Finally, the contest rising to a great height, the church withdrew from the care of Mr. Mastin, and chose Messrs. Waller and Pitman to attend them jointly. The ensuing year Mr. Waller was called to take charge of the church as a stated minister. Under him as their preacher they have been a happy people, and the church has increased.

Wilderness

This is a numerous church, in the upper end of Spotsylvania. They had for their first pastor Joseph Bledsoe. They were not happy under his care. When he moved to Kentucky, his brother, Aaron Bledsoe, became their stated minister. In 1788 they enjoyed the smiles of Heaven in a precious revival conducted chiefly under the ministry of Aaron Bledsoe. The church increased to one hundred and thirty. Mr. Bledsoe's labors were much blessed among them, until some unhappiness arising from his eccentric flights, he resigned his care.

Since that time Mr. Edward Elly has been an occasional pastor for them. Mr. Elly is a worthy man, and a sound preacher. The church has enjoyed peace and harmony under his ministry.

It was in this church that Thomas Bridges, now a prisoner in the penitentiary for horse-stealing, was baptized in 1788. Bridges began to preach soon after he was baptized; but being very illiterate, and of obscure parentage, he was not much noticed in his own neighborhood. He was, however, so far encouraged by the church as to obtain ordination. Having, from his youth, a propensity to lying, he was detected in this mean practice after he commenced preaching. The church, however, admitting his excuses, did not exclude him. Feeling restless under these charges, he asked and obtained a letter of dismission from the church. He now traveled off into Loudoun and the adjacent counties, where he became considerably popular as a preacher. He certainly had some talents. He was fluent in his delivery, and, for his education, spoke in handsome language. His memory was exceedingly retentive, and he had, after becoming a preacher, read a good deal. He had also a large stock of that kind of wit which pleases without profiting; but, in point of judgment, he was probably as deficient as ever man was. His opinions upon subjects that he had often studied and discussed were always incorrect; upon others, he was a mere child. After all, it is not likely that Bridges would ever have become so entirely abandoned had he not unfortunately married a wife with a considerable estate, by which his spirits being elevated far above their common level, he lost all the stock of prudence he previously possessed. Not accustomed to the management of property to any tolerable extent, he soon, very soon, spent what he had gotten by marriage. Still retaining the relish for his new sphere of action, but having lost all lawful resources, he strangely resorted to the shocking alternative of stealing horses; for which, being condemned in 1803, he was confined in the penitentiary, where he now is.

Guinea's Bridge

This church, so called from its vicinity to a bridge of that name, is a church of high standing, having a number of pious and worthy members. The Gospel was preached here in its power and purity at an early date after the rise of the Baptists. This place was not without persecutors also. At one time several preachers were apprehended by virtue of a warrant from a magistrate. Among them was Joseph Craig, remarkable for his eccentric manners. On their way to the magistrate's house Mr. Craig, thinking it no dishonor to cheat the devil, as he termed it, slipped off his horse and took to the bushes. They hunted him with dogs, but, Asahel-like, he made good his retreat.

The church was constituted under the care of Mr. N. Holloway. After various success, Mr. Holloway left them and moved to the county of Halifax. They then procured the stated ministrations of

Elder John Waller, under whose care they were prospered.

In 1797 the Lord poured out His Spirit abundantly, and many were turned to righteousness. More than one hundred were added. After the removal of Mr. J. Waller, in 1793, they were destitute of stated preaching for several years. So great was the decline that they had serious thoughts of dissolving their constitution, but finally, having obtained the regular ministrations of A. Waller, they again raised their heads. In 1800 they had the happiness to see a precious work of God among them. As many as 104 were baptized, and some of them were clever and useful men. Their meetinghouse is a very short distance from the county line, in Caroline. Mr. Waller still attends them.

Fredericksburg

This church, in the town of the same name, is a small but happy one. They have no resident pastor, but are supplied by Mr. A. Broaddus, who attends them monthly. If there is any objection to Mr. Broaddus's ministry in this city, it is that he is too popular with the irreligious. It may be said of him, as was said of Ezekiel, "Lo! Thou art unto them as a very lovely song of one that hath a pleasant voice, and can play well on an instrument; for they hear thy words, but they do them not." This remark by no means applies to the church, for although they hear with much pleasure, they practice with more. It is a young and rising church.

Zoar

This is a small church made up of certain members who felt themselves aggrieved by the conduct of the Salem and Black Walnut churches in the affair of Morris, and therefore formed themselves into a separate church.

The two churches out of which Zoar arose were originally the fruits of Mr. John Leland's labors. Mr. Leland was a native of Worcester, in Massachusetts, was baptized in 1774, and in the fall of 1776 he married and moved to Virginia and settled in the county of Orange in the neighborhood of those churches. He continued in Virginia about fourteen years, in which time he traveled and preached very extensively and very successfully. He baptized between six and seven hundred persons while in the State, and in January, 1791, he removed to Massachusetts, and settled in

Cheshire. Mr. Leland, as a preacher, was probably the most popular of any who ever resided in this State. He is unquestionably a man of fertile genius. His opportunities for school learning were not great, but the energetic vigor of his mind quickly surmounted this deficiency. His memory was so retentive that by a single reading he stored up more of the contents of a book than many would by a dozen careful perusals. It is probable that his knowledge derived from books at this day, taken in the aggregate, is surpassed by few. His preaching, though immethodical and eccentric, is generally warm, wise, and evangelical. There are not many preachers who have so great command of the attention and of the feelings of their auditory. In effecting this, his manner has been thought by some to approach too near to the theatrical. Cowper, the poet, says:

> *"He that negotiates between God and man,*
> *As God's ambassador, the grand concerns*
> *Of judgment and of mercy, should beware*
> *Of lightness in his speech."*

Here Mr. Leland and the poet are at variance; he does sometimes, and, indeed, not unfrequently, "court the skitteth fancy with facetious tales." If Cowper says, so did not Paul. Leland can say so did George Whitefield, Rowland Hill, &c., and they have been the most successful of modern preachers. Mr. Leland's free and jocund manners have excited the suspicions of some that he wanted serious piety. His intimate friends are confident that these are groundless suspicions. They believe that among his other singularities he is singularly pious.

While in Virginia he wrote several treatises, and was certainly very instrumental in effecting the just and salutary regulations concerning religion in this State. He has been similarly employed since his removal to New England. He has always been a zealous advocate for republican government. When Mr. Jefferson was raised to the presidential chair the ladies of Mr. Leland's congregation made a cheese of immense size[1] and sent it by Mr. Leland

---

[1] It was said to have in it 1,400 pounds of curd, and to have weighed 900 weight when taken from the press. The enemies of Jefferson called it the Mammoth Cheese. They also wrote poems and vented much wit upon the occa-

as a present to Mr. Jefferson. This affair made no little noise in the United States.

County Line

This church was a part of those who broke off from the Association with Elder John Waller, and were constituted into a separate church during his seclusion, having been previously an arm of the church called Waller's. After Elder Waller made peace with the Association this church was received as a member. At her constitution Mr. William Waller was installed as her pastor, but he moving to Kentucky in 1784, they procured the stated attendance of Elder John Waller. Under his ministry, in 1787, the windows of grace were opened and God rained down righteousness among them. The church multiplied. When Mr. John Waller moved away they procured the stated attendance of Mr. Absalom Waller. He still preaches for them once a month. This is a church of considerable respectability.

Bethel

This church is in the neighborhood of Bowling Green, Caroline County. There are not many, if any, churches in the Baptist connection more worthy of commendation than this. Though not large, they are, by all who know them, much respected for their work of faith and labor of love and patience of hope in our Lord Jesus Christ. If Paul said that the Thessalonians were ensamples to all that believe in Macedonia and Achaia, so may we say that most of the members of this church are ensamples to their contemporaries. Their meetings are solemn without austerity, and lively without any mixture of enthusiasm; their hospitality cordial without parade, and their manners simple and easy without affectation. They love without dissimulation, and therefore often meet, not only publicly, but from house to house, for social prayer and conversation.

Though they have no resident ordained preacher, yet several of their members have occasionally exhorted and preached in their assemblies. Elder A. Broaddus, pastor of Burris's, attends here monthly. He is viewed as their father, and from him, as children

---

sion. It was, however, received by the President with pleasure, and viewed by the impartial as a singular pledge of patriotism.—*Author's note.*

from a father, they receive that counsel by which they are nurtured up into everlasting life. Two of their most valuable members have already finished their short but happy course.

Mr. Charles Woolfork was a deacon at their first constitution. He discharged the duties of that office with great fidelity and promptitude. Having been accustomed to genteel society, and having an independent fortune, he had it in his power to do many good acts, and to do them likewise with a good grace. He was a man of God. Living in this spotless manner, in a few years he fell asleep, deeply regretted by all his acquaintance; but by his family and church in a more singular degree.

Mr. Thomas Jones, a relation of the deacon, was also a deacon of this church, and may be said to rank in the first grade. From the day he professed godliness until his death he appears to have devoted his whole soul to his Master's service. It is not likely that any private character ever did more good in so short a time. Though in affluent circumstances, he knew how to use this world as not abusing it. After a lingering illness he also fell asleep in 1805.

He was an israelite indeed in whom there was no guile. Here we must pause and consider why such men as these should run so short a course. To which we can only say, that all who understand much of the ways of Providence have plainly discovered that a high degree of prosperity is seldom of long duration. Things were too well in Bethel church to abide long in such a world as this.

Burris's

This church is in the southwest part of Caroline, having some members also in Hanover. It could be wished that favorable things could be said of this as of the foregoing church. But candor compels us to state that although they have some worthy and valuable members, there have been a more than common proportion of apostasies and fallings off. So much had the church declined at one time that the pastor had serious thoughts of proposing to them to dissolve their constitution, or rather to blend theirs with the Bethel. But God, who loves to surprise us with unexpected mercies, proclaimed a jubilee. This work of grace began in the summer of 1808, and in a few months some very valuable members were added. This church was first called Polecat, and the meetinghouse Burris's, after Rev. John Burris, who was once a preacher among them, but never was ordained.

Of Elder Andrew Broaddus, pastor of this church, much may be truly said. The next Association that was held after he took the ministerial care of the church entered upon their record the following eulogy: "In the midst of affliction, we have to mention with thankfulness to the great head of Zion, that Elder A. Broaddus, who has been a shining light in the churches these several years past, has, at the call of Burris's, consented to take the pastoral care of that church, and is consequently a member of our Association."

Williams's

This church, chiefly in the upper end of Goochland, is a church of long and high standing in religious society. For several years they were under the stated ministerial care of Elder John Waller. When he resigned some little time previous to his removal, they called Mr. Goodloe, who accepted the call, and accordingly preached for them statedly until the year 1796, after which Mr. John Poindexter, at their request, attended them occasionally. Under Mr. Poindexter's ministry they enjoyed a pleasant revival—a revival conducted with harmony, solemnity, and order, in which about ninety or one hundred were baptized. Of these, says their manuscript furnished us, only fourteen have been excommunicated in about ten or eleven years: and yet their discipline has been regular. A few years ago Mr. Elisha Purrington, who had been previously ordained, was chosen as pastor. Under him, as pastor, there have been peace and happiness in the church.

The church is much attached to Mr. Purrington, as a man of unaffected piety and mild and pleasant manners. As a preacher he is sound in doctrine, very lively and affectionate in his address, and has talents of the sort which are calculated to do good. He is a native of New England, and came to Virginia in the character of a teacher of psalmody or church music, in which he is excelled by none and equaled by few in the State.

In this church lives Thomas Waford, an old and faithful disciple of Christ, who was among the first to profess religion at the rise of the Baptists. He is not a preacher, but has done more good than a score of preachers of a certain description. When Waller and others used to travel off into strange places, Mr. Waford used to go on sometimes beforehand and publish their meetings and procure places for them to preach at; then he would return and accompany them. He would enforce by private arguments and admonitions what the preachers advanced from the pulpit. He also shared in their persecutions. Once he was taken up with them in Essex County and carried before a magistrate and examined and his saddle-bags searched, and then discharged, not having disturbed the peace by preaching, &c. At another meeting, when persecution ran high, he went to the spring to drink, and there meeting with one of the sons of Belial was severely whipped, the scars of which he will doubtless carry to his grave. Mr. Waford is now (1809), more than four-score years of age, and has professed religion more than forty years, during which time he has maintained a spotless reputation, not only for order and piety, but for steady and unabating zeal. Old as he is he misses very few Associations.

Licking Hole

This church, in the upper end of Goochland, is probably the largest church in the Goshen Association. It was planted under the ministry of Elder Ford and others. For several years after the constitution, Elder Ford was their occasional pastor, but at length they made choice of Rev. Hugh French for their pastor. Under his care they enjoyed peace and harmony. Until 1798 they were connected with the Dover Association; but being more convenient to the Goshen, they petitioned and obtained a dismission to join the Goshen, where they have been ever since. In 1804 they enjoyed one of the most heavenly revivals that ever was seen; four or five hundred were baptized, and among them some very respectable characters indeed. Elder Leonard Page, who was very active and useful in the revival, has been since chosen pastor. There are few, if any, churches in the State that possess a greater number of intelligent men than Licking Hole. Besides their pastor, Dr. John Morgan, a practitioner of medicine and a preacher of the Gospel, resides among them.

Here also died that amiable and beloved servant of Christ, Peregrine G. Smith. Mr. Smith was a native of Massachusetts, and at an early period in life professed vital religion. Having received a classical education, he began to preach the Gospel. After continuing a short time in New England he was advised to travel in the Southern States for his health, which was now very low. He came to Virginia, and after traveling through various parts of the State, and finding it, as he thought, more congenial to his constitution, he resolved to settle here. His residence and ministrations were much wished in many places. He, however, gave the preference to Licking Hole, and accordingly came here to live. Mr. Smith, it appears, had for several years been afflicted with the consumption, a complaint so flattering in its nature that few who have it ever think they have. He entertained some expectation of recovery until a few days before his death, which took place in 1807.

Mr. Smith was a preacher of fine talents indeed. His delivery was easy; his style very elegant; his action becoming, and his manner warm and animating. His knowledge of books was considerable, and having traveled very extensively for one of his age, he had also acquired considerable experience of men, &c. By these things, added to his mild disposition, his pious spirit and accomplished manners, his company and conversation were very attractive to all who had even a slight acquaintance with him. Licking Hole church did themselves much credit by their benevolent conduct towards his amiable and afflicted widow and child. So friendly were they towards her that when she passed through Richmond on her way to New England she said to a friend that she "had not believed there were such people in the world as she had found in this neighborhood."

Elder French, though not a man of distinguished talents, was esteemed a warm and experimental preacher. As a Christian he was very pious and exemplary; and as a man he was in high estimation in all the relations of social life. He only lived a few years after he joined the Goshen Association, and at one of the sessions he was made moderator. At the next Association his death is entered upon their records, with some commendatory remarks upon his character.

Thompson's or Goldmine

The preaching of the Rev. David Thomas, in Orange, made serious impressions upon some in this neighborhood who went there to hear him. This induced them to look out for preachers to come into their own vicinity, and accordingly they procured the services of Mr. Nathaniel Saunders and others. Finally, when Messrs. Hariss and Read came on in their circuit, this neighborhood participated in the blessing. Some were baptized. This induced Lewis Craig and other young preachers to visit them, so that in 1770 they were constituted as a church. They were much straightened to choose a pastor, being divided among three. At length they agreed to receive David Thompson. The church had now become large.

Under Mr. Thompson's care the church declined and fell into some unhappy contentions. He finally moved off, and the church obtained the stated attendance of Rev. Mr. Leland. Mr. Leland's ministry was greatly blessed. The church increased to a great extent. Few preachers were ever more popular in any place of their stated ministry than Mr. Leland was in these parts. But much to the regret of those without and within the church, Mr. Leland in 1791 removed to New England, his native country. This church then made choice of George Morris, one of their own members, who had been for some time preaching among them. The event of this choice may be seen in the account given of the Goshen Association. Morris, in the division of the church, gaining a majority, held on upon their meetinghouse. The minority, who were by the Association pronounced the church, built them a stage, and finally a meetinghouse, a few miles off, where, under the ministry of visiting preachers, in 1804 and 1805, they were revived, and have flourished greatly. Many of Morris's friends have left him and joined this church, who called themselves Goldmine church. In 1807 they chose Elder William Waller as pastor, who continues to attend them once a month.

Roundabout

This church, somewhat above the courthouse, and on the south side of Louisa, is a church of the first grade as to intelligent members and regularity in discipline. The Gospel was first brought into this neighborhood by several of the old preachers, particularly Mr. John Waller. In 1791, Mr. Poindexter, who had been baptized a short time before, began to preach. In 1792 he was chosen as pastor. As if God would clearly sanction the appointment, He granted a powerful revival of religion soon after he was called to the pastoral care. More than one hundred were baptized in the course of a few months. This work went on until they increased to more than three hundred. The revival began about Roundabout, but spread upwards, so that in 1795 a church was constituted about Foster's Creek called Siloam.

This church was raised chiefly under the ministry of Mr. Poindexter, and was an arm of Roundabout until constituted. He was chosen their stated preacher or occasional pastor. It was, when constituted, a considerable church, having nineteen or twenty white males and about thirty females, besides a great number of blacks. They continued to prosper until George Morris stirred up his schism in some of the neighboring churches. Having a brother a member here, he was too successful in forming a party in Siloam also. This brought on great distress, until they came to a determination, in 1802, to dissolve their constitution and rejoin the Roundabout. This measure also seemed to meet the divine approval; for immediately after their dissolution a small but comfortable revival took place, and about twenty were added to the church. Elder Poindexter had also extended his labors as far as Albemarle, and formed a church called Bethel, consisting of upwards of one hundred members. It being too far for Mr. Poindexter to attend them, they chose Mr. Robert Jones, a young preacher, who some time afterwards moved away, and Hephzibah church being constituted a little distance above, Bethel was dissolved, some of the members joining the new constitution, and some falling back into Roundabout. Thus these three churches were again united into one. No revival has appeared in Roundabout of late years. They are, however, in peace and harmony among themselves. Mr. Poindexter, their pastor, is clerk of the court of Louisa, and a man of high standing, both in civil and religious matters. He has made, and is still making, great pecuniary sacrifices for religion.

Scarrott's

This church, though not large, is of good standing. Nothing uncommon has occurred among them. They have moved on smoothly for many years under the stated ministry of Elder Henry Goodloe. Early after their constitution Mr. William Dawson was their pastor, but he did not continue long among them. Mr. Goodloe then became and has continued ever since to be their preacher.

Little River

Although this church has not lengthened her cords to as great extent as some others, she has passed through very few afflicting scenes, having generally enjoyed a considerable share of peace under her worthy and zealous pastor.

North Fork of Pamunkey

This is a large church, but has been much larger, having of late passed through not only cold but very afflicting times. Some of the old Baptist preachers labored in these parts at an early period of the rise of the Baptists. Mr. Aaron Bledsoe was among their first proselytes, having been previously a dissipated character. So soon as he believed himself to be a convert he began to persuade others. His zeal was unabating. He missed no opportunity to exhort, advise, and admonish any and every man he met with. He was really in season and out of season. Having a singular degree of boldness he would not be ashamed. Great man, little man, rich man or poor man, were all equal with him, as it respected his confidence. He was never to be swerved from his point or put to the blush. By his unwearied zeal, though far from being a man of knowledge or gifts, he made serious impressions upon many. A church was constituted and he chosen their pastor. The discipline of the church was by no means regular. No decision could be had without unanimity, which often clogged, often discouraged them. But the zeal and forwardness of their pastor surmounted many of these obstructions. The church increased. In 1788 they experienced an extensive revival; several hundred were baptized, so that in 1792, when they became a part of Goshen Association, they had about 350 members.

In the year 1806, Mr. Bledsoe was accused of fraudulent dealings, which he denied, though too plainly proven. The church excluded him, although there was a large minority in his favor who thought him innocent. No man probably ever felt more chagrin at being excluded than Mr. Bledsoe. He soon moved away out of the State, and is since dead. Many good men doubted whether Mr. Bledsoe ever designed anything improper.

Table of Albemarle Association

Name of churches	Year	Number at Consti-	Present Number	By Whom Planted	Former Pastors	Current Pastors	Counties
Abermarle	1773		78	William Woods	William Woods	J. Watts	Albermarle
Totier	1775	35	120	D. Tinsley, D. Patterson	M. Dawson George Eve	M. Dawson	Albermarle
Prethis Creek	1784	24	190	George Eve	H. Goss	M. Dawson	Albermarle
Hephzibah	1802	12	49	M'n Dawson	M. Dawson	M. Dawson	Albermarle
Whitesides	1788	25		B. Burgher	B. Burgher	B. Burgher	Albermarle
Buffaloe			120	M. Dawson	B. Coleman	J. Young	Amherst
Ebenezer	1773		80	O. Flowers	O. Flowers	W. Duncan	Amherst
Lyle's	1798	20	144	E. Craig, D. Thomson	P. Webber	William Basket	Fluvanna
Fork	1774	60	150			G. Anderson	Fluvanna

CHAPTER FOURTEEN:
History of the Albemarle Association, Including the Sketches of Churches

By reference to Chapter 12, it will be found that the Orange Association was in 1791 divided into three districts, of which one was called Albemarle. This was then, and is now, much the smallest of the three, having never had more than nine churches. They held their first session in 1792, and have continued to meet from year to year ever since. We have not been able to procure a full file of their minutes, but from such as we have seen, it appears that their business is conducted in Associations with the utmost harmony and love. Elder Martin Dawson has generally discharged the duty of moderator, and Elder Benjamin Burgher of clerk. The district included the churches in Amherst, Albemarle, and Fluvanna only.[1] Having given pretty full accounts of the proceedings of several Associations where the minutes were in our possession, it is the less necessary to enter into a detail of others, seeing the proceedings of one Association are very similar to all the rest in the same connection. We shall therefore proceed to give historical sketches of the churches in this Association, beginning with:

Albemarle

This is the oldest church in this Association. It was once under the pastoral care of William Woods, who is still a member. Mr. Woods resigned the care of the church, together with his credentials, in order to take off the disqualification from representing the county as a delegate in the General Assembly. If he were called of God to this work, it is hard to say how Mr. Woods will in the last day render an account of his stewardship. He is esteemed a useful and respectable man. Mr. Watts now labors for them as pastor, and is profitable in the ministry.

Totier

This church was planted by the labors of Rev. David Tinsley,

---

[1] Nelson has been stricken off from Amherst since our documents came to hand.—*Author's note.*

and watered by those of Rev. B. Burgher, William Woods and David Patterson. Tinsley preached in the bounds about 1770, but was not very successful. About 1773 Mr. Patterson, who was a resident of Buckingham, preached with much power, and baptized many in the neighborhood of Totier, who were considered as members of the church in Buckingham, of which Mr. Patterson was pastor. In 1774 Rev. Martin Dawson was baptized and soon began to preach. When the church was constituted he took the pastoral care and has continued ever since. Under his ministry the church has enjoyed great prosperity and peace, and has been favored with several precious revivals. Many of the members have at different times emigrated to the western country, so that the church has been more numerous than it is at present. Mr. Dawson, their pastor, is now (1809) about sixty-five years of age. He has always maintained a respectable standing, both in civil and religious society. He has been moderator to the Association for many years, a place which he fills with considerable propriety.

Prethis Creek

This church was for many years under the care of Rev. George Eve, who left them and went to Kentucky. During his continuance among them there was no extraordinary revival, but, in 1803, coming from the western country on a visit, the power of God revived in this church, under his temporary labors, and while he stayed there were added to the church upwards of one hundred. Elders Jones and Goss preached for them stately for some time.

Hephzibah

This church, for two or three years after her constitution, seemed to decline, but in 1805 a small revival was granted, when about twenty-five were added. Since that time they have been in peace and harmony under the stated ministry of Elder Dawson. Mr. Thomas Henderson, the clerk of the church, also exhorts and preaches at times.

Whitesides

This has been a prosperous church. Her pastor, Mr. B. Burgher, was in the ministry among the first that are now living, and is esteemed a sound and able preacher, especially when he feels what is called the liberty of preaching. He used to be more laborious in the ministry than at present; having been for many years very corpulent, traveling and preaching are not so practicable. Mr. Burgher has some poetical genius, having composed several songs and other small pieces of poetry. He has been clerk of the Association for many years and has composed most of their circular letters. The church has been generally happy under his ministrations, and has been favored with several comfortable revivals.

Buffaloe

Buffaloe church is now prosperous and happy; but for some time after her constitution there was considerable confusion, through the misconduct of Benjamin Coleman, their first pastor. In 1799, Elder John Young, who had moved from Caroline, settled in the bounds of this church and became their pastor the ensuing year, viz., 1800. In 1803 God smiled, and as many as eighty or ninety sinners were enticed to Jesus. Mr. William Duncan, a preacher of useful gifts, is a member of this church, and has been ordained to the ministry.

Ebenezer

This church was under the pastoral care of Elder Orson Flowers until 1805, when he was drawn into the vortex of Baptist preachers—Kentucky.[1] Since his removal they have been attended by Elder Duncan. They had a revival in 1804.

Lyle's

Lyle's church was planted by the united labors of Elijah Craig and David Thompson. These preachers were induced to visit this place in consequence of three or four persons in the neighborhood going, in the year 1769, some distance off to hear preaching, and being thereby awakened they invited the preachers to come and visit them. They did so. Their labor was not in vain. A few were admitted to divine favor and were baptized. Among these was their present pastor, Mr. Basket. As soon as God wrought in them they began to work for God, and held private meetings. The work progressed and a church was constituted. Their first pastor was Philip Webber, who moving to Kentucky, the care of the church

---

[1] It is questionable with some whether half the preachers who have been raised in Virginia have not emigrated to the western country.—*Author's note.*

devolved upon Elder Basket. In 1788 the Master of Assemblies paid them a visit and introduced a considerable number into the divine favor. It is a peaceable and prosperous church.

Fork

Fork church, in Fluvanna, was constituted off from Lyle's. They were at first tolerably prosperous, but, through the misconduct of their minister, they fell into great confusion, so far as to require the interposition of the Association in order to regulate them. But perhaps ere this Jesus has spoken the storm into calm.

Table of Culpeper Association

Year	Number at Constitution	Present Number	By Whom Planted	Former Pastors	Current Pastors	Counties
1803	72	62	W. Mason	W. Mason	W. Mason	Culpeper
1787	43	95	J. Koontz	J. Koontz	W. Fristoe	Culpeper
1772	30	85	S. Hariss, James Read, E. Craig	J. Garnett	J. Garnett	Culpeper
1774	47	247	D. Thomas	N. Saunders	W. Mason	Culpeper
1778	20	100	N. Saunders, G. Eve, W. Mason	G. Eve, W. Mason	L. Conner	Culpeper
1791	25	130	J. Picket, W. Mason	J. Picket	W. Mason	Culpeper
1771	27	47	J. Pickett, J. Johnson	J. Picket		Culpeper
1773	15	87	J. Picket	J. Picket		Culpeper
1773	37	114	E. Craig, J. Waller, S. Hariss, J. Read	G. Eve, J. Leather		Madison
1790	76	41	W. Mason	W. Mason	W. Mason	Madison
1769	66	100	S. Hariss, J. Read	E. Craig, G. Eve, H. Goss	R. Jones	Orange
1768	37	68	J. Picket	J. Picket		
1799	30	60	J. Picket	J. Picket	J. Koontz	Fauquier
1772	70	73	J. Picket, J. Koontz	J. Picket	J. Koontz	Fauquier and Culpepper
1774		48	J. Ireland, A. Moffett, J. Koontz	A. Moffett	A. Moffett	Shenandoah
1784		21	A. Moffett, J. Redding, J. Koontz	A. Moffett	J. Koontz, &c.	Shenandoah and Rockingham
1777	15	11	J. Redding, J. Taylor	J. Redding, J. Koontz		Hardy
1756	11	19	J. Alderson, &c.	J. Alderson (Sr. & Jr.), J. Redding, J. Johnson	J. Koontz	Rockingham

Name of churches
Bethel
Thompson's Gap
Crooked Run
Mountponey
F.T.
Gourdvine
Fiery Run
Battle Run
Rapidan
Robinson River
Blue Run
Carter's Run
Goose Creek
Mill Creek
Smith's Creek
Lost River
Lunie's Creek
Lynville's Creek

CHAPTER FIFTEEN:

History of the Culpeper Association, Including the Sketches of the Churches

Their first session was held at Smith's Creek meetinghouse, commencing on the fourth Friday in October, 1792. This session was occupied in organizing.

They met a second time at Thornton's Gap, on Friday, the 4th of October, 1793, and continued together three days. Letters from fourteen churches were received, stating their whole number to be 1,212. Rev. George Eve was chosen moderator, and Rev. Lewis Conner clerk. Nothing more than local matters were transacted at this session. The limits of our work will not admit of lengthy details of the proceedings of each Association in the State, nor indeed can it be desirable, seeing the proceedings of one Association are so similar to those of another, that by passing over the records of four or five of the largest and oldest and selecting such general matter as may have called their attention, we obtain everything, or nearly everything, worth regarding in any. A few general observations, therefore, as to the proceedings of the Culpeper Association will, we presume, be satisfactory; especially as a pretty full attention has been paid to the history of the churches in this Association.

Elder Lewis Conner acted as clerk of the Association from their first organization until a few years past. At present Mr. Richard L Tutt discharges the duties of that office. Mr. George Eve generally acted as moderator during his continuance in the State. Of late years Elders Mason and Conner—sometimes the one and sometimes the other—have filled the moderator's chair. Their course has been even and smooth; their business managed prudently and peacefully; their number of churches has increased, but their number of members rather decreased, owing chiefly to the great number of removals to the western country. This Association has never as yet joined the General Meeting of Correspondence, but it is hoped, when the principles and utility of that meeting are better understood, that not only this, but all the Associations in the State, will become members. Upon this short view of the Association, we shall now proceed to speak of the churches.

Upper Goose Creek and Bethel

These are churches of happy standing, but nothing has occurred among them necessary to be noticed here. Brother Koontz attends Upper Goose Creek with much success.

Thornton's Gap and Fiery Run

These two churches have furnished no historical account.

Crooked Run

This is a daughter of Blue Run, and was for about two years under the care of E. Craig, who was pastor of Blue Run. God having raised up ministers among them, viz., Elders J. Garnett and Thomas Ammon (the latter of whom was once imprisoned in Culpeper jail for preaching), Mr. Garnett was ordained as pastor. Under the ministerial care of this amiable man, the church has enjoyed peace and harmony. In 1788 and 1789 they had a glorious revival; 115 were added. In 1803 they were again blessed, and about thirty were baptized. By emigration, &c., their number is not so great as it has been. Mr. John Garnett, one of the ministers, has lately ascended the pulpit, and is said to be a young man of pleasing manners and promising talents.

Mountponey

This church was taken off from a church called Mountain Run, in Orange County, constituted in 1768 and since dissolved. The Rev. David Thomas was the first Baptist preacher that ever proclaimed the Gospel of Peace in the counties of Orange and Culpeper, which took place in the year 1763. His preaching was in power and demonstration of the Spirit. Mr. Nathaniel Saunders, who afterwards became a preacher, was among the first seals to his ministry. Many others were also baptized about the same time. In 1766, about two or three years after he was baptized, Mr. Saunders began to preach, and in 1768 was ordained to the care of Mountain Run church, which was constituted at the same time. Mr. Saunders held the care of this church until it was dissolved in 1782, and most of the members joined Mountponey.[1]

---

[1] Nathaniel Saunders, though not a preacher of great talents, was sound in the faith. He lived and died, in the estimation of all that knew him, a pious and

Mountponey, as will appear from the table, was constituted in 1774. Elder Saunders served them as a supply from a short time after their constitution until sometime in 1777. When the Rev. John Leland, from New England, came preaching among them, and became a member of Mountponey church, the church unanimously called him to the administration of the Word and ordinances without ordination by the imposition of hands. This being contrary to the established rule of the Ketocton Association, and indeed of the Baptists of Virginia generally, when the church sent her delegates to the next Association they were rejected. The habits of the Baptists in New England and of those in Virginia respecting apparel were also much at variance. Mr. Leland and others adhered to the customs of New England, each one putting on such apparel as suited his own fancy. This was offensive to some members of the church. The contention on this account became so sharp that on the 25th of July, 1779, about twelve members dissented from the majority of the church and were of course excluded. The dissenting members formed themselves into a church, and sued for admission into the next Association, and were received. The majority dismissed Mr. Leland in order, and soon after this he submitted to ordination by the imposition of the hands of a presbytery.

After Mr. Leland's departure Mr. Saunders resumed the pastoral care of the church. A reconciliation was effected. Mountain Run being dissolved, Mountponey had three preachers in her government, viz., Elder William Mason, who is now their pastor, and N. Saunders and John Price, all of whom labored together in great harmony until Mr. Price moved to Kentucky. In 1798, the set time to favor Zion having arrived, her gates were crowded with converts. To Mountponey church were added by baptism about two hundred, chiefly through the ministerial labor of Elder Mason. It was about this time that Elder Mason was chosen by the church as their pastor. Gourdvine and Bethel were constituted out of this church. Mountponey was a member of Ketocton also until 1803; they then joined Culpeper. Mr. Mason, pastor of this church, has

---

good man. After suffering a great deal, with a long and painful Illness, he finished his earthly pilgrimage towards the last of the summer, 1808.—*Author's note.*

been long laboring to turn sinners to righteousness, and under God he has turned many. To say much in favor of a living man has too much the appearance of flattery. We must, therefore, curtail; but our feelings will not permit us to be entirely silent. Suffice it to say that in all the relations of life he stands acknowledged through the whole circle of his acquaintances as one of the most exemplary men living. As a preacher, although he has no claim to learning or refined eloquence, he possesses gifts that are incomparably more valuable. Cowper's description of a Christian minister is realized in Mr. Mason:

> *"Simple, grave, sincere,*
> *In doctrine uncorrupt; in language plain,*
> *And plain in manner. Decent, solemn, chaste*
> *And natural in gesture. Much impressed*
> *Himself, as conscious of his awful charge,*
> *And anxious mainly that the flock he feeds*
> *May feel it too. Affectionate in look,*
> *And tender in address, as well becomes*
> *A messenger of Grace to guilty men."*

F. T.

This church is so called from its being contiguous to a place of that name. It was formerly called Ragged Mountain. Through the pious labors of Elders Saunders, Eve, Picket, &c., the Gospel was first successfully introduced within the limits of this church. A malignant opposition soon appeared to the Word. They threatened the preacher, but God bade them preach on; and so they did, until persecution was silenced. After the constitution of F.T., George Eve was their minister, whose labors were much blessed. Nothing notable, however, transpired until 1788, when W. Mason, in consequence of the resignation of Mr. Eve, became their minister. That was a year long to be remembered by F.T. A blessed revival appeared in all her borders. The work continued during that and the succeeding year. The heavens seemed to rain righteousness. Many of the votaries of Mammon and of Belial renounced their idols, and gave their hearts to their Redeemer. From this the Robinson River church was taken off. Benjamin Fewel was raised here, and afterwards moved to North Carolina, where he has been eminently useful, and is clerk of Mayo Association.

Gourdvine

This is another of the churches attended by Elder William Mason. The Gospel was first introduced into the neighborhood through the invitation of sundry persons to Mr. Picket and others to come and preach in their houses. Among others was a Mr. Sam Ferguson, a rich man, who had been an opposer; but God conquered him by His grace, and in return he made his house a house of prayer and preaching. The church has prospered moderately, with the enjoyment of peace and love.

Battle Run

This church is one of the daughters of Carter's Run, and for many years fed upon the heavenly manna dealt out by the Rev. John Picket. Their course has not been very remarkable. Their winters have not been more severe, nor their summers more fruitful, than those in their sister churches.

Rapidan

This is a daughter of Blue Run church. The Gospel was first carried into the bounds of this church by Messrs. Hariss and Read. The plant which they planted was watered by Mr. Waller and Mr. E. Craig. When the Gospel was first preached in the bounds of this church persecution ran high. Warrants were Issued to apprehend the preachers. E. Craig was taken out of the pulpit and committed to Culpeper jail. Thomas Maxfield, sometime after, was imprisoned for exhorting. Mr. Adam Banks about the same time was committed to jail for praying in the private house of a Mr. John Dulaney, and Dulaney himself, who was not a Baptist, for permitting it. Persecution often defeats its own cause. Men cannot be restrained from thinking, and they will think it a bad cause which requires force to support it. In the midst of these violent persecutions the cause of God flourished about Rapidan abundantly. In this church Rev. George Eve, one of the most successful preachers in these parts, was raised up, and about 1775 was ordained to the care of the church. During the years 1776—1778 they were much revived; as many as 130 or 140 were added under the ministry of Mr. Eve. By removals, deaths, &c., the church was again considerably reduced, but in 1788 a heavenly work commenced and went on until 1796, when, after having been about twenty-one years under his pastoral care, the church reluctantly gave Mr. Eve a letter of dismission, he being about to move to Kentucky. After a space of about eight years, in which they were supplied by visiting ministers, Elder Joshua Leather was appointed pastor, but he, after about two years, also went to Kentucky, since which time this church, which has been the nursery of several useful ministers, has been without a pastor.

Joseph Early joined the Baptists in 1772, and was a member of Rapidan church. He was a distinguished character in his sphere. Though not a preacher, he had his gift, and he did not neglect it. He was rich in this world, and he was willing to communicate. Viewing himself as a steward for God, he laid out his Lord's money according to His instructions. His hands were open to the poor and needy. He was the friend of the friendless. He also bestowed liberally for all religious purposes. When a meetinghouse was to be built or any other plan was in agitation that required money, Mr. Early's purse was easily commanded. His fellow-citizens elected him to represent them in the Legislature, but God had elected him to much higher honors. In 1783, after maintaining for about eleven years a most unblamable reputation for piety and goodness, he died in great peace, going forth to meet the Bridegroom, and has doubtless entered with Him into the marriage chamber.

Robinson River

Within the bounds of this church Mr. Mason preached for several years, having singular respect and attention shown him by all sorts of people; but to his great mortification, he could make no effectual interest for his Master. This was so discouraging to his soul that he had strong thoughts of turning his attention elsewhere. But an unseen power impelled him to the work until the set time for God to work; then were their mouths filled with laughing and their tongues with singing. A certain woman on her death-bed obtained a hope of eternal life, and when dying requested Mr. Mason to preach at her funeral, saying, at the same time, that it would be a great day. Accordingly at her funeral the revival commenced, and continued until many were turned to righteousness. Mr. Mason has ever since continued his ministrations among them, to the satisfaction of all; but through removals, deaths, &c., this church is not now as large as when constituted.

Blue Run

An account of the rise of this church may be seen in our account of the rise and progress of the Separate Baptists in Virginia. By recurring to that recital it will be seen that this was among the first places that the Gospel took effect, through the labors of Messrs. Hariss and Read, and that as early as the 4th of December, 1769, this church was constituted under the pastoral care of Elijah Craig. Her history since that period remains to be here inserted.

It appears that they prospered under the care of Elder Craig; many were added to the church, and it was large and prosperous for many years. In 1786 E. Craig moved to Kentucky, and then the church procured the services of Elder George Eve, who continued to officiate as minister until 1794. His ministrations were much blessed. During the years 1788 and 1789 the church was highly favored. Many precious souls were enlisted to fight under the banner of Christ and in the ranks of Blue Run church. In 1794 Mr. Eve resigned his care of Blue Run, having to attend two other churches. Elder Hamilton Goss was then called to the pastoral charge of this church. Under his ministry in 1802 they had a small revival. After continuing in the church for nine or ten years in love and peace, Mr. Goss removed to Harrison County, in the western part of Virginia. Mr. Robert Jones, then a resident of Albemarle, and unordained, was called to the pastoral care; having accepted the call, he was accordingly ordained for that purpose, and removed his residence to Blue Run. He is still their pastor and has been among them in love and harmony. Their number at present is one hundred, but they have been far more numerous, having been reduced by death and frequent removals. It is worthy of notice that there does not remain a single member in the church who was in it when first constituted.

Carter's Run

This church was the first fruits of the Rev. John Picket's ministry, and is the mother of most of the neighboring churches; for, from her were constituted the following, viz., Mill Creek, Battle Run, Hedgeman's River, Fiery Run and Upper Goose Creek.

Shortly after her constitution until his death, Carter's Run was under the pastoral care of the venerable Mr. John Picket. If anything remarkable has transpired within their limits it has not been communicated. See further account in the biography of Mr. Picket.

Mill Creek

This is also a mother church, being the first fruits of the labors of several old and faithful fathers in the ministry in that part of the district. Rev. John Koontz was the first that preached a pure gospel within the limits of Mill Creek. Having been baptized in Fauquier December, 1768, and living at the time in Frederick County, near Front Royal, he began in a few months after his baptism to exhort and preach in his own neighborhood. So he continued until November, 1770, when he resolved to go up to Shenandoah, into the neighborhood of Mill Creek, where his brother George lived. It is easy to conjecture that Mt. Koontz would hardly visit in a dark and unenlightened place without making some essay to spread the savor of the knowledge of Christ. He did blow the Gospel trumpet, and it gave no uncertain sound. Many were roused from their sleep, took the alarm and fled for refuge. Zion's gates were crowded with returning rebels. Soon after Mr. Koontz's labors began to be prospered about Mill Creek other preachers visited them. Among them were Lewis Craig, John Picket, &c. Mr. Koontz not being ordained, Mr. Lewis Craig baptized the first converts.

Among the first that were baptized was Martin Kaufman, who soon after became a preacher. The work went on. Mr. Koontz labored much. There were in the neighborhood many Dutch or Germans. Mr. Koontz being a German, could preach in either language, and would often preach twice to the same congregation, once in Dutch and once in English. But shall we say that this work of godliness progressed to so great an extent without any opposition? Far from it. Can the lion be ousted from his den and make no resistance? Can the bear be peacefully robbed of her whelps? Will the strong man armed give up his palace and his goods without a struggle? It is not so. Mr. Koontz found and sustained with fortitude no little opposition. At first they were contented to offer reproaches and threats, but as the work increased they resorted to more harsh treatment. Once Mr. Koontz was met on the road and beaten. On another occasion he attended a meeting towards Smith's Creek. When he arrived at the place he was met by a set of ruffians, who forbade his preaching. One Captain Leahorn, a respectable man, interfered and insisted he should preach, and prevailed. The persecutors, however, threw out heavy threats that if he ever came that way upon that errand again they would beat him severely. Mr. Koontz could not be deterred from coming, and they kept their word.

He went not long after. His enemies had thrown in money and hired a son of darkness to beat him. Accordingly, as soon as he arrived, the miscreant began to strike him with the butt end of a large cane, requiring him to promise never to come there again. This Mr. Koortz pointedly refused to do. The fellow continued beating until he had almost disabled him. Then he left him. While thus suffering Mr. Koontz felt nothing more than a firm determination not to yield. But the savage had left him but a few steps before he felt his soul exceedingly comforted. He could then thank God that he was counted worthy to suffer persecution for the name of Christ.

Sometime after this he and Martin Kaufman went to a place about six or seven miles from thence, and while they were preparing to preach he heard a man in a room adjoining that in which he and Mr. Kaufman were sitting inquire for John Koontz. When he heard the inquiry he immediately suspected that some mischief was in agitation, and stepped into a third room and got out of sight. The fellow, who had probably been instigated by some other persons, did not know either Koontz or Kaufman. When he came into the room he supposed Martin Kaufman to be John Koontz, and without asking any questions fell upon him with a stick, or something of the kind. It was not until after poor Martin had received many blows that he could convince the barbarian that he was not named Koontz. In the meantime the fellow's wrath was satiated and he went off without finding Mr. Koontz at all.

On another occasion he attended an appointment, but before he had begun to preach they took him off and said they would carry him to prison. At a small distance from the place they met a man coming to meeting. He said he had come to hear Mr. Koontz preach; that they should not carry him any farther, and attempted to rescue him, but the persecutors beat him off. When they had carried him a small distance farther he said to them: "Take heed what you do. If I am a man of God you fight against God." One of the party was immediately alarmed. The warning dropped was owned of God, working in him a repentance never to be repented of. They had proceeded but a little way, when the whole company began to relent and agreed to let him go. The man who first took the alarm, and two or three more of the company, afterwards became Baptists. This was the last violent attack made upon Elder Koontz. From the time of his initiation into the ministry until this day he has continued faithfully to declare the counsel of God. Among the Baptists there are and have been many active and laborious preachers, whose souls have glowed with seraphic ardor; leaning upon the sacred promises, they were willing to suffer with Christ here that they might reign with Him hereafter. But considering Mr. Koontz's unwearied labors in the ministry, the length of time in which he has been engaged (about forty years); considering that he has a constitution that has seldom or never failed him, requiring short and few intervals of rest, it may be fairly stated that few if any in the State have surpassed him as to the quantum of service devoted to the Lord's vineyard. He has been a laborer indeed, and no doubt will receive his full wages whenever the Lord of the Vineyard shall reckon with His servants. Mr. Koontz is still living, and, although grown old in service, he does not in any great degree slack his hand.

Mill Creek was a large church when first constituted. Most of the people in the neighborhood, previous to the preaching of the Baptists, were Dutch Mennonites, The Kaufmans and others who were of that sect being baptized, excited great displeasure among the Mennonites generally. In order to overturn the works of Satan, as they called it, they sent for preachers from Pennsylvania. In some short time four or five Pennsylvania Mennonite preachers came. They labored much to prevent the work then going on. They conceived that John Koontz was the chief cause of this disturbance, and thought if he could be convinced or overset by any means there would be no more of it, seeing he could preach in Dutch. To this end the preachers came to his house and labored much to convince him. They contended that Christians ought not to hold with going to war, with slavery, or taking legal oaths; that these were fundamental points. To this Mr. Koontz replied that the

Baptists, upon these points, left every man at discretion, wishing all to follow the dictates of his own conscience. He then questioned them as to the reason of their hope in Christ; whether they had felt the power of godliness in their hearts, or whether they relied upon their nursery faith. He found them entire strangers to vital godliness, denying the existence thereof. They left him and held meetings in the neighborhood two days, striving publicly and privately against the revival that was then happily progressing. Their labor was in vain. God still added to His people such as should be saved.

When the church, now called Mill Creek (then White House) was first constituted, there were two preachers in it, viz., Anderson Moffett and Martin Kaufman, for Mr. Koontz had not then moved from his residence near Front Royal. There being two preachers, inquiry was made which should be chosen as pastor. On this question they were divided, and being customary to have it unanimous, no choice could be made. So the affair stood until the year 1774 or 1775, when Mr. Koontz, having settled among them, he was ordained to the care of the church. About the same time Smith's Creek was constituted off, partly from the White House and partly from Lynville's Creek, and A. Moffett became their pastor.

Martin Kaufman having been a Mennonite previous to his conversion; retained most of their principles after he became a Baptist. When the American Revolutionary war broke out, most of the Baptists, being attached to the principles of the Revolution, took the oath of allegiance, and many of them joined the army. This gave great offence to Martin Kaufman and ten or twelve others who had been Mennonites. Some ineffectual attempts were made to satisfy them, in which it was urged that, inasmuch as they were not hindered in the enjoyment of their own opinions, they ought to leave others in the same enjoyment; that mutual forbearance in all matters of secondary importance was indispensably necessary to the happiness of society; that in our present imperfect state perfect coincidence of opinion in all matters was not to be expected, and that at least when it was found that so large a majority of the society to which they were united differed from them, they ought to suspect the correctness of their own opinions, so far as to yield the liberty of conscience to others, without pushing matters to extremes. To all these arguments they replied that to them it appeared that the points of difference were of primary importance, and that they could not in good conscience hold fellowship or communion with persons who allowed such unlawful practices. All attempts to reconcile them failed, and they finally broke off and formed a separate party.

From time to time others fell into their way of thinking, until their number ultimately swelled to sixty or seventy. Mr. Kaufman became their preacher, having been ordained by two of his own members. Their doctrine was not so Calvinistic as that of the Baptists generally. They professed to believe in universal provision and final perseverance. Their discipline was nearly the same as that of the Baptists. This party continued to increase moderately for some time, until some other churches were formed and preachers raised up. Mr. Kaufman, however, was the soul of the party, and when he became old and less capable of active exertion they declined fast. After his death, which took place in 1805, they dispersed. Some joined the old Mill Creek church and some Smith's Creek. Kaufman was generally considered a pious and inoffensive man, very zealous and indefatigable. His intellectual powers, however, were very small and his prejudices strong. He seldom or never adopted harsh terms in his opposition to the Baptists; always manifested considerable affection and friendship towards them when in their company. All things considered, it is most rational as well as most charitable to presume that Martin was actuated by pure motives, and that he conscientiously believed that he ought to do what he did.

At an Association held for the Orange District in May, 1809, an entry is made in the following words: "A letter came to the Association from the Menonist [Mennonite] Baptist church, at the White House, praying for a reconciliation; which church separated from us in the time of the war because they would keep no slaves, swear no oaths, nor bear arms in defense of their country. A letter was written by the Association in answer to the one received, and a committee appointed to wait on the church, who reported to the next Association that they attended and found that there was no probability of a reconciliation." Mill Greek church has had many ebbs and flows, but is now in good standing and about as numerous as when first constituted.

Smith's Creek

This church was constituted off from Mill Creek, formerly called the White House. The first dawn of divine light in this neighborhood arose from a few Baptists who had moved into its limits and adopted the practice of meeting at private houses on Sundays for the purpose of singing and praying and reading the Scriptures. By these means impressions were made upon the minds of many, so as to induce them to go a greater distance to hear preaching and to invite preachers. They were also favored with the divine mercy so far as to have preachers raised up among them. These were Mr. Ireland and Mr. Moffett, the latter of whom took the care of the church about two years after her constitution and has ever since retained it. They have had many revivals and declensions, but none of them were remarkable. Mr. Moffett, from the time of his first entry upon the ministry until this time, has been a steady, pious, and useful minister of the Gospel. Some years past, by an unfortunate fall from his horse, he got very much crippled, since which time he has been so lame as not to be able to move about without great inconvenience. He continues, nevertheless, to labor in the vineyard as far as he is able, and will probably ere long finish his course with joy.

Lost River

Lost River church has not been so large or flourishing as many others. At times, however, there have been some lively stirs, in which the church would increase considerably, but by frequent removals, deaths, &c., they were again reduced to a small number. At their first constitution they procured the stated ministry of Rev. A. Moffett, whose labors were owned of God. After Mr. Moffett left them they procured the attendance of John Koontz. In a few years Josiah Osborne commenced preaching, but after a little time moved to Greenbrier. Since that time they have obtained the occasional and stated services of Elders Moffett, Koontz, and Monroe just as they could. At present a promising preacher by the name of Sperry is among them.

Lunie's Creek

This church was planted by the united labors of Elders Joseph Redding and John Taylor, who, at the time of their coming among them, were young and unordained preachers. By the occasional visits of Elder Koontz and others, ordained ministers, a sufficient number were baptized to form a church, and they were constituted, under the care of Mr. Redding, who had now moved within their limits, and was ordained for that purpose. The church greatly flourished under his ministration, until some unpleasant dispute arising about Regulars and Separates, Mr. Redding moved away. The discipline of the church was thrown aside, and of course everything fell into confusion. No Baptist preacher preached among them for the space of four years. It fell to the lot of the faithful Mr. Koontz to restore order among them; after which he preached statedly for them during a considerable time, although he resided about seventy miles from them. A certain Mr. Walker, an excommunicated Baptist, imposed himself upon this church, and was by them imprudently received and ordained among them; which furnishes additional proof that more caution ought to be used in the ordination of ministers. This church is now destitute of a pastor.

Lynville's Creek

Called at first Smith and Lynville's Creek, this church is noticed in our general history of the origin and progress of the Regular Baptists. It will appear from what is there stated that this is among the oldest Baptist churches in Virginia, and that Elder John Alderson, Sr., was their first pastor. Under his care they went on very happily, having considerably increased, until the fall of 1757, when the indians invaded their country and scattered the church, many of whom moved forty or fifty miles below the Blue Ridge. After two or three years they rallied again, put their church matters in a regular train, and on the 12th of October, 1762, were received as a member of the Philadelphia Association.

In the summer of 1763 they were again disturbed by the irruptions of the indians, but returned again in a short time and continued their church state peaceably and tolerably prosperously for many years. In 1775, John Alderson Jr., son of their first pastor, was ordained and took the pastoral care of the church. In 1777 their beloved pastor moved into Greenbrier County, leaving the church destitute of any stated ministry; inconsequence of which discipline was neglected and everything fell into confusion, and so continued for about ten years. In 1787 they gathered the fragments of the church, set things in order, agreed to keep up regular discipline and obtained the stated services of Elder Anderson Moffett, a neighboring minister. They now went on smoothly and frequent additions were made to the church. In 1791 they received as member and pastor, Mr. James Johnson, hitherto a licensed preacher in Buckmarsh. The church flourished under his ministry. But, to the great loss of the church, Mr. Johnson also moved off into Kanawha County in 1794. Since that time they have had the stated and occasional services of the faithful but aged Elder A. Moffett. This has never been a large church, but can boast of several worthy and valuable members.

Silas Hart, a native of Pennsylvania, moved into the bounds of this church and became a member. He died and left by his last will to the Philadelphia Association property sufficient to yield an annuity of £50, to be kept in the hands of trustees and applied to the education of young preachers. The Philadelphia Association appointed the Rev. David Jones to receive the money in their behalf; but upon application the executors of Hart refused to pay it, upon the ground that the Association was not incorporated, and consequently not known in law or capable of maintaining an action. David Jones commenced a suit in chancery in Rockingham court, and in 1802 a decree was pronounced in favor of the executors. Jones appealed to the Staunton High Court of Chancery, when, in 1803, the decree was affirmed. He then appealed to the High Court of Appeals, where, in 1807, the decree was finally affirmed. Between the time of the decision in the Staunton Chancery Court and that in the Court of Appeals, the Philadelphia Association became incorporated. This, taking place subsequent to the commencement of the suit, did not avail as to the suit then depending. The Court of Appeals, however, made a reservation in the decree, stating that nothing done in this suit should affect any other suit which should be hereafter brought by the Baptist Association meeting in ordinary at Philadelphia; so that by resorting to another original action the Association will ultimately receive the money. This is certainly an important case to the Baptists of Virginia. From the decision above mentioned it would seem doubtful whether any property held by the Baptists as a religious society is safe. It remains, therefore, for them hereafter to decide whether it will be best to suffer their meetinghouses and other property to

continue thus jeopardized, or to become incorporated. If their becoming incorporated would be a dangerous precedent, leading in
any wise to religious oppression, it is better to remain as they are,
for it would certainly be more wise to jeopardize property than
principles. A fair and unprejudiced investigation of this subject is
desirable at this time, and would probably lead to beneficial effects.

Table of the Middle District

Year	Number at Constitution	Present Number	By Whom Planted	Former Pastors	Current Pastors	Counties
1765	40	60	Hariss, Walker	J. Walker, S. Walton		Nottoway
1771	81	150	W. Webber, J. Anthony	D. Tinsley, J. Dupuy, G. Smith, J. Wollridge		Powhatan
1774	30	300	I. Walker, R. Chastain	J. Garnett	S. Woodfin	Powhatan
1778	30	172	W. Hickman	W. Hickman	C. Forsee	Chesterfield
1777	13	71	S. Hariss, others	I. Hatcher, W. Hickman, G. Smith, J. Rucks		Chesterfield
1790	27	220	G. Smith, B. Watkins	B. Watkins	B. Watkins	Chesterfield
1778	20	200	E. Clay	E. Clay	E. Clay	Chesterfield
1802	117	156	E. Clay	T. LaPon	T. LaPon	Chesterfield

Name of churches
Nottoway
Powhatan
Muddy Creek
Skinquarter
Tomahawk
Spring Creek
Chesterfield
Salem

CHAPTER SIXTEEN:
History of the Middle District Association, Including the Sketches of Churches

When the General Association was divided, the lower district, on the south side of James River, assumed the name of the Middle District, being between the upper, which was called Strawberry, and the Portsmouth, which was then a part of the Kehukee. The Middle District included all the churches between the upper boundary of the Kehukee and the lower boundary of the Strawberry. The exact number of churches cannot be ascertained, as they were not entered in the Association minutes in those days.

The Middle District Association met in 1784 and organized themselves.[1] Their second session was held at Rice's meetinghouse, Prince Edward County, May 9, 1785. A general dearth in religion existed almost throughout the State. The names of fifteen delegates only are entered upon the minutes as sent from all the churches.

The business of this session related chiefly to state grievances, all of which are noticed elsewhere.

The Association continued to meet twice a year during this cold and wintry state; but they took up very few subjects except those that respected local matters.

In May, 1787, they met at Nottoway meetinghouse. The prospects began to be more auspicious; about four times as many delegates attended the Association. Many churches speak of revivals either already commenced or ready to break forth. As soon as there was sufficient warmth to put the churches in motion, so as to induce them to send their delegates to the Association, it was found that the district was too large to assemble in one body. Accordingly, when they met at Mossingford, May, 1788, they agreed to divide into two districts, or rather to strike off the upper churches in order to form a new Association, which was called Roanoke. The boundaries were fixed as follows: beginning where the Kehukee Association line crosses the Meherrin River; from

---

[1] The minutes of this session could not be procured.—*Author's note.*

thence upward by Lunenburg Courthouse to the Double Bridges; from thence to Charlotte Courthouse; thence the Lawyer's Road to New London to the upper line dividing Strawberry District, leaving it optional with churches near the line to associate in either district as might suit their convenience.

They held their first session, after the division, at Rice's meetinghouse, Prince Edward County, where they made some new regulations for the government of the Association.

During the different sessions between 1788 and 1791 nothing of any importance was done. The accounts received from the churches were interesting. It was a time of ingathering of souls.

In May, 1791, they met at Cedar Creek meetinghouse, in Lunenburg County. Here it appears that the revivals in some places had subsided, but in others were going on.

The circular letter for this session was a pleasing performance. It contains these forcible remarks upon ministerial support:

> *We fear covetousness and want of reasonable support of the ministry is one great reason why we are so languid in vital religion. When our ministers ought to be out and working in God's vineyard, behold they are forced to leave the flock, hungering for the bread of life, while they are struggling to provide necessaries for their families. When we consider the many pertinent publications on this subject, as well as the clear and obvious manner in which it is laid down in the Scriptures, it is somewhat astonishing that this duty is still so little attended to. What is man in his best estate?*

From this session until October, 1792, when they met at Appomattox meetinghouse, the business was altogether local. At the above session they made an arrangement of rather a singular nature. It was agreed that persons appointed by the Association should visit every church in the district, and "inquire into their state and standing; to see whether the Word and ordinances are duly administered; discipline kept up; gifts encouraged and licensed; a sufficient number of deacons ordained; pastors supported; flocks visited from house to house and their numbers known; churches destitute of pastors instructed in their duty; small constitutions not able to live to be dissolved; overgrown churches to be constituted for convenience."

From this, as well as many other proceedings in the different Associations, it clearly appears that the churches are often willing to depute to the Associations a portion of power as being necessary for the promotion of order and good government, and that when rightly used it is always productive of good effects. It is incumbent on the churches to inhibit them from the abuse of such powers.

From October, 1792, until October, 1797, they met, as usual, twice a year. Complaints of the cold state of religion during this season are universal. In 1797 the tone is much changed. At their session at Traylor's, in Chesterfield, they say in their circular letter, "How are our joys and sorrows heightened by turns, whilst we hear from some parts that God is magnifying the riches of His grace in the salvation of sinners, and from others that no symptoms of revivals appear!"

The sessions were as usual until October, 1800, when they met at Tarwallet meetinghouse, in Cumberland county. This is said to have been one of the most unpleasant, and, indeed, confused meetings that the Association had ever witnessed. The consequences did not subside for several years, as we shall presently show.

It was at this session that Mr. Conrad Speece (now a Presbyterian preacher), who had been baptized in the course of this year by Elder James Saunders, was introduced as a Baptist preacher, and was found both in the pulpit and in private conference agreeable and clever. He was a man of considerable learning, having been educated for a Presbyterian preacher. By reading some treatise on believers' baptism, as it is said, he became convinced of the impropriety of infant baptism. After some time devoted to the study of the subject, he offered himself a candidate for baptism, and was accordingly baptized by Mr. Saunders. Soon after this Association he professed to be again convinced of the validity of infant sprinkling, and wrote a letter to Mr. Saunders to that effect. He rejoined the Presbyterians and has since continued with them.

Of his motives it is difficult to judge. By some it was said that he was disgusted with the turbulent proceedings of the Association at this session; by others, that Mr. Speece was much disappointed on finding that Baptist preachers received little or no compensation for their ministerial services. It is, perhaps, more probable that he found the general tenor of the manners and customs of the Baptists quite different from his own and his former associates. Finding his temper soured at the loss of society to which his habits were assimilated, and not able at once to accommodate himself to that into which he had now fallen, he was the more easily persuaded of the truth of principles which but a few months previously he had announced as erroneous and false. It has sometimes been made a question in private companies whether it would not have been wiser on this occasion to have separated baptism and church

There were at that time several other eminent Presbyterian preachers halting between two opinions. It was thought they were perfectly persuaded of the impropriety of infant baptism, and therefore did not for many years baptize a single child, but were averse to joining the Baptists; or, however, from some cause did not do it. Now, say some, had one or more of these been baptized, without requiring them to become members of a Baptist church, they could have baptized the rest, and they might have formed a society to themselves, in which the ordinances would have been preserved pure, although their church government and general manners would have been different from the other Baptists. These suggestions were wholly speculative. One thing, however, is certain, that when Mr. Speece deserted the Baptists, the scruples of all the others were quickly removed, and they resumed the absurd practice of sprinkling children. Of Speece, we must say, we wish that he had either never submitted to baptism, or that being baptized he had not again turned away.

After their usual sessions, held twice a year, in which they only arranged local matters, the Association met, May, 1803, at Bethel meetinghouse, in Chesterfield County. Here they finally settled the confused business arising from the session of 1800. At the session of 1800 a censure was voted against a member of the Association, who had been appointed to attend the General Meeting of Correspondence, but who had not attended, alleging for excuse that he disapproved of the institution. The vote of censure gave great umbrage to the delinquent member. After considerable confusion the vote of censure was rescinded. This did not prove satisfactory. He complained to the church of which he was a member, and they remonstrated to the next Association. The matter was agitated from session to session, but not effectually settled until the Bethel meeting. It seems the church required of the Association to make concessions for having maltreated their delegate. When the thing was taken up at Bethel the deputies from the churches[1] made their remonstrances, and the Association made concessions. This manifested on the part of the Association a pacific disposition, which is highly commendable when applied to suitable cases. Whether the censure was unmerited or the remonstrance just or not, the mode of proceeding was surely highly incorrect. To ask one Association to make concessions for the acts of another is virtually to require of one set of men to repent for the sins of another, seeing no two Associations would probably be composed of the same individuals, and especially at the distance of two or three years from each other. The most that one assembly of representatives in any case can properly do towards making reparation for the offences of another is to rescind their offensive measures. For an Association to make direct concessions to an individual or a set of individuals is too great a prostration of dignity ever to be thought of.

October, 1803, they met at Walker's meetinghouse, in Prince Edward County. Here a proposition was made to divide the district. In answer to this it was agreed to call a convention consisting of two members from a church, and that an invitation be given to the Roanoke and Portsmouth Associations to unite in the convention, so that they might, if agreeable, strike off a part of their churches in order to make the Associations by this new arrangement more convenient for all parties. The convention accordingly met and formed two new Associations, leaving to the Middle District only nine churches. For further account of this division see Appomattox Association.

The Middle District continued to meet twice a year until 1807, when they resolved to have only one session in each year. No business worthy of historical notice has been transacted since they were thus reduced. They have hitherto refused to become members of the General Meeting of Correspondence.

From the time of the division in 1783 until this time Rev.

---

[1] Two or three other churches had united in the remonstrance.—*Author's note.*

Eleazer Clay has generally acted as moderator, a few sessions excepted. Until Roanoke was stricken off, Rev. John Williams acted as clerk. From that time until he removed to Kentucky, in 1795, Rev. Simeon Walton acted. Since that period Rev. Benjamin Watkins has discharged the duties of that office. The continuation of the same clerk without reappointment at each session seems to be a wise and prudent measure. The papers being lodged in his hands, he would feel it more incumbent on him to be in place, as well to qualify himself more expertly for his office, when he knows there is no uncertainty as to his appointment.

Nottoway

The first origin of vital religion in this neighborhood began with a Mr. Samuel Thompson. He was not a preacher, yet, willing to do what he had talents for, he read publicly to such as would come to hear him Whitefield's and Davies's sermons. By this means some of his neighbors obtained a hope of eternal life. These new converts hearing that there were persons on Dan River that preached these doctrines, they traveled off to look for them. This took place about 1768. They procured the attendance of Hariss and Walker. Their speech and their preaching while among them was in demonstration of the Spirit and power. A great work broke out in those parts; insomuch that the above church was constituted in 1769, and called Nottoway, which may be said to be the mother church of all others for many miles in circumference. Jeremiah Walker moved from North Carolina and took the pastoral care of them. Few men in so short a time did more good than Walker did round about Nottoway. Besides his labors in the adjacent neighborhoods, by which many churches were planted, his success in this church was very extensive. Within about two years from its constitution they rendered an account of 260 members to the Association, and it was the largest church in Virginia; and two years after that, when several others had been taken off, their number was 196. In 1784 Simeon Walton was chosen pastor, who faithfully discharged the duties of that office until 1795, when he moved westward. Simeon Walton, Charles Anderson, David Ellington, William Mullen, Robert Foster and William Ellis were preachers raised in this church. She is now at low ebb.

Powhatan

This has been long a flourishing church. The Gospel was first carried here by Elders Webber and Anthony, at that time very young preachers. They were followed by Waller, the Craigs, and finally by David Tinsley, who agreed to settle among them. The Word took a rapid spread; many were added, of whom several became preachers. Tinsley was very laborious among them until the year 1774, when he was clutched by the iron hand of persecution, and immured in Chesterfield prison. The forlorn state of the church through his absence, stirred up the spirit of John Dupuy, who commenced first as exhorter and then preacher; and a few years afterwards, when left by Tinsley, the church chose him for their pastor. Under his ministrations the church was blessed with a revival, in which there were large additions. Like many other sister churches, they fell into a declension in the time of the war. Soon after the war Mr. Dupuy moved to Kentucky. The church then chose Mr. George Smith for their pastor, who was a popular and useful preacher. Under his care they were happy and united. But him they also lost through the fertility of Kentucky soil. He moved in 1804. The next year they chose their present pastor, Elder Wooldridge. Of late years they have but few additions. Few churches have raised more preachers than the above. Their number is no less than fourteen, viz.: John and James Dupuy, Edward Maxey, George Smith, George Stokes Smith, Lewis Chadoin, B. Watkins, Noah Lacy, Thomas LaFon, Isaac Lookado, Josiah Gayle, John Wooldridge, William Rousee and Samuel Roper.

Muddy Creek

The Gospel was first carried into this neighborhood by Jeremiah Walker, Rane Chastain and others. After meeting with some opposition it so far prevailed as to bring about twenty or thirty persons into the liberty of the sons of God. With these materials a church was built. Having no stated pastor, however, they did not go on so well as could be desired. They dwindled until about 1784. Elder Samuel Woodfin, their present pastor, was called to preach for them. Under his ministry they soon revived, and additions were made from time to time amounting in all to about forty. They have had small additions at different times, though no remarkable revival. For some time back they have, like many other churches, severed a wintry season, Richard Stratton, a pious preacher, was raised here. His race was short. He was arrested by death at an early period.

Skinquarter

This is a large, respectable church of long standing. Elder William Hickman was their first pastor, and was also the father of the church. He served them about six years, and then moved to Kentucky. Under his care they enjoyed some prosperous seasons. They also felt the bitterness of some adverse scenes. Mr. Hickman was succeeded in the pastoral office by Elder John Goode. In 1785 they were favored with a revival which continued about two years. Many persons during that happy season bowed to the divine sceptre. In 1790 they were bereft by death of their beloved pastor. Mr. George Smith and other neighboring ministers attended them statedly. In 1799 Elder Charles Forsee, their present pastor, was installed in that office. His labors were blessed during the years 1799 and 1800. As many as seventy or eighty were baptized into the church. After this revival, wading through various difficulties from apostasies and other causes, the church at length settled down in peace and happiness. God again visited them in 1807 with a small revival.

Besides the pastors mentioned, this church is owned as the mother of several other preachers, viz., Josiah Rucks, James Rucks, Walthal Robertson, Edmund Goode, and Williamson H. Pittman. All these are still living, and are all still members of Skinquarter except Josiah Rucks and Walthal Robertson, who have moved away.

Tomahawk

Tomohawk has passed through many revolutions as to preachers, but by prudence and caution on the part of the active private members they have been a very happy people. Elder Jeremiah Hatcher was their first pastor, who, after serving them about two years, moved to Bedford. They then chose Elder William Hickman, who, in about three years, moved to Kentucky. They were then served by Elder George Smith as an occasional pastor for about fifteen or sixteen years, during which time they had not only calm and peaceable times, but precious revivals. He also resigned about 1791. They then chose Mr. James Rucks, who, being ordained, acted as pastor about six years, and declined through sickness. They then chose their present faithful minister. A small and unprosperous church, called Wintercomack, was once a part of the Middle District also, but was dissolved a few years past.

There was also once a flourishing church called Fine Creek, in Powhatan County. Mr. Maxey was their first pastor. He, though not a great man, was a good and useful preacher. In the midst of his course he was arrested by the small-pox and carried to an early grave in the year 1781. The church declined after his death, until, in 1793, they dissolved their constitution, and the greater part, with their pastor, Elder Samuel Woodfin, fell into Muddy Creek, where Mr. Woodfin is now pastor.

Spring Creek

This church was planted chiefly by the labors of Elder Benjamin Watkins, their present faithful pastor. After getting as many as were thought necessary for a constitution, they were organized in 1790; Mr. Watkins pastor. Few churches have seen more prosperity than this. For some years after their organization there were some added every year. About 1799 some members, feeling impressions to pray for a revival, proposed that stated prayer meetings should be kept up. This was acceded to, and proved very efficacious. Fast days were also observed and were thought to do much good. The revival commenced and continued about two years, during which time more than two hundred were baptized. Since that happy period they have passed through some afflicting scenes, yet out of all God has and will deliver them.

They have another meetinghouse besides Spring Creek, called Bethel. Here, it is expected, will be another church at some future day.

The following preachers were sons of Spring Creek; Francis Hancock, Reuben Short, Jordan Martin, and Peter M. Carey. Of these, the two last are still members. Mr. H. is dead, and Short has moved to Patrick, where he is useful. Mr. Martin is ordained, and travels and preaches considerably. His neighbors say he preaches also by example.

Mr. B. Watkins, their present pastor, is one of the most indefatigable preachers in Virginia. Though often laboring under severe infirmities of body, with other obstacles, he halts not at dangers or difficulties. He makes long preaching journeys, in which he every day, and sometimes on nights, proclaims his Master's gospel in its simplicity and power. He is, indeed, a wise workman and diligent laborer. For more than twenty years he has kept a diary, a custom productive of so many benefits that it is somewhat strange that so few have fallen into it.

Here the two fires from above and below met; Chesterfield was considered as an arm of Nottoway, Dupuy's of Goochland.

Chesterfield

The first preachers who had the honor of preaching the Gospel within the bounds of this church were William Webber and Jo. Anthony. For this they were counted worthy of a prison. Their labor was not in vain in the Lord. When they first preached there was not a Baptist in the county. In the course of a few years E. Clay, the pastor of this church, having obtained a hope, was baptized. It seems Mr. Clay had heard the Baptist preachers some years before up in Halifax. He had heard, and was wounded by the two-edged sword; but, having come out from among them, his wounds were measurably healed, until about this time, being visited by an acquaintance who had become a Baptist, his conversation opened his wounds afresh. In a few months they were effectually and radically cured by the balm of Gilead.

Mr. Clay commenced laboring in the Lord's vineyard soon after his baptism, and has continued therein from that time, faithfully testifying to the truths of the Gospel which he had felt. Being rich, he was very attentive to the preachers who were imprisoned in Chesterfield. With some interruptions he has been moderator to each of the Associations of which he has been a member. His labors for many years have been confined chiefly within his own and the adjacent congregations. He is now an old man, being sixty-six years of age, and will doubtless ere long receive the fruits of his labor.

Salem

Salem was an arm of Chesterfield church. Thomas LaFon, the present pastor, having entered upon the ministry, and being thought to have promising gifts, a church was constituted and he ordained to the pastoral charge. Under his ministry the church has increased by a comfortable revival, in which fifty-nine were added.

This makes five Baptist churches already mentioned in the county of Chesterfield, and most of them large and respectable. It is worthy of remark that, generally, the Baptist cause has flourished most extensively where it met with the severest opposition in the outset. In Chesterfield jail seven preachers were confined for preaching, viz., William Webber, Joseph Anthony, Augustine Eastin, John Weatherford, John Tanner, Jeremiah Walker, and David Tinsley. Some were whipped by individuals and several fined. They kept up their persecution after other counties had laid it aside. They have now in the county more than 500 in communion, among whom are four magistrates, two majors and five captains of militia.

[The Association above described has enlarged its boundaries by the addition of most, if not all, of the churches of Amelia County. The nine churches of 1809, with about 1,400 members (of both races), had increased in 1892 to twenty-four churches and 3,090 white members. The statistics are not at hand as to the increase of colored Baptists within the bounds of the Middle District Association. An admirable "History of the Middle District Association," by Rev. L. W. Moore, was published by the Virginia Baptist Historical Society in 1886.]

Table of Appomattox Association

Year	Number at Constitution	Present Number	By Whom Planted	Former Pastors	Current Pastors	Counties
1792	55	65	Obe, Echols		J. Weatherford	Campbell
			W. Dodson	C. Cobb	Ed. Johns	Campbell
	50		Ed. Johns	Ed. Johns	Ed. Johns	Campbell
1804	30	78	J. Jenkins	J. Jenkins	R. Dabbs	Charlotte
1771	18	90	S. Hariss	J. Weatherford	B. Todd	Charlotte
1803	15	60	H. Lester	H. Lester		Charlotte
1772	12		S. Hariss		P. Matthews	Prince Edward
1773	35	200	S. Hariss, J. Read	J. McLeroy	J. Saunders	Prince Edward
1781	12	280	J. Walked	R. Foster	A. Watkins	Prince Edward
1788	27		T. Crymes	T. Crymes, H. Lester	A. Miller	Prince Edward
1771	25	200	C. Clarke	R. Chastain	R. Chastain	Buckingham
1774	45	50	S. Hariss, J. Read	D. Patterson		Buckingham
1784	42		T. Hargett, R. Chastain	R. Chastain	W. Flowers	Buckingham
1786	26	110	R. Chastain	R. Chastain	J.L. Abraham	Buckingham
1806		31		I. Garret		Buckingham
		200	S. Hariss, J. Read	D. Ellingtone	J. Scurry	Amelia

Name of churches
Lower Falling
Ebenezer
New Chapel
Staunton River
Cubb Creek
Ash Camp
Rocks
Appomattox
Sailor Creek
Mountain Cross
Buckingham
Providence
Wreck Island
Union
State River
Sandy Creek

CHAPTER SEVENTEEN:
History of Appomattox Association, Including the Sketches of Churches.

It has already been shown in the preceding chapter that from the Middle District were struck off two new Associations, called Meherrin and Appomattox. By reference to the different tables, the bounds of these may be tolerably understood.[1] Besides the churches contained in the Middle District, several from Roanoke and Portsmouth fell into the new Associations. Of the Appomattox we purpose now to treat.

The first meeting after the division was at Walker's church, in Prince Edward County. Letters and delegates from eleven churches were received.[2] This meeting was chiefly employed in forming a constitution and rules of decorum.

The constitution in one of its articles is rather singular. It declares that the moderator shall not speak to any subject; nor any person be chosen to that office longer than two sessions successively. The design of these restraints, without doubt, was to prevent any from acquiring too much influence. But when we guard against one possible evil we ought not to be unmindful of another. The office of moderator does not appear, in its nature, to afford presumption that it would be often abused for arbitrary purposes. Therefore, to deprive an Association of the counsel and skill of one of her most intelligent members to guard against so distant an evil, has the appearance of excessive caution. It is much better to give the power and watch the use of it.

The next Association was held at Ash Camp church, in Charlotte County, in October, 1805. A query respecting the propriety of admitting unbaptized persons to communion was introduced at this session. The question was answered by a large majority that none but persons baptized upon a profession of faith were proper communicants. The subject of open communion has been more

---

[1] We had not the minutes designating the bounds— *Author's note.*

[2] It does not appear certainly from the minutes how many churches were in the Association at this time; but it is probable there were thirteen.— *Author's note.*

agitated among the Baptists in this part of Virginia than in any other, arising, as was supposed, from the high opinion which they entertained of the piety of some other Christian sects in the adjacent parts. Some respectable Baptists were induced from this consideration to think favorably of a mixed communion. It was certainly a very erroneous mode of forming an opinion. If open communion be wrong in itself, it cannot be made right by the practice of men, however exemplary they may be in other respects. Their proceedings, from the last-mentioned Association until our accounts close, appear to have been prudent and peaceable, but chiefly of a local nature.

The moderator's chair was filled alternately by Elders Rane Chastain and James Saunders. Elder Bernard Todd uniformly acted as clerk.

Having given a brief account of the proceedings of the Association, we shall now proceed to give short sketches of the churches of which she is composed, beginning with:

Lower Falling

This has, like many other churches, passed through various scenes. Since Mr. Weatherford has attended them they enjoy better times than formerly. The downfall of Obadiah Echols was very affecting to all the churches to whom he had ever ministered. This church participated in the distress.

Ebenezer

This church was raised under the labors of William Dodson. Dodson was a man of active zeal, but rather destitute of prudence; he did much good, but he also did much harm. For many years Rev. Charles Cobb was pastor of this church. He had been an elder in a Presbyterian congregation during several years of the early part of his life. It was not until he was advanced in age that he ascended the desk. This prevented his ever making considerable attainments in ministerial talents. However small his ability in the pulpit, he did much good. His life was exemplary, and a hint from such a man is more convincing than labored discourses from learned doctors who neither feel nor practice what they say. After a life of usefulness, Mr. Cobb fell asleep. Since his death Rev. Edmund Johns attends them statedly and usefully.

New Chapel

The information respecting this church has been small. It appears however, from such accounts as can be gathered, to be a church of not many years' standing. Mr. Johns, their minister, though regular in his duties about home, traveled but little to propagate the Gospel, and is therefore not extensively known. The church under his care is said to enjoy peace and harmony.

Lower Falling and New Chapel were members of the Roanoke Association from the time of the constitution until 1806. Finding it more convenient, they had themselves dismissed from the Roanoke, and May, 1805, joined the Appomattox.

Staunton River

There had been some few professors of religion in this neighborhood for many years, but until some little time previous to the constitution of the church the bulk of the people were unusually immoral and wicked. Rev. John Jenkins commenced stated preaching among them, aided by an invisible hand. They received the Word of God which they heard of him, not as the word of man, but (as it is in truth) the Word of God. A reformation of manners ensued. Some enlisted under the Gospel banner; in 1804 a considerable church was constituted. They procured the stated services of Rev. Richard Dabbs, and under his ministry they continue to be a flourishing church. Some of the members live in Halifax. From the time of her first constitution until 1807 she was a member of Roanoke. At that time she was dismissed to join Appomattox.

Cubb Creek

Now under the pastoral care of Rev. Bernard Todd, this is a church of long standing. Early after the rise of the Baptists there were some in this neighborhood who embraced religion. They became sufficiently numerous in 1771 to form an independent church. They were, a few years after the constitution, placed under the care of Micajah Hariss, in 1779. Mr. Hariss resigning on account of difference of sentiment, Rev. John Weatherford became their pastor. Under his ministry they prospered moderately. Several respectable and useful men joined them, and among them some preachers. Mr. Todd, their present pastor, is a man of education, and, at the time of his becoming a Baptist, was a man of high standing in civil society. He had for several years represented the county as a delegate in the Assembly and was among the most active and useful magistrates in the county. But all this he counted as dross that he might win Christ Jesus and be found in Him. He ascended the pulpit at a late period. He is, nevertheless, a sound and useful preacher. Under his ministry the church has flourished.

Ash Camp

This is a young but prosperous church. It was raised under the ministerial labors of Rev. Henry Lester, who was their pastor until 1808. He then moved to the western country, since which time they have had the service of Rev. Richard Dabbs. There are some very respectable characters who are members of this congregation.

Mr. Lester embraced religion at a very early period of the rise of the Baptists, when about eighteen years of age. He soon began to preach, and was acceptable as a young preacher. Marrying, however, when quite young, his ministerial labors were somewhat curtailed. He continued still to blow the Gospel trumpet, but not to such an extent as some who were less entangled with the affairs of this life. He is now (1809) about fifty-seven years of age, of good constitution, &c. In point of talents as a preacher, Mr. Lester may be considered as occupying a respectable grade.

Rev. Richard Dabbs has been a member of Ash Camp ever since its constitution. He had been baptized for several years before he began to preach. Since he commenced, few persons have risen into notice as rapidly as he, and at present, in point of popularity as a preacher, certainly none in those parts surpass him, if any can be said to equal him. He is, surely, the most indefatigable of preachers. He travels almost incessantly, and is thought by some of his intimate friends for some years past to have preached more sermons than there are days in the year. He does not preach in vain. There are seals to his ministry wherever he goes. His talents do not consist in deep investigation or close reasoning; not in full and fair explanations of mysterious texts of Scripture or of abstruse points of divinity. He says clever things, and he says them in a winning manner. Besides, his voice is harmonious, his person agreeable, and his manners, both in and out of the pulpit, affectionate and pleasing. He sings well, and is fond of it. His exhortations are warm and pathetic. With all these advantages, it would not, indeed, be strange if Mr. Dabbs's talents were somewhat overrated by many. Be that as it may, unquestionably, such gifts as he really possesses he improves to the greatest possible advantage; and if he should not become biased by excessive popularity, nor be weary in well doing, he will reap a plenteous harvest in that day.

Rocks[1]

This is among the oldest churches in this Association. The Gospel was first brought here by Samuel Hariss in 1771, who in some short time baptized Robert Jennings, a Presbyterian, a man of respectable standing, and who was for many years afterwards an ornament in the church. Other preachers watered the seed sown by Mr. Hariss, and about the year 1772 a church was constituted which fell under the pastoral care of William Johnson. He was succeeded in a few years by one Mr. John McLeroy, an Irishman, who turned out badly, and then moved to Georgia. In 1790 Elder John Weatherford became their pastor and continued for many years; and he also removed. Of late years they have had Elder P. Mathews for pastor.

Appomattox

This is an old church. When first constituted they were cursed with the services of a wretched traitor to the cause. One McLeroy, a foreigner, having specious talents as a preacher, became their pastor. After some years of confusion and distress he left them and moved to Georgia, having been previously excommunicated. They then called their present pastor, Rev. James Saunders. Under his ministry they have been a flourishing people. Of late, however, they have passed through very lamentable scenes.

Sailor Creek

This is a large and respectable church. They have for many years been under the ministerial attention of Rev. Abner Watkins. He has grown old in the vineyard, but he has not grown weary.

---

[1] This account was taken from an old manuscript of Mr. John Williams. From some circumstances it is doubtful whether there were not two churches of the same name, one in Charlotte and the other in Prince Edward.—*Author's note.*

God has been with him here, and doubtless, if he is faithful until death, he will receive a crown of life. If the temper of a whole people may be understood from that of a few, few ministers are more beloved by their congregation than is Mr. Watkins. As a preacher he is considered plain and practical, not aiming to rise very high, nor ever falling very low. In the vicinity of this church was once a church called Liberty, which flourished for some years, and then declining, was dissolved, the members falling chiefly into Sailor Creek.

Robert Foster, the first pastor of Sailor Creek, was brought to the knowledge of the truth under the ministry of Jeremiah Walker, was baptized June, 1769, and began to preach the following year. He was not considered a preacher of talents, but was respected as a good man and faithful to his trust.

Mountain Creek

This church was raised through the faithful and indefatigable labors of Rev. Thomas Crymes. He attended them as minister for some time. When he was no longer to be had, they were ministered to by Mr. Lester. Under his ministry they were favored from above. The church grew. When Mr. Lester removed they obtained the attendance of Elder Armistead Miller, who still discharges the duties of that sacred office. About the year 1791 there were in this church seventy-eight members; the present number has not been received.

Buckingham

A mother church, in the county of the same name, this is one of the largest and most flourishing churches in the Appomattox Association. The first successful preacher in these parts was Christopher Clarke. It was not long before Mr. Chastain, their present pastor, commenced preaching. He has been their pastor, their only one, from the beginning. Surely no people need ask to be more blessed in a pastor. Under him the church has prospered almost uniformly. If they have had their wintry state, from which none are exempt, yet, under the prudent management of this venerable pastor, they have not passed through such severe conflicts as some other churches. Mr. Chastain is now an old man, and ripe for the crown that awaits him. As a preacher he is held in high estimation for soundness, simplicity and usefulness.

Providence

This is not a very prosperous church at present, having been for some years without a pastor. They have but few male members, some of whom, however, are useful men. David Patterson, their first pastor, was part of the first fruits of the Gospel in these parts. After his conversion he quickly commenced preaching, and was distinguished for his steady zeal and exemplary piety. Being a man of independent property, he received no compensation for ministerial labors, which, by the by, is very much the case, either voluntarily or involuntarily, with a large proportion of Baptist preachers in Virginia.

Wreck Island

This church has for her minister Rev. William Flowers, a preacher of acceptable gifts. They are a church of good standing so far as information has been received. The church was first constituted at a place called Bent Creek, in 1775, but neglecting discipline, they declined until 1784. They were reconstituted at the place called Wreck Island or Rock Island. Mr. Chastain then attended them statedly and they prospered under his care. He was succeeded by William Johnson, and he by James Saunders as a visitor. Mr. Flowers, their present pastor, was a laborer in the church for some time before he was appointed pastor. Since his appointment he has conducted himself so prudently as to leave them no grounds to regret their choice. James Doss was also for many years an ordained minister in this church.

Union

This church, planted by the successful labors of Rev. Rane Chastain, has for some years been under the pastoral care of Rev. Jacob Abraham. With some afflictions they have also had some favorable seasons. At present they are a united and happy people.

Jacob Levi Abraham, the minister of this church, was a native of the county of King William and of Jewish parentage. He may be considered as a rare instance of the conversion of a Jew. Mr. Abraham quotes Scripture with great readiness, but some think that he shows something of the Jew still, in his preaching, by leaning more to the Old Testament in his quotations. Considering that he had but very small opportunities in point of education, he certainly possesses gifts of no inconsiderable grade.

Slate River

This is a small church in Buckingham County. We have not received any remarkable particulars respecting them. Their pastor, Mr. Isaac Garret, has the reputation of a faithful laborer, who mainly designs the advancement of Zion's prosperity.

Sandy Creek

This is a large church in Amelia County. They were formerly under the watchful care of David Ellington. After he moved southward they procured the services of Rev. John Scurry. Under his ministry they have been doing well. Mr. Scurry has the reputation of being an able minister of the New Testament. God has hitherto stood by him, and he has only to lean upon His omnipotent arm to the end, when God will not forget his patience of hope. In this church once lived John Pollard, a preacher of very considerable talents. In the early part of his ministry he was very popular and apparently very useful; but suffering his brains to be addled by some unfortunate bias, he fell into the doctrine of hell redemption, or the non-eternity of future punishment. He has since dragged on, rather a nuisance in the religious world.

"Oh, popular applause! What heart of man is proof against thy sweet seducing charms? "

TABLE OF THE MEHERRIN ASSOCIATION

Year	Number at Constitution	Present Number	By Whom Planted	Former Pastors	Current Pastors	Counties
1785	53	70	J. Williams	J. Williams	W. Richards	Charlotte
1791	77	48	J. Williams, W. Creath	W. Creath	R. Dabbs	Mecklenburg
1772	16	115	J. Walker	J. Marshall, J. Williams	W. Richards	Mecklenburg
1773	40	39	J. Walker	J. King	W. Creath	Mecklenburg
1799	14	54	W. Creath	W. Creath	W. Creath	Mecklenburg
1771	108	21	J. Walker	J. Williams	J. Shelburne	Lunenburg
1775	36	119	J. Walker	J. Shelburne	J. Shelburne	Lunenburg
1779	35	55	J. Walker	S. Jones		Lunenburg
1777	25	70	J. Walker	T. Crymes	W. Ellis	Lunenburg
1805	59	59	J. Shelburne	J. Shelburne	J. Shelburne	Lunenburg
1789	19	36		J. Lee	P. Wynn	Dinwiddie
1773	20	30	J. Walker, S. Hariss	P. Wynn	P. Wynn	Dinwiddie
1784		26	T. Hargett, R. Chastain	W. Creath	W. Creath	Brunswick
1776		57	Z. Thomson	Z. Thomson	W. Dossey	Brunswick
1787		160	Z. Thomson		W. Garner	Greenesville
1806	30	30	W. Creath	W. Creath	W. Creath	Greenesville

Name of churches
Sandy Creek
Allen's Creek
Bluestone
Maloan's or Geneto
Wilson's
Meherrin
Reedy Creek
Cedar Creek
Tussekiah
Flat Rock
Cutbanks
Harper's
James's
Reedy Creek
Fountain's Creek
Zion

CHAPTER EIGHTEEN:
History of the Meherrin Association, Including the Sketches of Churches

This Association was constituted in the year 1804 (see Chapter 16). October, 1804, the churches designated to compose the Meherrin Association assembled by their representatives at Ebenezer meetinghouse, Mecklenburg County, in a convention for the purpose of forming a constitution and rules of decorum. Twelve churches sent deputies. The constitution which they formed is somewhat more energetic than is usually avowed by Associations. By one article the Association can withdraw from a church which is not in orderly standing, which is only a soft word used for exclude or excommunicate; for it unquestionably amounts to the same thing, as is plain from the circumstance. A church thus ejected or withdrawn from by the Association is not admitted to the communion of the remaining churches. All things then fairly considered, it cannot be prudently denied but that Associations ought to possess the power of inspecting both the principles and practices of the churches within their connection. There is no better proof of the necessity of this power than the practice of Associations, most of which, if not all, have at times found it necessary to resort to this measure in order to preserve uniformity.

The next session was at Bethel meetinghouse, in Mecklenburg County, in August, 1805. At this meeting they agreed to adopt the abstract of principles set forth by the Roanoke Association some years before. This is in substance the same as the Baptist confession of faith. To exhibit something of this sort as a specimen of their principles is a proof of wisdom in a religious assembly. To wish to give it the authority of Holy Writ, or to ascribe to it anything like infallibility, is the absurdest folly and superstition.

This Association has continued to meet and transact business in a prudent and judicious manner until the present time. Nothing of a general nature not noticed elsewhere has been agitated since the last-mentioned session, except that they have joined the General Meeting of Correspondence. We shall now proceed to treat of the churches, beginning with:

Sandy Creek

This is in the lower end of Charlotte, and is a Baptist church of happy standing. They were taken off from the Meherrin church, in the fall of 1785. Rev. John Williams, being in their bounds, became a member and their pastor. So he continued until his death, in 1795. After this sorrowful event, Sandy Creek was for a long time without any stated ministry; but (to their praise be it said) they kept up regular meetings, and preserved order and discipline. At most of their meetings the question which seemed to occupy their attention was: *How shall we preserve true religion undefiled amongst us? How shall we advance its interest?* It seemed to be the general opinion that a faithful preacher would be the most likely to effect their object. Accordingly, God directed their attention to Elder William Richards, then pastor of Bluestone, and who lived about twelve miles from their meetinghouse. On the 20th of October, 1798, Elder Richards accepted their call, and has been their stated minister ever since. Under his care they have been a lively and thriving church. Spring, 1802, a work of grace commenced, and continued about eighteen months, during which time about sixty persons were received and baptized. Four preachers have been raised in this church since Elder Richards had the care of them, viz.: John Ashworth, who, with several private members, moved to the county of Franklin, and there became a separate church, under the name of Pig River (Mr. Ashworth, pastor), which church is a member of Strawberry Association; Robert Portwood, who has also moved away; David McCargo and George Petty, who are now ordained preachers, residing in the church.

Allen's Creek

The Gospel was carried here about 1770, and many persons embraced the truth under the preaching of Mr. John Williams. They were united and happy until Mr. Williams, in 1790, moved away. Being left destitute of ministerial instruction, and having a considerable number of black people in their society, of whom there were some preachers of talents, they commenced the administration of the ordinances without ordination. They were persecuted by some of the community and protected by others, equally respectable. They increased rapidly, so that in a few years more than one hundred blacks were baptized by them. These branched out into different companies, or churches, if they may be so called. When Mr. Williams returned to these parts he had no little difficulty in settling them into order. Many refused to give up their independent state, but the most orderly joined Mr. Williams; and he leaving it to the choice of those who had been baptized by the blacks to be rebaptized or not, more chose to be rebaptized. Their affairs went on not very well until the year 1790. Mr. William Creath, then a young man and active minister, recommenced the preaching of the Gospel among the people of this vicinity. God owned his labor. A goodly number were baptized, and constituted into an independent church, 1791. Mr. Creath was unanimously chosen pastor, which office he accepted and discharged the duties of for ten or twelve years, when, moving out of the bounds, he resigned his charge. Since then they have had no regular pastor, but at present are supplied with stated preaching by Mr. Richard Dabbs, whose ministrations have been very successful.

Bluestone

It seems the Gospel was first carried into the neighborhood of Bluestone by William Murphy and Philip Mulkey about 1756. Their labors were very successful, and in 1758 or 1759 they were sufficiently numerous to exercise the rights of a church. There were several white members besides a large number of blacks, belonging chiefly to the large estate of Colonel Byrd, in that neighborhood. Many of these poor slaves became "bright and shining Christians." The breaking up of Byrd's quarters scattered these blacks into various parts. It did not rob them of their religion. It is said that through their labors in the different neighborhoods into which they fell many persons were brought to the knowledge of the truth, and some of them persons of distinction. The remains of this church continued in a dwindled state until the Gospel was preached in the neighborhood of Meherrin. They then revived, and others being added, and a preacher, Mr. John Marshall, being raised up, they were constituted December, 1772.

Bluestone was chiefly taken off from Meherrin, but is at present much larger and more flourishing than the mother church. When first constituted, Elder John Marshall was installed as pastor, but he leaving them about the year 1786 or 1787, they obtained the stated attendance of Mr. John Williams, who supplied them until 1794, when Elder Richards, their present pastor, moved from North Carolina into their bounds. He was then chosen to go in and out before them, and has so continued to this day. Elder Richards, in his manuscripts furnished us, states that the cold and languid state of this church was cause of great grief to his soul, and that he often sought the Lord for a blessing. Accordingly, in the year 1799, the heavenly work began and continued for two or three years. More than one hundred members were baptized. Although since that time they have mourned under their leanness, yet order and love have mostly prevailed; not many of their new members have visibly apostatized.

Elder Richards, pastor of Bluestone, was a native of Essex County, and of genteel connections. He professed religion and was baptized when quite young. His relations being greatly opposed to it, caused him many severe trials at first; but he finally removed their opposition by his correct deportment. When he first commenced preaching his gifts were rather unpromising. By slow degrees, however, he improved his talents, until he now ranks among preachers of distinction. All sorts of persons in his own parts are found to attend his ministry. For, if there are some persons who do not think him the best of preachers, there are certainly none but what admit him to be the best of men. He has acted as moderator to the Meherrin Association for several years, and fills the post with great propriety.

Malone's or Geneto

This church was composed of members partly from Nottoway and partly from Meherrin church. Elder E. Baker was their first pastor, who soon left them and traveled off. Then Elder King took the chair. During his residence among them prosperity attended them; but to their great mortification he left them and moved to Henry County. Elder Balaam Ezell then preached for them statedly until he moved. Since his departure they have been blessed with the stated ministry of Rev. William Creath. Nothing very remarkable has occurred among them. Their present number is almost the same as when they were first constituted.

Wilson's

This church was planted by the labor of Elder William Creath while he was pastor of Allen's Creek. At first they were small, but in 1802 God sent them a time of refreshing, when about forty were baptized. Since then there have been deaths, removals and exclusions sufficient to counterbalance their additions, so that their number at present is only fifty-four. Although they have not for some years been blessed with a revival, yet under the care of their active and laborious pastor they enjoy peace, love, and good order.

Elder Creath is a man of strong mind and deep research in matters of divinity, and were his manner equal to his matter he would be among the greatest of preachers. He is thought by some to be too fond of polemic points, so as to lessen his usefulness by exciting unnecessary prejudices. One thing is certain, that in subjects of dispute there is a time to speak and a time to be silent, and when we speak unseasonably, and especially if intemperately also, we damage the very cause we profess to espouse. But with this, if this be so, Elder Creath is a very useful man. He seems willing to spend and be spent for the honor of his Master.

Meherrin

As early as the year 1757 or 1758 Mr. Dutton Lane, a preacher from Pittsylvania, preached occasionally among the people of this neighborhood. Some impressions were made, but the leading men in the neighborhood opposed. Mr. Joseph Williams, a magistrate, charged him before the whole congregation not to come there to preach again. Mr. Lane mildly replied, that as there were many other places where he could preach without interruption, he did not know that he should come there again shortly. After wishing peace to the rest of the company he gravely addressed Mr. Williams and said: "Little, sir, as you now think it, my impressions tell me that you will become a Baptist—a warm espouser of that cause which you now persecute." This prediction came to pass. In about twelve years Williams embraced religion, was baptized, and became a zealous member and useful deacon in the church that was afterwards formed at that place.

In 1768 the Gospel was preached here by S. Hariss and Jeremiah Walker. The heavenly work was prospered from year to year until a considerable number were baptized in this vicinity, all of whom were considered as members of Nottoway church, at this time the only constituted church within many miles. Being considered sufficiently qualified they were pronounced a separate church November 27, 1771, consisting of 108 members, several of whom became afterwards able ministers of the Gospel, viz., John Williams, Elijah Baker, John King, and James Shelburne. Of the two first of these, see biography of Elder John King, see the historical account of Strawberry Association. Elder James Shelburne is still living in the neighborhood of this church, and is their occasional pastor. When they were first organized as a church they received their ministerial instruction from Jeremiah Walker, who attended them statedly, and was then pastor of Nottoway. In December, 1772, John Williams was ordained to the ministry, and he became their pastor. The number of disciples increased greatly, insomuch that as many as five or six other churches were taken off Meherrin and formed into separate churches, Meherrin being the only Baptist church in the counties of Lunenburg, Mecklenburg, and Charlotte.

From deaths, removals, &c., this large and prosperous church is now reduced to twenty-one members, and, indeed, she has been lower than she is at present, her prospects being more auspicious at this time (1808) than they have been for some years. The four preachers mentioned above will always stand as monuments of honor to this their mother church. The Baptist cause has probably not been more advanced by any four preachers in Virginia.

Reedy Creek

This church in Lunenburg, was constituted in June, 1775. Soon after their constitution they made choice of Mr. James Shelburne as their pastor. He has discharged the duties of that office until this time, being still a diligent and useful preacher of the Gospel, though about seventy years of age. They have been favored with several comfortable revivals of religion, so that although there have been frequent removals and deaths, their number is still more than 100.

They have four meetinghouses within their limits, at each of which there is stated preaching once a month. The following account taken from the venerable Mr. Shelburne himself, as well as from Mr. Richards, who was present, is worthy of note. Mr. Shelburne is one of the most religious men living. He seldom talks on any other subject. It is easily conceived, then, that whenever Zion languishes, he feels his portion of sacred sorrow, expressed by the prophet Jeremiah, ninth chapter, first verse. It will also be admitted that of this mourning the church to whom he stood committed, in the solemn office of pastor, would share her full portion. Such was the case for several years. The state of religion in Elder Shelburne's church was truly lamentable. He felt it, and mourned. God heard his groans and removed his complaints. He is often pleased, however, to take strange ways (strange to mortals) to effect his purposes. It was deeply impressed upon Elder Shelburne's mind that if he would make a religious feast; or, in other words, if he would invite his neighbors generally to come to his house, and there, for three or four days, entertain them with such as he had, and at the same time employ every opportunity in exhorting them to repentance, &c., that the Lord would thereby begin a goodly work. He tried it and succeeded. He first appointed meetings at the meetinghouse, and from thence invited them, one and all, to his own house. Many went. The time was occupied in the most devout manner. Singing, prayer, exhortation, and conversation were all in their proper season attended to. The heavenly shower descended. The souls of many were refreshed, and from that time the work went on to the conversion of great numbers. After this revival declined, and times again became unpleasant, Mr. Shelburne had the same exercises, made the same experiment, and had the indescribable joy to find that the same blessed consequences ensued. Some superficial observers will say, "Indeed, then, this old gentleman could stir up a revival as easily as make a feast." No; far from it. He never attempted it in any case until urged to it by the spirit of grace deeply impressing his mind. And when divine wisdom points out the way it is as easy to accomplish a revival as it is to bend the knee or open the lips. But all the devices of man are of little avail unless the hand of God be superadded.

Cedar Creek

First planted by the labors of Rev. Jeremiah Walker, Cedar Creek church was for many years under the care of Rev. Stephen Jones, a pious, faithful and useful preacher of God's word.

After having fought a good fight Mr. Jones finished his course around 1806 aged about sixty-three. His death was much regretted by all classes of his acquaintance. Just before he died he called his family together and prayed with them and for them, saying "it was the last time, as he should in a few hours pass over Jordan." Since his death the church has been destitute of a pastor. It is not so flourishing as it has been.

Tussekiah

This is an old and numerous church. Thomas Crymes was chosen minister at the time of constitution, having been previously engaged in the ministry among them. He was a faithful and diligent servant of God. By saint and sinner he was esteemed a good man. His constant and unremitting labor in the ministry was supposed to have contributed to the disease of which he died in the year 1789. He was willing to be spent in his Master's work. Oh! Let me live the life and die the death of the righteous.

After the death of Mr. Crymes, the church, being destitute of a preacher, resolved, notwithstanding, to keep up the monthly meetings, and when met, to wait upon the Lord to see whether any would be divinely impressed to exercise any public gift, leaving to each member to sing, pray, exhort, or preach as were his impressions. In some short time William Ellis, a man well reported of for piety and zeal, became a preacher. In May, 1790, he was called to the pastoral care, and has continued ever since. Under his ministration the church, though not blessed with any important revival, has had frequent additions, and is a prosperous and happy church.

Flat Rock

This is a new church. They are the effects of Mr. Shelburne's labors. From the present prospects they are likely to be a united and happy people.

Cut Banks

Nothing has been received respecting this church, except what may be learned from the table.

Harper's

The Gospel was first carried hither in its purity and power by

Elders Hariss, Childs, and Walker; great effects ensued. The hearts of many being wrought upon, produced a great reformation among the people. Finally, in 1773, a church was constituted. They were for some time attended by Mr. Walker. After his downfall they were destitute until, in 1787, Rev. Peter Wynne was ordained to the care of them. They have never been a very numerous church, but have had some useful members. At present, however, through deaths, removals, &c., they are not so flourishing as they have been. Mr. Wynne is still their pastor; a man that fears God and works righteousness.

James's

This is a young church, concerning which nothing worthy of notice can be had. They live in peace and love with one another.

Reedy Creek

This church in Brunswick County, together with Fountain's Creek, Geneto, Cut Banks, and Harper's, were members of the Portsmouth Association until Meherrin Association was constituted. Hence we may account for the circumstance of there being two churches of the same name in this Association.

Reedy Creek was planted by the ministerial labors of Mr. Zachariah Thomson, who continued to visit them stately for some time. After living many years without any regular pastor, they at length called and obtained the services of Elder William Dossey, who is a young man of talents, piety, and very amiable manners. He has hitherto resided, when in these parts, at the house of Mr. Joseph Saunders, clerk of the Meherrin Association. "Mr. Saunders," says the History of the Kehukee Association, "with other members of this church, is remarkable for virtue, piety, and usefulness." He was also clerk of Portsmouth. Since Mr. Dossey has had the care of them the church has been looking up.

Fountain Creek

This is a large church, first planted by the ministry of Elder Zachariah Thomson. Mr. William Garner took the care of them at their organization and has continued ever since. They have had their ebbs and floods, but have generally been a prosperous church. In the year 1802 the rich clouds of mercy gathered and they had a pleasant shower. A considerable number was added.

There is an arm of the church in North Carolina, who assemble at Vasers meetinghouse, Northampton County.

Zion

Zion is also some of the fruits of Mr. Creath's ministry. Having been lately constituted, nothing more need be said except that they are in peace and harmony among themselves and bid fair to prosper. Mr. Creath still attends them statedly.

TABLE OF ROANOKE ASSOCIATION.

Name of churches	Year	Number at Constitution	Present Number	By Whom Planted	Former Pastors	Current Pastors	Counties
Catawba	1773	100	60	S, Hariss	J. Hill, N. Hall, W. Dodson	P. Hurt	Halifax
Buffaloe	1776		87	S. Hariss	T. Gilbert, N. Hall, O. Echols, J. Hurt	C. Hubbard	Halifax
Mayo	1774	100	250	R. Picket	R. Picket	R. Picket	Halifax
Wynn's Creek	1773	35	40	O. Echols	O. Echols, T. Dobson		Halifax
Hunting Creek	1775	8	80	T. Dobson	T. Dobson	T. Dobson	Halifax
Musterfield	1779	13	38	O. Echols	L. Baker	L. Baker	Halifax
Childrey	1783	30	160	O. Echols	O. Echols, J. Owen	J. Jenkins	Halifax
Millstone	1787	35	81	W. Dodson	W. Dodson, S. Brame	J. Jenkins	Halifax
Arbor	1785	35	81	W. Dodson	W. Dodson	J. Atkinson	Halifax
Polecat	1790	20	17	O. Echols	O. Echols, S. Brame	J. Atkinson	Halifax
Miry Creek	1803	40	34	J. Atkinson	C. Lovelace	C. Lovelace	Halifax
Liberty	1802	50		J. Atkinson			Halifax
Daniel River	1802	60	84	J. Jenkins	C. Lovelace	C. Lovelace	Halifax
Twelve Corner	1803	25	30	C. Hubbard	C. Hubbard	C. Hubbard	Halifax
Mossingford	1785	11	196	J. Williams	J. Williams	R. Dobbs	Charlotte
Buffaloe	1778	30	90	J. Read	H. Lester, J. Read, J. Watkins	B. Ezell	Mecklenburg
Seneca	1804	60	128	J. Jenkins	N. Lovelace	N. Lovelace	Campbell

Name of churches	Year	Number at Constitution	Present Number	By Whom Planted	Former Pastors	Current Pastors	Counties
Mill church	1770	19	103	J. Creel	J. Creel, J. Burgess, J. Atkinson	E. Dodson	Pittsylvania
Upper Banister	1773		40	S. Hariss	W. Bailey, O. Tarrant, R. Elliot	W. Blair	Pittsylvania
County Line	1771		47	S. Hariss	S. Hariss, O. Echols, W. Dodson, S. Brame, M. Bates		Pittsylvania
Birch Creek	1787	55	93	R. Elliot	R. Elliot		Pittsylvania
Union	1780	35	60	R. Elliot	R. Elliot, J. Tompkins	D. Nowlen	Pittsylvania
Bennett's	1790	22	67	J. Kenney	J. Kenney, G. Dickenson	J. Jenkins	Pittsylvania
White Thorn	1791	80	53	M. Bates	M. Bates	W. Hopwood	Pittsylvania
Lower Banister	1798	32	277	J. Jenkins	J. Jenkins	J. Jenkins	Pittsylvania
Stinking River	1800	40	52	M. Bates	G. Dickenson	G. Dickenson	Pittsylvania
Shokoe	1803		60	J. Jenkins	D. Nowlen	D. Nowlen	Pittsylvania
Double Creek	1803	35	48	J. Atkinson	W. Moore		Pittsylvania
Zion's Hill	1807	35	35	J. Jenkins	J. Warner	J. Warner	Pittsylvania

CHAPTER NINETEEN:

History of the Proceedings of the Roanoke Association from Her Constitution until 1807.

It has already been shown that Roanoke was stricken off from the Middle District in May, 1788. Their first session was held in October, 1788, at Miller's Ferry, Dan River—Watkins's meeting-house; in which, according to custom, they were chiefly employed in forming a constitution or rules of government. This constitution possesses more energy in some of its provisions than will be found in the form of government adopted by most of the Associations. It has stood more than twenty years, and under it the Association has prospered to an unusual extent, as will be seen hereafter. By this constitution the Association is made the medium to procure suitable presbyteries in the ordination of preachers, and likewise to obtain seasonable aid in all matters of distress to the churches.

They[1] met for the second time in May, 1789, at Grassy Creek meetinghouse, in North Carolina.

Letters were received from twenty churches, the state of which is described in the following extract from the circular letter: "Excepting a few instances, we had agreeable accounts from the churches touching the advancement of Emmanuel's interest, and from some parts very much so."

The business with which this session was occupied displays a noble and enterprising spirit, and proves that if they could have effected their intentions they would have done much towards advancing the respectability of the Baptist society. But, alas! What are the most noble views without means to accomplish them?

The erection of Baptist seminaries of learning and the publication of a history of the Baptists in Virginia were the subjects of the greatest importance to which they attended. For further infor-

---

[1] After the separation from the Middle District they were joined by several churches in North Carolina.—*Author's note.*

mation as to their proceedings on each, see the History of the General Committee and other places.

A copy of the minutes of this Association, accompanied by a letter from Rev. John Williams, was sent by him to Mr. Rippon, London, who published extracts therefrom in his Annual Register of the Baptists.

October, 1789, they met again at Catawba meetinghouse, Halifax County. Letters from twenty-eight churches were received. Their tidings were pleasing.

About this time Henry Pattillo, a Presbyterian preacher of distinction, had preached several times in favor of infant baptism, in which he had degraded the Baptists in the most scurrilous manner. The Association, in order to rebut his calumny, appointed John Williams to answer him on a certain day, which they determined should be a day of fasting and prayer. Accordingly, Mr. Williams fulfilled the appointment to the general satisfaction of the Baptists and their friends, and to the annoyance of their enemies. A David can slay a Goliath when he comes to him in the name of the Lord of Hosts.

Their next session was at White Oak Mountain, Pittsylvania County, June, 1790. Letters from thirty-four churches were received, affording no singular intelligence. The business of the Association was not interesting.

October, 1790, they met again at Picket's meetinghouse. Letters were received from thirty-one churches.

At this Association some debate arose as to the authenticity of the Christian Sabbath; but was at length unanimously determined in favor of its being observed as a sacred day. This subject has been not unfrequently taken up among the Virginia Baptists, both in public and private, and the divine authority of the Sabbath day disputed by some. In consequence of such debates, it has been thought that the Sabbath has not been as religiously observed in some places as duty would require.

An abstract of principles, containing twenty articles, was published by this Association. They are substantially the same as the confession of faith.

They met at Dobson's meetinghouse, Halifax, June, 1791. Letters were received from thirty-four churches. They detail nothing singular. It was determined that in future the district should be divided into two; the one to be called Dan River Association, and the other to retain the name of Roanoke. It is unnecessary to detail the particulars of this division, seeing after two sessions they determined to reunite.

October, 1791, the Roanoke Association met at Catawba meetinghouse, Halifax.

April, 1792, they met at Allen's Creek meetinghouse, Pittsylvania.

October, 1792, they met at Mill meetinghouse, Pittsylvania. No business worthy of notice was transacted at these sessions.

May, 1793, they met at Grassy Creek meetinghouse, North Carolina. Letters were received from twenty-seven churches, from which it appeared that the state of religion was very adverse indeed, only twenty having been baptized since the last Association.

October, 1793, they met at Hart's chapel, North Carolina. Letters from thirty-six churches were received, detailing unpleasant tidings as to the low state of religion.

The following query was introduced and answered, viz.: "Whether the excommunication of a minister does not make his credentials null and void?" Answered in the affirmative.

This is a subject of general interest. Many evils have been produced from excommunicated preachers availing themselves of their former credentials, yet it is difficult to find a remedy.

May, 1794, they met at Bluestone meetinghouse, Mecklenburg. Letters from twenty-six churches were received, the language of which was lamentable. In all, forty-four had been baptized. The total number in all the churches was 3,148.

October, 1794, they met at Catawba meetinghouse, Halifax. Letters from thirty-six churches were received. They still lament their languid state. The only business transacted at this session worthy of notice was the division of the district. The State line became the boundary between the two districts. The churches in North Carolina were constituted under the name of the Flat River Association. The Roanoke appointed their next session to be held at Banister meetinghouse, Pittsylvania County, on the Saturday before the first Sunday in May, 1795.

Saturday, May 2, 1795, they met at the appointed place. Letters from twenty-five churches were received, all of which bemoan the dark and gloomy state of religion among them. The circular letter to the churches on this subject speaks in this wise: "We have read your letters which give us the doleful tidings of the declension of religion in this district, and also how few there are added to the borders of Zion. O, brethren! What counsel shall we give you in this distressing situation? We can only say that the cause must exist among the professors of religion. God has not changed. It must be, therefore, certain that we have changed, and that our transgressions have raised a wall between God and our souls." This letter was composed by Samuel Brame. The whole number of churches now remaining in this district is thirty-four. The whole number baptized in the corresponding churches is eight only. The whole number in all the churches is 2,085.

October, 1795, they met at Reedy Creek meetinghouse, Halifax.

May, 1796, they met at Sandy Creek meetinghouse, Charlotte.

October, 1796, they met at Buffaloe meetinghouse, Mecklenburg.

May, 1797, they met at County Line meetinghouse, Pittsylvania.

October, 1797, they met at Musterfield meetinghouse, Halifax.

May, 1798, they met at BufFaloe meetinghouse, Halifax.

October, 1798, they met at Emmerson's meetinghouse, Pittsylvania.

May, 1799, they met at Millstone meetinghouse, Halifax.

October, 1799, they met at Allen's Creek meetinghouse, Mecklenburg.

May, 1800, they met at Arbor meetinghouse, Halifax.

October, 1800, they met at Whitethorn meetinghouse, Pittsylvania.

May, 1801, they met at Childrey meetinghouse, Halifax.

October, 1801, they met at Mossingford meetinghouse, Charlotte.

The business done during this long wintry state is not of sufficient importance to command attention, except as to their mode of proceeding respecting the languid state of Zion. An industrious and careful shepherd watches and feeds his flocks in winter, guards them from wolves and dogs, shelters them from storms, cherishes the weak, stays the wandering, separates the contagious, puts out the troublesome, &c., &c., and has them in spring strong and lively to bring forth and raise their young. So acted the Roanoke Association towards the churches. As a mother nourishes her children, so she nourished her people. Her conduct during this period is worthy of lasting remembrance. Frequent days of fasting and prayer were appointed and observed through the churches, to bewail their declension and to strive for a revival. Every circular letter contained some exhortation to the churches to search for the cause, to endeavor to rouse up from their lethargy. In 1797 they laid off two districts and appointed two ministers and two laymen for each, to travel through the churches, to examine their state and standing, to stir them up to duty and to inquire if there was no accursed thing in the camp that caused the frowns of the Lord upon the armies of Israel. This measure was faithfully executed, and at the next Association the church letters expressed great approbation of its beneficial effects.

In 1798 a query was sent from one of the churches proposing an examination of the ministers as to the performance of their duty, and more particularly as to family worship, suggesting that to some neglect of this kind might be ascribed their languid state. The examination was agreed to, and each minister rose up in his place and rehearsed his exercises. Some, with great contrition, acknowledged their neglect and promised future diligence. It was a solemn season. The proverb, "Like priest, like people," though often used in ridicule, is a serious truth. The spirit of the living creature is in the wheels. Seldom do we see a dull preacher and a lively church, or *vice versa*. Therefore, for the most part, to reform the ministry is to revive the church. The ministerial examination mentioned above is said to have made great changes. It operated like Paul's epistle to the delinquent Corinthians. They sorrowed after a godly sort. It wrought in them great carefulness, &c. It was not a great while after this, viz., the middle of the year 1799, that the dawning of one of the bright days of the Son of Man appeared. The work, however, was confined to a few churches until the beginning of the year 1802, when it became general. Fair and refreshing gales are not more welcome to sea-worn sailors than these breathings of the Holy Spirit were to the precious sons of Zion in this Association. In some churches the numbers were more than doubled; in some, two hundred were added.[1] In their circular letter, May, 1802, they publish an account of this work, and state that one thousand three hundred and forty-one had already been baptized, and that the work was still going on.

The Association for May, 1802, was held at Buffaloe meetinghouse, Mecklenburg.

October, 1802, they met at Rieve's meetinghouse, Pittsylvania.

Notwithstanding the blessed state of the Gospel in this district at this time, they had a severe trial in the malconduct of a certain James Tompkins, and in the opposition made to the prudent discipline exercised towards him by a presbytery united to the churches of which he was a member and minister. The presbytery consisted of ministers appointed by the Association at the request of the churches immediately interested. When the presbytery met, the Upper Banister and Stewart's Creek churches united, and with the presbytery formed a council to investigate and decide on Tompkins's conduct. On a fair and impartial trial they judged him guilty of the crimes alleged against him, and excluded him. Tompkins, however, denied the allegation; and being a man of address, formed a considerable party in his favor in some of the churches, who very incautiously and prematurely expressed their disapproval of the proceedings in their corresponding letters to this session. To these churches the Association sent committees to remonstrate. The churches and individuals who had caused the distress conceded, and a report to that effect was made to the next Association.

A committee was also appointed, at the request of some of the churches, to attend the churches with which Tompkins had been connected and to give him a further chance to exonerate himself from the charges laid against him, or of making satisfactory concessions. They met and reinstated him, with partial concessions on his part. Of his guilt, however, many who were well acquainted with the whole ground entertained very little doubt. In a little time after his restoration he professed to be convinced of the truth and propriety of infant baptism, and actually joined the Presbyterians.

---

[1] The churches in this Association are confined within much narrower limits than in almost any part of Virginia, so that two hundred was a very large number indeed, all things considered.—*Author's note.*

Mr. Tompkins did not live long in the enjoyment of his new principles. The scythe of time, that sweeps down without distinction the good and the bad, brought him to the dust in a short time.

James Tompkins was a young man of considerable talents, and until suspected of disorderly behavior, was very popular as a Baptist preacher. It would seem that his downfall was a species of adversity permitted of God to be set over against the prosperity of the Baptists in this Association. It happened in the height of the revival.

April, 1803, they met at Ebenezer meetinghouse, Campbell County. Letters from twenty-seven churches were received. As far as the state of religion can be conjectured from the minutes, it appears that the revival, as it respects the conversion of sinners, was somewhat on the decline, the harvest being nearly over. But as it respects the state of the churches, it seemed that Christians were in the lively exercise of vital piety; a number of young and promising laborers thrust into the vineyard; several new churches constituted; and, with very few exceptions, peace and love reigned throughout Zion's borders.

A minister of considerable talents, misled by ambition, having about this time set up as a candidate for Congress, created some distress among the brethren. In consequence of which the following query was offered to this Association:

Query. Will the Word of God tolerate a minister of the Gospel in suing for a post of honor and profit in legislation and retain the privileges of his ministerial office at the same time?

For reasons unknown the Association never answered the query. We will offer a few reflections. For a real minister of God's Word to become a candidate for political office seems to us more absurd than for a man made prime minister to sue for the office of constable. Doubtless, in the view of a sound mind, the disparity between the office of prime minister and that of constable is not so great as between a legitimate stand in the pulpit and a seat in Congress. As the heavens are higher than the earth, so are God's honors above man's.

October, 1803, they met at Meherrin meetinghouse, Lunenburg. Letters from thirty-two churches were received. The state of religion was nearly as described at the last Association. No less than nine young preachers had been ordained from the last Association, as appears by the returns of presbyteries. For some sessions back there had been some in the Association who advocated a division of the district. On a fair trial now it was found that a large majority were decidedly opposed to it. It was, however, agreed that any churches lying on the extremity might be dismissed for the purpose of combining with others appertaining to other Associations to form a new Association. By these means it fell out that the Associations now called Meherrin and Appomattox were established. A committee of seven able and experienced ministers was appointed on Saturday to examine the amendments made to the confession of faith, and reported on Monday that they were of opinion that "the amendments and alterations are much for the better." To which the Association consented.

May, 1804, they met at Bethel meetinghouse,[1] North Carolina. Letters from thirty-one churches were received. Religion seemed not to be so warm and prosperous as at the last Association, yet there were several applications for the constitution of new churches and for the ordination of young ministers. It was determined that a summary of church discipline should be prepared for the advantage of the churches in their government and sent by the composer to the churches for inspection. This summary was finally ratified by the Association, and two hundred copies were printed. This was certainly a wise and prudent measure, calculated to preserve order and uniformity among the churches.

October, 1804, they met at Stinking River meetinghouse, Pittsylvania. Letters from twenty-eight churches were received; the state of religion nearly as at last session. No business worthy of notice was taken up in this Association.

May, 1805, they met at Catawba meetinghouse, Halifax. Letters from thirty-four churches were received; and if any judgment can be formed from the ordination of ministers and the constitution of churches, we may venture to pronounce that the state of religion was by no means very adverse in this district at this time. The circular letter, however, calls it a sifting time. No other except

---

[1] The meetinghouse is in North Carolina, but it belongs to Mayo church; the larger part of which is in Virginia.—*Author's note.*

local matters commanded the attention of the Association.

October, 1805, they met at Hunting Creek. Letters from thirty churches were received. The Association appointed the Saturday before the first Sunday in December for humiliation, fasting, and prayer for an increase of grace and a revival of God's work. This practice is surely worthy of imitation. In no Association have the appointments of fast days and such like means for the promotion of the prosperity of Zion been oftener resorted to than in Roanoke District; and it may with safety be said that within her limits the Baptist cause has flourished more than in any section of the State of Virginia, not to say of the United States. They prayed the Lord of the Harvest to send forth laborers, and they were sent. They abound in preachers, some of whom are able, and most are useful.

May, 1806, they met at County Line meetinghouse, Pittsylvania. Letters from twenty-nine churches were received. It was resolved to adopt as a circular letter for this session a letter of Mr. John Newton on the doctrine of election and final perseverance. This is certainly an admirable composition. But when we consider the prepossession of most readers in favor of authors with whom they have personal acquaintance; when we consider the improvement which these annual compositions might afford to some of the sons of genius in the Association, we are of opinion that it is impolitic to borrow, especially from old and known writings which they could easily get without printing.

October, 1806, they met at Upper Banister meetinghouse, Pittsylvania. Letters from eighteen churches were received. Their style is that of complaint on account of the dead state of Zion.

It is stated in the minutes of this session that in the churches that compose the Roanoke Association there are twenty-five ordained and five licensed ministers. There are in all twenty-nine churches, having on an average more than one preacher for each church. In this session the following query was introduced: *"Has a minister of the Gospel any more power in the government of a church than an individual of the laity?"* Answered in the negative.

This decision must doubtless carry the principles of free government beyond all Scripture example provided by ministers of the Gospel—pastors of churches are intended. Nothing can be clearer than that through the whole tenor of the New Testament they are recognized as having authority of some sort. They are called rulers, and are promised a reward if they rule well. They are called elders, alluding no doubt to elders under the Mosaic economy, who surely had authority in the nation. Paul writes to the different churches in the language of authority, and advises Timothy and Titus as ministers whom he considers as having power. It will then be asked, "What kind of authority do they possess?" To which it may be answered, "They have a power similar to that of fathers—the authority of love." Hence they are charged by Peter not to lord it over God's heritage; not to act and feel as if they were lords and masters. This sentiment, while it embraces the plain tenor of the Word, is by no means repugnant to republican church government, seeing pastors are chosen by the churches, and cannot, therefore, have any kind of power until given by them. They are, therefore, representatives of the churches exercising various branches of power, in the name and for the benefit of the church, and for the glory of God.

If this were not the case, how could the pastor be responsible for the standing of the church, as is evident from the addresses to the angels of the seven churches of Asia?

May, 1807, they met at Seneca meetinghouse, Campbell. Letters from twenty-four churches were received. The accounts, as usual of late years, represent the churches as in a wintry state. Nothing except local matters was attended to in this session.

October, 1807, they met at Millstone meetinghouse, Halifax. Letters from twenty-seven churches were received. No revival. The love of many waxing cold.

Considerable agitation of mind was excited at this session in consequence of a query introduced from a church in the county of Charlotte: *Whether it was a maxim, firmly established among the Baptists, that "human learning is of no use."* This query arose out of an illiberal assertion contained in a letter from Mr. Rice, a Presbyterian preacher of Charlotte, to the chairman of the committee of missions, and which was published in the *Assembly's Missionary Magazine* of May, 1807, in which Mr. Rice declares that among the Baptists of this neighborhood it is a maxim, very firmly established, that human learning is of no use. The Association took up the business and appointed a committee of certain brethren to answer and explain the subject. The answer, which was strong and energetic, composed by Mr. Kerr, was printed. No reply, or attempt to establish the assertion, has been made by Mr. Rice as yet.

It will easily be discovered by a judicious reader that the administration of this Association has been, from the beginning, marked with prudence, moderation, zeal, and piety, and that to her wise and watchful measures, under God, may be ascribed much of the great success which has attended the Baptist cause within her limits. Her ministers, though not blessed with classic educations, seem well versed in that wisdom which descendeth from above.

At their first constitution Rev. Samuel Hariss acted generally as moderator. Since his relinquishment and death, Rev. Reuben Picket has commonly filled the moderator's chair. Their first clerk was Rev. John Williams. He was succeeded by Rev. John Atkinson, and since his resignation Rev. John Jenkins has acted as clerk. These offices have been temporarily filled by others, but the above named were their stated servants. A number of excellent circular letters were found in the minutes of this Association. But our limits are becoming too narrow to publish the extracts which we at first intended; and in particular, one annexed to the minutes of 1801, composed by Rev. James Hurt, being an address to young preachers, and so well calculated to do good that it is with real regret we feel compelled to omit it.[1]

---

[1] Would not a volume made up of circular letters, judiciously selected, be a pleasing and profitable publication at this time? The compiler would gladly furnish a friend disposed to publish such a volume materials (to a considerable extent now in his possession) from which the selections might be made.—*Note by the author.*

CHAPTER TWENTY:
Historical Sketches of the Churches in Roanoke Association.

Catawba

The people of this neighborhood had the proclamation of peace made to them soon after the rise of the Baptists in Virginia. Samuel Hariss was the first successful preacher. His plants were watered by the succeeding labors of himself and others, until a church was constituted, and James Hill, a preacher, raised up among them. He was inducted as their first pastor, and continued for some years. In 1777, Elder Nathaniel Hall became pastor, and continued faithfully to discharge the duties of his office until 1785, when, believing himself to be supplanted by William Dodson, a preacher of popular talents, he moved to the State of Georgia, where he lived and died a faithful minister of God's Word. He, though a sound preacher, was not a minister of distinguished abilities.

Dodson having insinuated himself into the favor of the congregation, was chosen as Mr. Hall's successor. Being of a restless spirit, after a few years he left them. In 1793 they made choice of their present pastor, who has continued to serve them steadily until this time. Catawba has been a flourishing church from the beginning. They have generally had among them several private members of intelligence, piety, and prudence that were rich in this world and willing to communicate, hence they have so frequently had the Association at their meetinghouse.

Mr. Philip Hurt, their pastor, is a sensible, sound, and solemn preacher, a friend to discipline and order, and has done much good in his day and generation. God has bestowed upon Mr. Hurt one of the greatest of blessings ever enjoyed by a pious father in this vale of tears. He has the happiness to see his own son, living in the bounds of his church, a pious Christian and an eminent minister of the Gospel.

Robert Hurt was one of the firstfruits of the great revival. He commenced preaching soon after his conversion, and rose into notice as a young man of amiable manners, pious life, and very promising talents. Although he lives in the bounds of Catawba, he acts as minister for some of the neighboring churches.

Buffaloe

This was also the fruits of the venerable S. Hariss. Thomas Gilbert, a preacher of zeal and usefulness, was their first pastor. They had also the ministerial services of Nathaniel Hall and Obadiah Echols at different times; but we have not had information sufficiently distinct to be able to say at what periods these men served them. Their present pastor, Elder Clarke Hubbard, is a warm, zealous, and persevering preacher. Although his opportunities for acquiring literary culture were very small in his early life, yet as soon as he was arrested by divine grace he devoted his mind to the improvement of his gifts, and his profiting appears to all who know him. Buffaloe participated in the revival of 1802, and seventy-six were added.

Mayo

This is one of the largest churches in Roanoke Association, yet has been much larger than it is at present. From the beginning they have been a very respectable people: in 1790 they had one hundred and forty members. At subsequent periods they increased by small additions, but in 1802 they enjoyed the outpouring of the Spirit in large portions; one hundred and twenty were added, after which the church had as many as four hundred members, but by frequent removals, &c., they are now not so numerous.

They have had but one pastor, and no other can they wish, so long as he is enabled by divine goodness to perform the duties of his office. Rev. Reuben Picket, their pastor, was born in the year 1752, embraced true religion in the year 1769, and was baptized by Samuel Hariss, in Orange County, not far from his place of residence, a few months after his conversion. Although only about eighteen years of age, his mind led him to appear in public in order to persuade sinners to repentance. Hearing of a great work of God in Shenandoah County, he could not be kept back, but went into the midst of it. There he commenced, first as exhorter and then preacher, and soon became very successful in inducing his fellow-men to turn to God. He and Elder Koontz traveled together; Koontz preached in Dutch, and he in English; many of each language, through their labors, were initiated into divine favor. About this time, Mr. S. Hariss coming on a preaching visit through those parts, Mr. Picket felt great desire to travel with him; but knowing that he was not rich, and that his embarrassment would be great, unless he followed some calling for a livelihood, he was very unhappy for some length of time. Spreading his case, however, before his invisible instructor, this text came forcibly to his mind: "Go ye, and preach my gospel;" which was succeeded by the promise: "Lo, I am with you always." He immediately forsook all earthly employment, and traveled on with Elder Hariss towards the south, expecting to go to an Association in South Carolina. He was, however, stopped by a severe spell of sickness, and left by his brethren in a strange part of the world. His sufferings both of mind and body were now extremely severe. But it was only the refiner's fire purging off the dross, and leaving Mr. Picket, like tried gold, to shine with seven-fold splendor. After he was fully recovered from his afflictions, he felt the smiles of God in a more abundant manner than he had ever done. He then commenced his ministerial travels in North Carolina and Virginia, disseminating evangelical seed in various parts. He was still only about twenty years of age. Young as he was, his talents were extensively useful. Many acknowledged him as the messenger of peace to their souls; and several churches were constituted through the instrumentality of his labors. He, at length, in 1773, was ordained and took the care of Reedy Bottom, a church raised under his ministry. The work afterwards spreading to Mayo Creek, a church was constituted by the name Mayo; and, soon after, Reedy Bottom was dissolved. To Mayo, Mr. Picket has been the constant and faithful pastor from its constitution until this day. Mr. Picket stands in the highest estimation wherever he is known. Although old and very infirm, he is unremitting in his labors, and not only continues his ministrations to his own congregation, but often visits neighboring churches, especially in matters of distress. For, as a disciplinarian, he is surpassed by none. His talents are more distinguished for warm and searching addresses to the heart than for deep investigation. He has been for many years the moderator of the Association, and doubtless fills the chair with as much dignity and propriety as any man in Virginia. When he shall fall asleep his survivors will say: "Mark the perfect man, and behold the upright; for the end of that man is peace."

Mayo has also two other ordained preachers within her limits, viz., John Brookes and Abner Harrilason.

Winn's Creek

It does not appear that this was ever a thriving church. Her members have not for many years, if ever, exceeded what they are now. Planted by the labors of Obadiah Echols, his downfall in all likelihood proved a shock to the church not easily recovered from. An inveterate distress existed in this church for a long time, which drew the attention of the Association. There were several presbyterial committees sent before they could effect a remedy. They did not participate in the great revival of 1802.

Obadiah Echols, the planter and first pastor of this church, was, for many of the first years of his ministry, the most indefatigably laborious preacher anywhere in these parts; and being a minister of considerable talents, he advanced the cause of religion to a very great extent. But, alas! being a man of impetuous passions, and not keeping them under proper restraint, he fell into gross immorality. The mischief arising from his fall was commensurate with the good which sprung from his former labors. Not long before his death he professed repentance and was reinstated.

Hunting Creek

This church was planted by the labors of Rev. Thomas Dobson, and he has continued, from first to last, their pastor. Their course has been as smooth and regular as most churches. They began with eight members, and now have ten times that number.

Elder Dobson, their pastor, is now an old man. He was a native of Essex County, but moved to Halifax when young. He embraced religion in his youthful days, and soon lifted up his voice to invite wanderers into the right way. He has traveled little, but in his small vineyard he has willingly worked, and will, ere long, find his reward, according to the deeds done in the body. He is esteemed by his neighbors of every description, whether saint or sinner, a man of gravity, sincerity and usefulness.

Musterfield

This has always been a small church; yet under the care of their faithful pastor they have enjoyed love and peace. Elder Leonard Baker, who has been the pastor of this church ever since they had any, is the brother of Elijah Baker, who was so distinguished in planting churches in the early rise of the Baptists. He frequently traveled with his brother, and aided him in many of his useful labors, especially on the Eastern Shore. For many years Elder Baker has confined his labors chiefly to his own vicinity. By those who have a right to know him, he is valued as a man of sincere piety and a minister of genuine worth. Musterfield did not partake of the great revival.

Childrey

This has been a church of no small prosperity. She had not arisen, however, to so distinguished a state until the revival in 1801 and 1802. In that work from first to last about one hundred were added to Childrey. They have no regular pastor, but are blessed with the stated services of Elder Jenkins.

Millstone

This was planted by William Dodson, who also assumed the pastoral care at their constitution. Dodson was a man of ardent zeal, some talents, and but little prudence. Although he did good, he did it in such a way that it was often evil spoken of.

Their next pastor, Samuel Brame, was probably one of the most amiable, precious young men that ever ascended the pulpit. He was a native of Caroline (see Reed's church) and embraced religion when very young, under the ministry of the celebrated Mr. Leland. He married in Halifax, and moved into the bounds of Millstone church. He was a great preacher, and bade fair still to be much greater, but for reasons unknown to man, his Maker called him to Himself, when quite young. How unsearchable are the ways of God! He was brother to William Brame, mentioned in our account of the church in the city of Richmond.

Arbor

This was taken off from a church called Miller's Ferry. William Dodson took the care of it at her first constitution; but in a very short time John Atkinson was ordained, and then chosen pastor. He has continued to discharge the duties of that office ever since. They have had several revivals of religion, the most remarkable of which began in 1801, and lasted about two years. Upwards of one hundred and fifty were baptized, by which the church was swelled to a larger number than she ever had previously. Two churches, Liberty and Miry Creek, were taken off from this church since the revival, by which her numbers are considerably lessened. Arbor church has never had less than two preachers within her borders; and some of them men of the most conspicuous talents. Charles Lovelace and William Dossey were raised in this church. At present, besides their pastor, John Kerr, a preacher of celebrity, resides among them.

Elder John Atkinson, who has been their pastor about twenty-five years, is a preacher of popular and very useful talents. He travels far and near, and has been the instrument in God's hand of turning many to righteousness. He is a leading man in the Association, and for many years acted as clerk.

Elder John Kerr is a native of North Carolina, and at about nineteen or twenty years of age believed and was baptized. It was not long after his baptism before he commenced public speaking. He soon commanded attention. His speech and his preaching were in demonstration of the Spirit and of power. He shortly began to travel, and wherever he went he was highly acceptable. His labors were blessed. Marrying within the limits of Arbor church, he became a permanent resident. Although he is a member here, he preaches statedly for a church at some distance from him. If Mr. Kerr's attention should not be divided by attempting plans irrelevant to his ministry, he will probably live and die one of the brightest lights of the present age, and receive in heaven a correspondent crown.

Polecat

This is a small and rather declining church, attended at present by Elder Atkinson. A few were added in the revival of 1802.

Miry Creek and Liberty

These are two churches taken off from Arbor soon after the great revival. We are not informed of anything remarkable among them.

Elder Charles Lovelace, pastor of the former, is spoken of by his acquaintances as a good man and useful preacher.

Dan River and Twelve Corner

These are churches not distinguished for anything remarkable. They have no regular pastors, but have the stated attendance of neighboring preachers, mentioned in their proper places.

Dan River enjoyed a portion of the refreshing showers of 1802.

Mossingford

We extract from the manuscript[1] of Mr. Williams, the father of this church, the chief of what we shall say respecting it. "They were an arm," says he, "of Sandy Creek church until 1805, but being too remote to attend regularly, they were constituted in December, 1805, with eleven members. They prospered from the beginning, and really excel in harmony and union of the Spirit. And although they are situated so as to mingle continually with Presbyterians and Methodists, a number of whom are in these parts, yet, to the praise of each be it spoken, that, notwithstanding the diversity of sentiments touching externals with the former, and externals and internals with the latter, no rancor nor root of bitterness seems to be encouraged by either party, but a friendly intercourse maintained by mingling in social and private worship. It is no strange thing to see a Presbyterian and Baptist preacher in the same pulpit, each in their turn addressing the congregation. This union and sociability, carried as far as conscience will admit, is an ornament to religion." These are the words of Elder Williams, and his actions squared with the principles here professed. He was a man of catholic temper.

Mossingford sustained a great loss in the death of Mr. Williams. After some years, however, they obtained the pastoral services of Rev. Richard Dabbs, whose ministry among them has received many seals.

Buffaloe

This church lies in Mecklenburg, and may be said to be a church of happy standing. They enjoyed, at different times, the pastoral labors of James Read in his last years, of Henry Lester, of

---

[1] Many of our historical relations of the churches on the south of James River are extracted from manuscripts written by Mr. Williams, aided by Mr. Asplund, and which were taken for the purpose of publishing a history of the Baptists of Virginia.—*Author's note.*

James Watkins, and now of Balaam Ezell, a man of God and a faithful servant of his people. Buffaloe was one of the favored places in the time of the great revival. Ninety were added.

Seneca

This is a young and thriving church, under the ministerial care of Nathaniel Lovelace, a young and promising preacher.

Mill Church

This church was planted by the labors of Rev. John Creel, a Regular Baptist preacher, who about 1765 moved from Fauquier into these parts. In 1770 the church was constituted according to the mode of the Regular Baptists, under the name of Birch Creek, and in the same year joined the Ketocton Association. They continued to send delegates to that Association until 1773, when, finding it inconvenient to attend at so great a distance, and the prejudice between Regular and Separate wearing away, they were dismissed, and joined the Separates. The names Mill and Birch Creek appear to have been often confounded in the minutes of the Association. They had additions to the number of one hundred in the revival of 1803.

John Creel, their first pastor and planter of the church, was a most amiable man, and a very successful preacher. His talents, though not conspicuous, were solid, and being well occupied with his five he gained other five. He was universally loved by all descriptions of people. At about fifty-two years of age, while assisting in raising a house, he was accidentally killed by the falling of a log. Time and chance happeneth to all men.

Upper Banister

This church has been much more numerous than at present. William Blair, their present pastor, is a preacher that holds fast the faithful Word as he has been taught. He has already done much good, and being in the vigor of life bids fair to do much more.

County Line

This is an old church and was once a very flourishing one. Rev. Samuel Hariss was their first pastor. Although she is represented in the table as having commenced her church state in 1771, which is substantially correct, yet the name is not to be found in any of the Associational minutes for many years after that time. Fall's Creek appears to have been her original name, which was probably changed by the constitution of new churches. She is the offspring of old Dan River church, now dissolved, and is herself the mother of many others. Each of her pastors is mentioned elsewhere.

Union and Birch Creek

These were the offspring and care of the pious and faithful Richard Elliott, who lived respected and died lamented. He was succeeded in the care of Union by James Tompkins, mentioned in the preceding chapter. After Tompkins's dereliction they were happy enough to procure the pastoral labors of Elder David Nowlen. Birch Creek was a partaker in a small degree of the revival of 1802; thirty were added.

Bennett's

This church was the fruit of Elder James Kenny's ministry, who also was their first pastor. Elder Griffith Dickenson succeeded Mr. Kenny, and Mr. Jenkins succeeded Mr. Dickenson. The two last were not regular pastors, but attended them as supplies.

Rev. James Kenny, their first pastor, was a Methodist preacher previous to his being baptized. When he first joined the Baptists he retained some tinctures of Arminianism. This created some obstacles in his ordination as a Baptist preacher. He, however, was ordained, and continued many years as pastor. The question whether an Arminian preacher ought to be ordained was agitated here with some warmth; and not only here, but in many other places. It is certainly a question of no small difficulty. The doubt, we conceive, is not whether it is lawful, but whether it is expedient. To decide questions of expediency, much regard ought to be paid to circumstances. Exactly the same decision might not be proper in different places. Paul circumcised Timothy at Lystra; but would not circumcise Titus at Jerusalem.

Whitethorn

Of this church, we have no information of anything very remarkable.

Elder Matthew Bates, their father and first pastor, was an amiable and eminent minister of God's Word. The few years in which

God permitted him to work in his vineyard were well employed. He died at an early period of life, lamented, just as far as he was known.

Willis Hopwood, their present pastor, is a young man of strong and ingenious mind. May he have a double portion of his predecessor's spirit!

Lower Banister

This is one of the largest and most respectable churches, not only in Roanoke, but in any other place.

Mr. Jenkins, who has been their pastor from the beginning, is a minister indeed. He was a native of Fauquier County, and was baptized previous to his removal to Pittsylvania. He was ordained to the ministry in 1794, and has been one of the most successful preachers ever since. Several churches have been planted by his labors, and all those which he attends seem to prosper more or less. He has a mind susceptible of great improvement; and although for want of opportunity when young, his education was rather small, yet his literary attainments, acquired by dint of close attention, are very considerable. A few years past he published a treatise on "Infant Baptism," and one on "Final Perseverance," both of which display considerable ingenuity, and the last of which was much admired.

Lower Banister enjoyed the revival of 1801 and 1802, beyond any of her sisters. Two hundred and fifty newborn sons and daughters were added to her former family.

Stinking River

This is the offspring of the excellent Mr. Bates. Elder Griffith Dickenson, their present pastor, though a man of some age, has not been a great many years in the pulpit. He is an old Revolutionary soldier. He spent his time when young in honorably fighting for his country; his last days he devotes to the still more honorable occupation of marshaling the host of Israel. His present weapons, though, are not carnal, but mighty. As a preacher, when ardently engaged, he displays talents and animation, by which his hearers "take knowledge of him that he has been with Jesus."

Shockoe

This is a rather thriving church. They have had from the first, as pastor, Elder David Nowlen. If we may judge of him from the various appointments for presbyteries, committees, &c., thrown upon him by the Association, we must say he appears to be a servant ready to every good word and work.

Double Creek, Zion Hill, and Stewart's Creek

These are small churches in this Association, concerning which we have not been able to learn anything remarkable.

Elder George Roberts, now a resident of North Carolina, in Flat River Association, and who acts there as moderator, was once an active and successful preacher in Virginia. He professed religion shortly after the rise of the Baptists in Virginia, and putting hand to the plow, has never yet looked back. He greatly assisted in procuring the great ecclesiastical revolution in the State. He often attends the Roanoke Association and is useful in their councils.

TABLE OF STRAWBERRY ASSOCIATION

Year	Number at Constitution	Present Number	By Whom Planted	Former Pastors	Current Pastors	Counties
		100	N. Shrewsbury	J. Williams, J. Preston	W. Leftwitch	Bedford
1797	90	200 .	N. Shrewsbury	I. Fuqua	J. Moorman	Bedford
		100	J. Anthony	J. Anthony	J. Anthony	Bedford
			J. Hatcher	J. Hatcher	G.Rucker	Bedford
		40	W. Johnson	W. Johnson	J. Black	Bedford
1801	86	160	J. Preston	J. Preston	J. Burnet	Bedford
1805	28		I. Fuqua	J. Carter, I Fuqua		Bedford
1805	40	90	I Fuqua	I. Fuqua	I. Fuqua	Bedford
		12	A. Weeks	A. Weeks	A. Weeks	Bedford
		26	N. Shrewsbury	W. Moorman		Rockbridge
1804	30	35	W. Moorman	W. Moorman		Botetourt
1804	32	28	W. Moorman	W. Moorman		Botetourt
	20	30	W. Johnson	J. Fears	W. Turner	Franklin
			Mr. Douglas	Mr. Douglas	J. Pedigo	Franklin
1801	18		J. Pedigo	J. Pedigo	J. Ashworth	Franklin

Name of churches
Goose Creek
Little Otter
Otter
South Fork of Otter
Staunton River
Beaver Dam
Suck Spring
Timber Ridge
Difficult
Buffaloe
Rock Spring
Mill Creek
Gill's Creek
Chapel
Bethel

Number at Constitution	Present Number	By Whom Planted	Former Pastors	Current Pastors	Counties
62	65	W. Turner	W. Turner	W. Turner	Franklin
28		R. Hall	R. Hall	J. Pedigo	Franklin
		R. Stockton	R. Stockton	J. Pedigo	Franklin
				J. Ashworth	Franklin
		R. Hall	R. Hall	J. Pedigo	Patrick
		J. Pedigo	J. Pedigo	S. Hubbard	Patrick
		R. Stockton	R. Stockton	J. King	Henry
			J. Anthony	J. King	Henry
30	30	J. Anthony	J. Anthony	J. Anthony	Campbell

230

Name of churches	Year
Black Water	1804
Pig River	1773
Snow Creek	
Snow Creek and Pig River	
Smith's River	
Jack's Creek	1804
Leatherwood	1772
Beaver Creek	
Burton's Creek	1806

CHAPTER TWENTY-ONE:
History of the Strawberry Association, Including the Sketches of the Churches.

It appears from the most authentic documents that this Association was constituted previous to the dissolution of the General Association, and about the year 1776. For, at a meeting of a General Association in the year 1782, as appears from the minutes, the Strawberry Association corresponded. The entry is made in the following words, viz., "Robert Stockton, a messenger from the Strawberry Association with a letter, was admitted to his seat." And again, towards the close of the minutes, is the following entry: "The clerk is directed to write a letter to the Strawberry Association in answer to theirs, with a copy of our proceedings."

The first laborers in the ministry in this district appear to have been the two Murpheys (William and Joseph), Samuel Hariss and Dutton Lane. Soon after the rise of the Baptists in these parts there were several preachers called to the work, the most distinguished and the most useful of whom was Robert Stockton. Through the indefatigable labors of him and others the cause of religion flourished to a considerable extent. The churches from the bounds of this Association met in the General Association until the division in 1776, after which they probably continued as an independent Association and corresponded with the General Association only by messengers sent from the Association.

When this district first became independent it must have had very few churches, for in 1787 there were only eleven churches and ten ordained preachers. From 1787 to 1793 the increase both of churches and preachers was very great; for, after striking off the New River District, there remained sixteen ordained ministers in Strawberry. In 1798, after Mayo was takeu off, there remained twelve churches and eight ordained preachers. In 1808 they had twenty-four churches and sixteen ordained preachers. From which it appears they just doubled their number, both of preachers and churches, in ten years.

While Mr. Stockton was among them he generally acted as moderator. Of late years that office falls sometimes to one and sometimes to another. Richard Stockton is at present their standing clerk.

This Association, when first constituted, included all the churches in Virginia on the south side of James River and above the upper line of Roanoke (then Middle District). When New River was taken off, it was agreed that the Blue Ridge should be the dividing line between that and Strawberry. When Mayo was taken off, it was agreed that the boundary between that and Strawberry should be as follows, viz.: "Beginning at Elder Stephen's church, leaving it on the south side; thence to Smith's River at the mouth of Beaver Creek; thence up the said river to the Tarrarat mountain." They have not printed their minutes of late years. This circumstance, added to some other causes, prevented our obtaining as full documents as were necessary in order to give as perfect a relation of her proceedings as of other Associations. The proceedings of the Association, however, as far as we can learn, have been regular and peaccable. We must now proceed to the sketches of churches, beginning with:

Goose Creek

The great revival in the churches of Roanoke Association in 1802 spread into Strawberry, and continued four or five years. Goose Creek shared largely in the divine blessing. It commenced among them in 1802 and continued about two years, in which time about one hundred were added to the church. Their number, however, was lessened by the constitution of Beaver Dam in 1804. Two young preachers were raised in the revival, viz., William Leftwich, their present pastor,[1] and Joshua Burnet, both of whom have been since ordained.

Otter

This is a church of respectable standing. In 1804 a great revival arose in this church and continued about two years. Many were baptized and a new church constituted from them called Burton's Creek. Elder John Anthony has been the pastor of this church for

---

[1] In treating of churches it is very desirable to exhibit short characteristics of their ministers, and, indeed, of distinguished private members; but our information of this Association is so contracted that there are few ministers of whom we can say anything.—*Author's note.*

many years. Although he has done much, he is not yet weary in well doing. He does not travel extensively, but is desirous to keep his own vineyard well dressed.

Little Otter

The revival seems to have been more extensive here than in any church. The windows of heaven were opened towards the close of the year 1801; abundant showers of refreshing rain were poured forth upon them during the years 1802 and 1803, As many as two hundred and twenty-five persons were baptized; three preachers thrust into the harvest, viz., John Carter, William Moorman and James H.L. Moorman, and two new churches constituted, viz., Timber Ridge and Suck Spring. The members of Little Otter live in and about the town called Liberty.

North Fork of Otter

No information has been received respecting this church, except what may be seen in the table.

Staunton

This church, though now small, participated in the revival. Elder John Black and Elder John Jenkins were chief agents in the work.

Beaver Dam, Suck Spring and Timber Ridge

These are all new churches constituted since the revival, and all mentioned in treating of the mother churches.

Difficult Creek

This is a small church of which we know nothing more than what may be seen in the tables.

Buffaloe

This is the only Baptist church in Rockbridge. A part of her members formerly lived in Botetourt. In 1803 God lifted up the light of His countenance upon them and continued to be gracious in adding to them such as should be saved for about two years and a half, until about seventy were baptized. Rock Spring and Mill Creek were taken off from Buffaloe. A good preacher is one of the best gifts of heaven to a pious people, but if he unfortunately forgets his sacred character, and neglects to keep his body under, and thereby becomes a castaway, the affliction is then more than commensurate with the former blessing. Buffaloe found it necessary to exclude her once useful minister.

Rock Spring and Mill Creek

These were constituted from Buffaloe, and were attended statedly by her pastor, and who was also in a degree father to these churches. His backsliding was, of course, very afflicting to them. Their prospects are not promising.

Gill's Creek

This church was also revived in 1802, under the ministry of Elder Wilson Turner. A considerable number were added. The church called Blackwater was a daughter of Gill's Creek.

Pig River and Snow Creek

This is a church of good standing, attended by Elder John Ashworth. The reader will recollect that in our account of Sandy Creek church, Meherrin Association, we mentioned that John Ashworth, a preacher, moved with a party from Sandy Creek into Franklin County, and there formed a new church, composed chiefly of those that had moved with him. Mr. Ashworth has continued to be a steady and useful minister.

Chapel, Bethel, Blackwater, and Pig River

Of these four churches we know nothing more than can be found in the table, and in what is said of them in treating of other churches.

Snow Creek

This church has now no resident pastor, but was for many years under the pastoral care of Elder Robert Stockton, now residing in Kentucky.

Mr. Stockton is a native of Albemarle County, and was born December 12, 1743. He became religiously impressed while a young man, and had joined the communion of the Presbyterians, among whom he was brought up; but afterwards, forming an acquaintance with some of the Baptist preachers, he was convinced of the impropriety of infant baptism, and was baptized by Rev. Samuel Hariss, 1771. After his baptism, he quickly commenced preaching. His labors were blessed; and many churches either directly or indirectly arose through his instrumentality. In his communications to the editor he states that he was at the constitution of eleven churches in the Strawberry Association. Although his usefulness was so obvious in this country, and although he was among the richest men in those parts, his mind was not at rest. From some cause not known to the compiler he moved to Kentucky and settled within the limits of Green River Association. To leave a people among whom his ministry had been manifestly and extensively owned of God is a hazardous thing for a preacher of the Gospel, and ought never to be done upon slight or trivial grounds, or for the sake of worldly emolument, or without strong marks of the divine approval. Mr. Stockton had always an inclination to travel, and perhaps no man ever traveled to greater advantage, for, possessing an invincible boldness, it was quite unimportant to him what kind of house he went to, whether saint's or sinner's, friend's or opposer's. He never failed whenever he went to enter largely into religious conversation, and having great command of his temper and great presence of mind, he often made religious impressions upon minds previously swallowed up by prejudice. It was also an invariable rule with him to propose, and if permitted, to perform family worship. In doing this he would often exhort a half hour or more to the family. It is very entertaining to hear Mr. Stockton relate the various adventures of his life respecting things of this sort.

His talents as a preacher are hardly up to mediocrity, and no man thinks less of them than himself; but his talent for exhortation is very considerable. The way, by the by, that he has done so much good has not been through his great or numerous talents, but by occupying such as he had in an industrious manner. If his strokes were not very heavy he gave the more of them; if the iron was dull he put on more strength.

Smith's Run and Jack's Creek

Very little, unnoticed in the table, has reached us respecting these churches.

Joseph Pedigo, the pastor of Smith's Run, as far as we can hear, is a man of weight in religious matters in those parts. He sometimes acts as moderator of the Association.

Leatherwood

This church was formerly under the care of Robert Stockton, but now of John King.

Elder King has been already mentioned in treating of Meherrin church in Meherrin Association. Few men open their mouths in the pulpit more to the purpose than Mr. King. His language is strong and nervous, his ideas clear and perspicuous, his manner warm and animating, and his countenance grave and solemn. Though modest and unassuming out of the pulpit, when he ascends the sacred stand he speaks as one having authority; he lifts up his voice and commands all men to repent. His life has been an honor to his Master's cause; and when he has ceased to suffer here, doubtless his death will be glorious.

Beaver Creek and Burton Creek

Of these churches we have no information not already detailed.

TABLE OF NEW RIVER ASSOCIATION

Year	Number at Constitution	Present Number	By Whom Planted	Former Pastors	Current Pastors	Counties
1774	21	78		S. Goodwin , W. Howard	J. Black	
1784	25	35		N. Hall,	W. Howard	Roanoke
1789	16	13	R. Jones	R. Jones	R. Jones	Montgomery
1785	28	27	J. Lawrence	J. Lawrence	W. Howard	Montgomery
1801	27	28	J. Matthews	J. Matthews	I. Rentfro	Montgomery
1803	30	28	J. Jones	J. Jones	J. Jones	Montgomery
1803	40	51		W. Howard	P. Howard	Montgomery
1796	17	33	J. Stanley		J. Stanley	Giles
1790	20	55		S. Goodwin		Roanoke

Name of churches
Bethel
Salem
Gready Creek
Meadow Creek
N.F. Roanoke
West Fork
Pine Creek
Stinking Creek
Catawba

CHAPTER TWENTY-TWO:
History of the New River Association, Including the Sketches of Churches

This Association was taken off from the Strawberry and formed into a separate Association in 1793. They met for the first time in October, 1794, and organized themselves. Their number of churches at first was only seven or eight. The dividing line between this and the Strawberry is the Blue Ridge. It may be seen by the table in what part of the State the district lies. The business of the Association has been conducted in prudence, peace, and harmony. It appears that the Baptist interest prevails more than that of any other religious society, there being only two or three Presbyterian congregations in the district and but few Methodist classes. Between these and the Baptists a good understanding subsists, insomuch that a considerable party were of opinion in the Association that they ought to invite the Presbyterian and Methodist ministers to sit with them in their Associations as counsellors, but not to vote. This subject underwent a lengthy investigation, and finally was decided against inviting. This was assuredly a very prudent determination—first, because it might tend to confusion; and secondly, because it would probably rather interrupt than promote friendship. Seeing, in most cases, as it respects the intercourse between man and man, too much familiarity often ends in strife. We should be more likely to continue in peace with a neighbor whom we treated with the distant respect due to a neighbor than if we were to introduce him to our private domestic concerns. It cannot, however, but be earnestly desired that party animosity should be mollified by every rational method. Party rage is never the effect of true religion. Well might Paul ask the Corinthian partisans, "Are ye not carnal?" Steadfastness in our own principles and charity towards those of others are not inconsistent with each other.

The minutes of the New River Association have never been printed. Hence it was not possible to procure them for every session, nor indeed is it important. We have them for four years, from which the character of the Association may be understood. The Calvinistic sentiments are the doctrines of this Association. Yet there are not wanting some who hold some or all of the Arminian tenets. Their views upon this point may be gathered from the following query, with its solution, viz.: *Is it right to license any man to preach the Gospel who holds with Arminian tenets? Answer. By no means.*

At an Association held at Pine Creek meetinghouse, second Saturday in October, 1803, William Howard was appointed moderator and Joseph Rentfro clerk.

The following query was introduced, viz.: *Ought not experienced ministers of the Gospel to take under their patronage the young and illiterate preachers?* To which it was answered, *"Yes; and teach them true principles and sound doctrines, and set good examples before them, and say, 'Be ye followers of us as we are of Christ Jesus.'"* Could the principle contained in this solution be carried into effect by some regular and methodical plan, it would produce the most sovereign relief to the Baptist ministry in Virginia. It has been a general complaint against the Baptists of Virginia that they sanction men for the ministry who do not possess the necessary qualifications. These complaints without doubt have often sprung from a corrupt taste, and also from men of refined minds, who did not make the proper allowance for hearers of less refinement. Yet, with all due allowance the complaint is sometimes well founded. The evil has arisen partly from not making proper distinctions as to gifts, so as to authorize men to preach, who at most only had the gift of exhortation; and partly from a false delicacy in setting up weak preachers, where the people were in expectation of hearing others more capable. If, then, some regular mode of examining and introducing young preachers could be devised, many weak gifts would be improved and become respectable. Add to this some regulation as to the kind of qualifications each man may properly claim, as well as the time and manner of exercising his talents, and it is not unlikely the inconvenience would be lessened, if not quite removed. In England, and, indeed, in some parts of America, no man is allowed to preach unless he first makes his wishes known to some of the elders of the church; they then give him a private hearing, and encourage or stop him, according to their opinion of his qualifications. A middle course between that and the Virginia rule might be useful. At least inhibit any from preaching at other than an appointment

241

made for himself, until he be licensed by the church; and, indeed, as to licensed or ordained preachers, the wishes of an audience ought to be consulted in preference to the sensibility of an individual. At their Association for October, 1804, the knotty and intricate doctrine of supporting preachers, or farther of ministerial contributions, was brought forward in the following query: *Are the poor bound by the Gospel to give to the rich for preaching the Gospel?* Answer: *The Lord loveth a cheerful giver, according to what he hath, and not according to what he hath not.*

All things considered, a better answer could not probably have been invented.

The circular letters annexed to the minutes of this Association are very excellent, and but for the want of room, extracts from some of them would have been inserted.

Rev. William Howard has generally acted as moderator, and Mr. Joseph Rentfro as clerk.

We will now attend to the churches in this district, beginning with:

Bethel

This church was the first constituted, and, of course, the oldest in the Association. We have not learned by whose labors this church was first planted. It is quite probable that it was by removal of the first members from some of the interior counties. It had no regular supplies or pastor for seventeen years after the constitution. The presumption is that if the church had been raised by the labors of any minister visiting those parts, that such minister would have supplied them regularly. Their first regular preacher was Mr. Samuel Goodwin, who moved into their bounds and became their pastor. He continued among them about ten years and then returned to Catawba, from whence he first came to Bethel. Bethel then obtained the attendance of Mr. Howard, who preached for them once a month until a few years past, when old age and infirmities put it out of his power. While Mr. Howard had the care of the church, about the year 1804, a comfortable revival took place, when the church increased from sixteen to seventy-eight. Since Mr. Howard has declined his visits to them, they have procured the services of Rev. John Black, who, it is said, is an able preacher.

Salem

This was constituted, as may be seen from the table, in 1784, and fell under the care of Mr. Nathan Hall. He retained the charge about six years, and was then silenced for misconduct. After about four or five years the church turned their attention to Mr. Howard, who has been their pastor ever since. In the year 1802 God visited them with a goodly time. Many precious souls were turned to righteousness. When Mr. Howard took the care of them their number was thirteen; the revival raised them to seventy-nine. In 1803 they dismissed forty members for the purpose of forming a new church, which was called Pine Creek.

Rev. William Howard, pastor of Salem church and moderator of the Association, is a venerable man, who seemed resolved to exert the last remains of life and strength in advancing the glory of Him who has called him from darkness to light. How useful are such men to go out and in before the young and less experienced.

Greasy Creek

Greasy Creek was raised under the labors of Rev. Robert Jones. About the year 1803 God revived His work among them, chiefly through the ministry of Mr. Jesse Jones, son of Robert, a young and ardent preacher, whose labors were accepted of his Master, so that their number increased to forty-three members. Thirty of these were taken off in order to form a new church, which was called West Fork, to which Jesse Jones became pastor. Mr. Shadrach Roberts is a licensed preacher in this church.

Meadow Creek

This church was formed partly out of members who moved hither from the State of New York and partly of natives. Rev. John Lawrence became their pastor. He had been a minister for many years in the State of New York, was an eminent servant of Christ and a pious and sensible man. His labors were not very much blessed after he moved to Virginia. Some disturbance happening in the church, and Mr. Lawrence being obviously in dotage, was rather indiscreet in espousing one of the parties so as to give some discontent to the body of the church, in consequence of which, added to his incapacity through dotage and infirmities, the church dismissed him from his pastoral charge. Soon after he was taken ill, and God dismissed him to the church triumphant. He was eighty years of age when he died. After his dismission Elder Howard preached for them statedly, and God poured out His Spirit upon them. The church increased from sixteen to sixty-four. Elder Howard, through infirmity, is not able to visit them statedly, as formerly, but he attends them occasionally and administers the ordinances. Robert Simpkins is a licensed preacher in the bounds of this church.

North Fork of Roanoke

This church was planted chiefly by the labors of Rev. James Mathews. He some years past moved to Tennessee. After the removal of Mr. Mathews they had Mr. Isaac Rentfro for their minister. He moved to Kentucky in 1798, since which they have had no pastor. In 1802 there was a general revival in Montgomery County. This church partook of the blessing. Nineteen were added.

Sinking Creek

This church was raised under the ministry of Mr. Joseph Stanley, who is still their pastor. Under his labors the church has prospered, having increased from seventeen to thirty-three.

Catawba

When first constituted, Catawba had no pastor. Samuel Goodwin was their first pastor, who took charge about 1781 or 1782. He retained his charge for about ten years, and then, having moved away to Bethel, after about ten years came back and resumed his care of Catawba. About 1805 he was excluded for intemperate drinking. He until that time had borne a most amiable character for piety and integrity, and was esteemed an excellent preacher, and very active and useful. Gracious heaven! How many thousands of the professed sons of Zion are overturned by this deadly evil! This church partook in the revival.

West Fork

(See Greasy Creek.)

Pine Creek

This is a flourishing church, chiefly taken off from Salem. It has a promising arm on Brush creek, where Henry Beal lives and labors in the ministry, and who is an ordained minister.

TABLES OF HOLSTON AND MOUNTAIN ASSOCIATIONS *

Year	Number at Constitution	Present Number	By Whom Planted	Former Pastors	Current Pastors	Counties
			HOLSTON ASSOCIATION			
1783	12	36	J. Frost	M. Foley	C. Pennington	Washington
1791	45	69	A. Baker	A. Baker	M. Foley, Jr.	Washington
1799	8	65	M. Foley, W. Brudrage	W. Wilson	W. Wilson	Washington
1802	20	27		M. Foley	J. Foley	Washington
1788	30	170	T. Burgess, S. Goodwin	T. Hansford, D. Kelly	E. Kelly	Russell
1805	12	32	J. Wilson, S. Hilton	S. Hilton	S. Hilton	Russell
1802	12	65	E. Kelly	E. Kelly	W. Wells	Russell
1805	16	16	D. Jesse, W. Nells, E. Kelly	R. Kilgore	R. Kilgore	Russell
1806	51	51	E. Kelly, W. Wilson	D. Jesse	D. Jesse	Russell
1797	11	60		J. Flanery	J. Flanery	Lee
			MOUNTAIN ASSOCIATION			
1795	13	13		W. Porter	W. Porter, D. Kieth	Grayson
1797	18	100		A. Mitchell	A. Mitchell	Grayson
1782	15	77		T. Evans	A. Baker	Grayson

Name of churches
N. Fork of Holston
S. Fork of Holston, or St. Clair's Bottom
Mill Creek Valley
Rich Valley
Glade Hollows
Russel
Stony Creek
Copper Creek
Castlewoods
Deep Spring
N. Fork of New River
Meadow Creek
Cedar Island, or Fox Creek

CHAPTER TWENTY-THREE:
History of the Holston and Mountain Associations, Including the Sketches of Churches

The Holston Association was constituted about the year 1785, according to Asplund's Register. They have adopted the confession of faith. They had eighteen churches in all, in 1791. We are informed from an authentic source that they had twenty-five churches in 1807, viz., fifteen in the State of Tennessee and ten in Virginia, and their whole number of members, 1,619; averaging not quite sixty-five to a church. Those churches that are in Virginia average a little more than fifty-nine. There were two Baptist churches in this district at a much earlier date than any mentioned in the table, but they were broken up by the Indian war. We have no account of the Holston Association. We must therefore proceed to speak of the churches, beginning with:

North Fork of Holston

Two large companies have emigrated from this church, in each case taking off their pastor, viz.: Joshua Frost, their first pastor, moved into Knox County, Tennessee, carrying with him thirty-three members, and there they became a church. This happened about 1794 or 1795. In 1798 they got another pastor, Moses Foley; but in 1803 Foley and twenty-six members moved to Abraham's creek and formed another church. In 1808 they procured the pastoral care of Charles Pennington. It is a church of good standing.

Glade Hollows

This was taken off from Clinch River church, which is one of the two old churches mentioned above as broken up by the war. A few members returning after the war, the church was reconstituted. But shortly after Glade Hollows was taken off, the mother church was dissolved. Glade Hollows has always been a prosperous church, but particularly the year 1801, under the ministration of Edward Kelly, they had a blessed revival, when the church, in the course of eighteen months, swelled to three hundred and sixty. After this three other churches were taken off, viz., Stony Creek, Sandy Creek, and Castlewoods.

South Fork or St. Clair's Bottom

This church was for many years without a pastor, and then really flourished; but, aiming to choose a pastor, they could not be unanimous. The majority chose Mr. Baker, but a party adhered to Mr. William Brundrage, an emigrant from the North. They were a divided, and consequently an unhappy people, until Brundrage moved to Ohio, in 1805. They then became united; proving that preachers may be the greatest curse, as well as the greatest blessing.

Mill Creek

This has been a happy church. Beginning with only eight members, they have increased to sixty-five.

Rich Valley

This was at first a thriving church, but through the misconduct of their pastor, Moses Foley, they have had cloudy and unpleasant seasons.

Russell

There is nothing remarkable of her, except that her members are in union and good understanding.

Deep Spring

They had a comfortable revival in 1801, and increased to their present number. They are doing well.

Stony Creek

This church was also revived about 1802 and 1803, and increased to about eighty-five. Since then, although they have had cold times, they have preserved order, &c.

Copper Creek[1]

As at the beginning, so now they enjoy union and peace.

---

[1] Deep Creek, Stony Creek, and Copper Creek had not joined any Association in 1808. It was expected they would join at the next session.— *Author's note.*

Castlewoods

Nothing remarkable is said of her in our manuscripts. We would gladly exhibit the character and talents of the preachers and distinguished private members of this and the Mountain Association, but for the want of information we are unable to do so. The documents we have procured at all respecting the different Associations on the Western waters, have all been obtained through the friendly attention of Rev. Josiah Osburn and John Alderson. Our numerous letters written to the ministers residing within the limits of the Association were not attended to.

Mountain Association

This Association was constituted August, 1799, the churches having been previously dismissed from the Yadkin Association, and is composed of churches in North Carolina, Tennessee, and Virginia. Three only are in Virginia, of which we will say a few things, beginning with

North Fork of New River

William Porter was the pastor of this church, but being unable, through old age, to go through the duties of the ministry, the church associated Daniel Keith in the pastoral care. This circumstance often occurs in England, but very rarely in Virginia. It much oftener happens in Virginia that one minister is pastor of three or four churches than that the same church has more than one pastor. The committing the ministerial authority of the church to more than one elder has in this country often been found upon experience to be bad policy. It often creates parties. In some cases such as the above, however, it is very well.

Meadow Creek

God has showered down His grace upon this church. They have a happy and increasing people.

Fox Creek

They were at first a flourishing church, but, their preachers becoming disorderly and eventually excluded, they fell into confusion and distress.

The removal of Elder Andrew Baker among them in 1803, under God, healed all their backslidings. God turned their mourning into joy by turning many to righteousness. For several years Mr. Baker had the gratification to see his Master's work prosper in his hands.

TABLE OF ACCOMAC ASSOCIATION

Year	Number at Constitution	Present Number	By Whom Planted	Former Pastors	Current Pastors	Counties
1790		135	E. Baker, G. Layfield		G. Layfield	Accomac
1785	20	105	E. Baker		G. Layfield	Accomac
1786		132	E. Baker	G. Layfield, S. Marshal	T. Waters	Accomac
1779		124	E. Baker	G. Northun, G. Layfield, E. Shav	T. Waters, J. Benston	Accomac
1778	5	219	E. Baker	E. Baker	J. Elliot	Northampton
1783		126	E. Baker	F. Baker	J. Elliot	Northampton
1807	27	50	E. Baker	C. Fisher	A. Fisher	Northampton

Name of churches
Pungoteague
Matompkin
Chingoteague
Mesongoes
Lower Northhampton
Hungo's
Machipongo

CHAPTER TWENTY-FOUR:
History of the Accomac Association, Including the Sketches of the Churches.

The Accomac Association district lies altogether on the Eastern Shore of Virginia. The Gospel was first carried thither by Elijah Baker. After Mr. Baker had planted a number of churches both on the Eastern Shore of Maryland and Virginia, and had been joined by other preachers from different parts, as well as by young ones raised under his ministry, he proposed that the churches should meet by their delegates and form an Association. This they did the year 1784. They took the name of the Salisbury Association from the town of that name in Maryland where they met. They also became a fostering mother to the churches. They increased from year to year, and many useful preachers were raised up. The business of the Association was conducted with great decorum, and their decisions were wise and prudent. Dr. Robert Lemon, a practitioner of medicine, but not a preacher, acted as moderator from shortly after their organization until the division of the district, in 1808. During many years it was customary for them to hold their annual Associations in Maryland near Salisbury, but they held also an occasional Association in Virginia, every August. This arrangement was not satisfactory to the Virginia churches, and they petitioned to be dismissed, in order to form an Association out of the churches wholly in Virginia. This was done; and the new Association, called Accomac, met for the first time at Pungoteague, August, 1809, at which session they were chiefly employed in forming a constitution and rules of decorum. They also agreed to join the General Meeting of Correspondence. At this session Elder George Layfield was chosen as moderator, and Mr. William Costen as clerk. As this is the first and only meeting they have had since the division, nothing more can be said as to their proceedings. The historical sketches of the churches must now be attended to.

Pungoteague
This is a large and happy church. For some time after their con-

stitution they had no regular pastor, but for a good many years they have been under the pastoral care of Rev. George Layfield, to whom they listen as children to a father.

Mr. Layfield is indeed a father in Israel. He has long professed to know the way of life, and has never since departed from it, either to the right hand or to the left. He was a Presbyterian previous to his hearing the Baptists, and could not, for some time after he heard them and loved them, bring his mind to be willing to give up his infant sprinkling. He finally yielded to the force of truth, and being baptized, commenced as preacher. His first residence was in Maryland, where he continued for many years before he became a preacher. In point of talents Mr. Layfield may be considered as standing on respectable ground. He does not aim to speak in the enticing words of man's wisdom, but in simplicity and godly sincerity commends himself to every man's conscience. He is a man of grave deportment, yet cheerful manners. He is liberal in his sentiments towards those who differ with him on religious subjects.

Matompkin

This church has also the stated services of Elder Layfield, and are peaceable and harmonious. They never had any regular pastor.

Mesongoes

This is a church of good standing, but has seen better days than the present. Their first preacher was George Northam, who was not distinguished for anything singular. He was succeeded by Mr. Layfield, and he by Elijah Shay. Shay was a preacher of popular talents; but after raising himself to considerable distinction he sold his birthright for a mess of pottage. He became a drunkard and was excluded from the church. Failing thus of the grace of God, he sought to supply the deficiency by art and deception. He moved off to Alexandria, where also he conducted himself so disorderly as to incur the censures of all those who made pretensions to seriousness. From thence he traveled off under the name of a Baptist preacher, until the brethren near Alexandria thought it their duty to advertise him as an impostor, which they did in the minutes of the Ketocton Association. What mischief do such traitors do to the best of causes!

Chingoteague

The Gospel was first carried into these parts by the indefatigable E. Baker. His labors were not at first extensively blessed immediately in the neighborhood of Chingoteague. The seed, however, sown by Mr. Baker and others was cultivated by Mr. Layfield, and a church was constituted under the care of Elder Layfield. After some time he yielded the care to Elder Solomon Marshall, who attended them stately, but not as an abiding pastor. They now have the pastoral services of Elder Thomas Waters, whose labors among them have been highly blessed. Mr. Waters is a loving, zealous, laborious, and successful servant of the Most High God. Having a warm heart, he enjoys nothing more than to see divine love spreading from heart to heart, warming and animating the souls of saints. On such occasions he seems willing to be spent in praising and adoring his Gracious Redeemer.

Lower Northampton

Within the bounds of this church was the place where Mr. Baker began his evangelical career on the Eastern Shore. Here also were the first persons baptized that ever submitted to that sacred ordinance on this coast; and here was constituted the first church. When first organized Elder Baker became their pastor, and so continued until the day of his death. The church soon after her constitution became large and flourishing, and continues so to this time. There are some very respectable private members among them. Elder John Elliott preaches for them stately since the death of Elder Baker.

Isaac Broughton is an ordained preacher in this church, esteemed by all who know him a pious and venerable man, but of very infirm health.

Hungar's

This has been for some time a declining church, having sustained great losses by the death of many of her most valuable private members. They were once a numerous people.

Elder Elliott, their pastor, commenced preaching in 1783, when about thirty years of age, but he had been a professor for some time before. Seeing how much laborers were wanted in the harvest, his spirit was moved within him. He stepped forward, and the Lord smiled upon his services. He is esteemed by all his acquaintances a pious and exemplary man, as well as a steady and useful preacher.

Machipongo

This is a young and somewhat increasing church under the care of Elder Caleb Fisher. Previous to his profession of religion Mr. Fisher was very fond of the fashionable vices of the age. Racing, dancing, gambling, and keeping wild and wanton company were the objects of his most intense pursuit. Serious reflections, though sometimes forced upon his mind, were never welcome. God, in the midst of his wild career, marked him as an object of invincible grace. The arrows of the Almighty stuck fast in him, and although he was at first as an ox unaccustomed to the yoke, he finally found that the yoke of Jesus was easy and His burden light. He found rest to his soul, and was baptized the year 1792. To his vicious associates he now became as obnoxious as he was before agreeable. After some years—in 1802—he began to preach. This gave many of the sons of Belial an opportunity to insult him. While he preached they would mock, and sometimes openly. On one occasion they stirred up so much disturbance that he thought it his duty to prosecute them. In return a Mr. Henderson, under some frivolous pretense, swore the peace against him and dragged him before a magistrate. While there he lavished out the most unlimited abuse against Mr. Fisher; when lo, he fell speechless by a paralytic stroke! He lost the use of one side and suffered more than common pain in such cases. This display of divine vengeance had an awful effect upon the minds of the surrounding people, and, indeed, all who heard of it.

Mr. Fisher was upwards of forty years of age when he began to preach. It is not to be expected that under those circumstances he should make any great advancement in improving his gifts. He is esteemed, however, a man of strong mind, and as a preacher sound and animating.

The cause of the Baptists is not thought to prevail as much on the Eastern Shore as it did some years past. When they first came into this country they had to combat with the Established Church, armed with the civil sword. Clothed with a heavenly panoply, they went forth in the name of the Lord of Hosts and prevailed. The

Established Church here, as well as in most other places in Virginia, declined rapidly after the rise of the Baptists. Of late they have other opponents that are much more successful. For many years past the Methodists have been a very increasing people on the Eastern Shore. Whether their prosperity is only temporary until the set time to favor Zion shall arrive, or whether for some cause God is disposed to permit His people to be led into captivity and to become subservient to the neighboring nations, we cannot determine. As this state of things has occurred in many other places as well as in these parts, it will not be improper to offer a few remarks by way of conjecturing the cause; not because it is believed that the remarks apply to this or that particular place, but with a design to offer a caution to all. Baptist principles, under right views, have no tendency to paralyze the efforts of man or retard his activity. But how often do these effects follow the misinterpretation of these principles! How frequently, where error thrives through the industry and zeal of its supporters, do the friends of truth lie still under a mistaken confidence that truth cannot be hurt, and instead of opposing zeal to zeal, industry to industry, and all lawful means in a good cause against all lawful or unlawful ones in a bad one, they too often permit the hearts of the people to be stolen and their prejudices set against sound principles before they take the alarm! Truth is often injured by an unsuitable application of its parts. Strong meat should not be given but to men. To preach the deep, mysterious doctrines of grace upon all occasions and before all sorts of people is the sure way to preach them out of their parts. To give to any one doctrine more weight than the proportion found in the Scripture defaces the beauty of the whole and retards its progress. Unguardedness respecting preachers, in various ways, but especially as to impostors, has injured the Baptists in many parts, but in none more than on the Eastern Shore. They have probably suffered more by impostors than any other people in Virginia. The most distinguished of these was Joseph Flood. He was for eight or ten years a Baptist preacher of great popularity in those parts, and by many was thought pious. His brilliant talents seem to have blinded the people to his faults. He had married a wife in early life, with whom he lived peaceably. She dying, he married a second, who proved a heavy curse. He left her and employed his time altogether in preaching. For this he was not much blamed by those who knew all the circumstances. But he would not stop there. He came down into Accomac and actually persuaded a young woman of respectable connections to go to Philadelphia and there to be married to him. It is difficult for any at a distance to conceive what a deadly stab this gave the Baptist cause upon the Eastern Shore. Flood sent his credentials to the church, and in many respects acted a candid part. He has since settled in Bedford County, Va., and has occasionally preached, but not as a Baptist.

Soon after Flood's downfall came one Samuel Counsel, under the name of a Baptist preacher; and being a man of considerable ingenuity, became popular. He was, indeed, a wolf in sheep's clothing. He was an Arian in principle, and used great subtlety in maintaining his opinions. He was thought by some to have made impressions on some respectable professors, and that if his bad life had not betrayed him he might have formed a party in the churches. The Salisbury Association noticed him and guarded the churches against him, which, with some other things, drove him off.

About the same time came one Carey (as he called himself) and pretended that he was a Baptist preacher. Carey was far from possessing distinguished gifts, and indeed could not be said to have any one qualification for making good his way under his assumed character, except an indescribable stock of impudence. Still, however, he imposed upon many, and was noticed in several places as a preacher of gifts. Against him also the churches were cautioned, and he went off elsewhere; and if not hanged is perhaps still imposing upon the credulous somewhere.

After these repeated slams, it is not strange that the Baptist cause has rather declined of late years in this Association. But, peradventure, these dark scenes are but the preludes of a bright and glorious day, for which, no doubt, many precious and pious souls are daily lifting up their hearts to God; for, indeed, the Baptists of these parts are a tender, loving, affectionate and pious people, anxious for the welfare of Zion. For hospitality and kindness the Eastern Shore people, both saints and sinners, are surpassed by none.

This is the last Association in Virginia that can be said to have arisen from the labors of Separate Baptist ministers.

CHAPTER TWENTY-FIVE:
Of the Origin and Progress of the Regular Baptists.

We have already informed our readers that one of the three original companies of Baptists that emigrated to Virginia came from Maryland. From these arose the Regular Baptists, as they were for a season called in contradistinction to the Separates. These, though not so numerous as the Separates, are a large and very respectable body of people; for, with very few did they come into Virginia, and now they are become several Associations. Besides the Ketocton, which is a very extensive Association, the Red Stone, Greenbrier, and Union all sprung from the same source.

Our papers do not exactly agree respecting the date at which the first Baptists made their appearance in these parts; but upon a full examination of the different documents it is probable that we shall give a correct statement.

In 1743, Edward Hays and Thomas Yates, members of a Baptist congregation in Maryland, moved with a company and settled at Opequon, in Berkeley County, Virginia. Their minister, Mr. Henry Loveall, soon followed them. His preaching was attended with success, and in a short time he baptized fifteen persons. They continued their church state until 1751; but it is probable they were rather remiss in their government, for we are informed that in that year certain ministers of the Philadelphia Association came among them, and new-modeled the church, forming it, as our manuscript says, upon the Calvinistic plan, sifting out the chaff, and retaining the supposed good grain. From which it may be presumed that the first preacher and his party were either Arminians, or inclined that way.

In 1754, when Stearns and Marshall were among them, their minister was Samuel Heton, who was probably their first preacher, after they had been new-modeled as above. What became of either Loveall or Heton we are not informed. The next preacher that lived among them, and far the most distinguished, was Elder John Garrard, probably from Pennsylvania. The precise year in which he came is not ascertained, but it was probably about 1755.

From the time that they were purified, in 1751, this church was in connection with the Philadelphia Association. They were very zealous, had much preaching, and were remarkably warm in their religious exercises, and more particularly so after Mr. Daniel Marshall came among them. They went to such lengths that some of the more cold-hearted lodged a complaint in the Philadelphia Association. Mr. Miller was sent to see what was the matter. When he came he was highly delighted with the exercises, joined them cordially, and said if he had such warm-hearted Christians in his church he would not take gold for them. He charged those who had complained, rather to nourish than complain of such gifts. The work of God revived among them, and considerable additions were made to the church. The country in which they had settled was but thinly inhabited, and was subject to the inroads of the Indians. Some of these savage irruptions took place not long after Mr. Garrard had settled among them; in consequence of which he and many of the church moved below the Blue Ridge, and resided for some time in Loudoun County, on Ketocton creek. He was not while there forgetful of his duty, but labored night and day for the instruction and salvation of sinners. God turned the hearts of many, who, believing, were baptized.

A church was constituted called Ketocton, to which Mr. Garrard was appointed pastor. It is probable that this church was organized in the year 1756; for on the second Sunday in June, 1757, the Mill Creek, Ketocton, and the Smith and Lynville's Creek churches held their first yearly meeting, at the meetinghouse of the last-named church; so that we shall probably be correct if we date the constitution of the Ketocton church in 1756; of Mill Creek in 1743; her first revival in 1751, and her reinstatement after the Indian irruption in 1757.

Having briefly shown the origin and progress of the Baptists who first settled in Opequon, we shall now attend to another company on Smith and Lynville's Creek, in Rockingham.

The Smith and Lynville's Creek church was constituted August 6, 1756, under the pastoral care of John Alderson, Sr. There had been some Baptists living in this place for about eleven years previous to the constitution of the church. These were probably a party of private members from some of the churches in the Philadelphia Association, or perhaps some of them from New England; for it is stated that one John Harrison, wishing to be baptized, went as far as Oyster Bay, in Massachusetts, to obtain that ordinance. As there were Baptist churches and ministers much nearer, the presumption is that he had been led to that measure in consideration of some, if not all, of the Baptists of his neighborhood having come from thence.

During the eleven years, from the time the Baptists first came to this neighborhood until the constitution of the church, they were visited by several preachers from the Northern States, among whom were Mr. Samuel Eaton, Benjamin Griffith, John Gano and John Alderson, the last of whom afterwards settled among them and became their pastor.

The three churches above named became members of the Philadelphia Association soon after their constitution and so continued until they formed an independent Association. Previous to this, however, they met in an annual or yearly meeting, alternately at the three meetinghouses. In their yearly meetings preaching was kept up for several days, ministers from distant parts attended and consultations were held respecting the propagation of the Gospel, as well as advice offered for the good government of the infant churches. These meetings greatly accelerated the spread of the Gospel, and also ripened the churches for a separate Association.

About 1760 Rev. David Thomas, from Pennsylvania, came to Berkeley, in Virginia, on a ministerial visit. A small time previous to this, two men in the county of Fauquier, on Broad Run, had, without any public preaching, became convinced of the reality of vital religion, and that they were destitute of it. Wrought upon by such convictions, and hearing of the Baptists in Berkeley, they traveled thither, a distance of about sixty miles, to hear them. When they arrived and heard the Gospel, it proved a sweet savor of life. They returned home; God built them up by His Spirit, and in a short time they made a second visit to Berkeley, offered an experience of grace to the church, and were baptized. It so happened that these men and Mr. David Thomas came to Berkeley at the same time. They invited him to go down to Fauquier and preach, and he accepted the invitation. It was said of Martin Luther that, if the Pope had given him a cardinal's cap, he would never have propagated the principles of the Reformation. It might be so. And it could also be said that, if they had made Paul high-priest, instead of sending him to Damascus, he would not have spread the Gospel among the Gentiles. So also, if Mr. Thomas had not happened to meet with these men, who were hungering for the bread of life, he might never have gone to Broad Run, and from thence over a great part of Virginia, by which thousands were turned from darkness to light. These things in the eye of mere reason look like contingencies; but by the eye of faith they are all plainly viewed as the contrivance of infinite Wisdom and executed by an infallible though invisible hand.

After Mr. Thomas had labored awhile at Broad Run and in the adjacent neighborhood his labors were so much favored that he resolved to become a resident among them. Many professed faith and were baptized. A church was quickly constituted, to which Mr. Thomas was chosen as pastor. This took place a little after the year 1760. He did not confine his ministry to one neighborhood. He traveled through all the surrounding country, lifting up his voice as the voice of God commanding all men to repent. He was in deed and in truth a burning and shining light. There were few such men in the world as David Thomas was at that time. Having by nature a strong and vigorous mind, he had devoted his attention with diligence to the acquirement of a classical and refined education. In this few if any of his contemporaries succeeded better. He graduated at an early period. Besides the endowments of his mind he had a melodious and piercing voice, pathetic address, expressive action, and, above all, a heart filled with the love of God and sympathy for his fellow-men, whom he saw overwhelmed in sin and misery. God bade him speak on, and much people believed through him.

Mr. Thomas drew the attention of the people for many miles around. They traveled in many instances fifty or sixty miles to hear him. It is remarkable that about the time of the first rise of the Gospel in Virginia there were multiplied instances of persons who had never heard anything like evangelical preaching that were brought through divine grace to see and feel the want of vital goodness. Many of these, when they would hear of Mr. Thomas and other Baptist preachers, would travel off to hear them and invite them to come and preach in their neighborhood. By this means the Gospel was first carried into Culpeper. Mr. Allen Wyley, a man of respectable standing in that county, had been thus turned to God, and not knowing of any spiritual preacher, he had sometimes gathered his neighbors and read the Scriptures and exhorted them to repentance; but hearing after a while of Mr. Thomas, he and some of his neighbors traveled to Fauquier to hear him. As soon as he heard him he knew the joyful sound, submitted to baptism, and invited him to preach at his house. He came, but the opposition from the wicked was so great that he could not preach. He went into the county of Orange and preached several times, and to much purpose. His labors were blessed. Having, however, urgent calls to preach in various other places, and being much opposed and persecuted here, he did not attend here as often as was wished. On this account it was that Mr. Wyley went to Pittsylvania for Mr. Hariss. Mr. Thomas and Mr. Garrard, sometimes together and sometimes apart, traveled and propagated the pure principles of Christianity in all the upper counties of the Northern Neck. Mr. Thomas was far the most active. It was not to be presumed that the friends of the Establishment would feel themselves disinterested in these proceedings. Their Dagon was fast falling before the Gospel. They therefore resolved to stir themselves to prevent this calamity. They adopted various methods to accomplish this object. The clergy often attacked the Baptists from the pulpit; called them false prophets, wolves in sheep's clothing, &c., &c. But, unfortunately for them, the Baptists retorted these charges by professing to believe their own articles—at least the leading ones—and charged *them* with denying them, a charge which they could easily substantiate; for the doctrines most complained of as advanced by the Baptists were obviously laid down in the common prayer-book.

When they could not succeed by arguments they adopted more violent measures. Sometimes, when the preachers came to a place for the purpose of preaching, a kind of mob would be raised, and by violent threats they hindered the preaching.

Sometimes the preachers, and even some that only read sermons and prayed publicly, were carried before magistrates, and though not committed to prison, were sharply reprimanded, and cautioned not to be righteous overmuch.

In one instance only it appears that any person in these parts was actually imprisoned on account of religion. He, it seems, was a licensed exhorter, and was arrested for exhorting at a licensed meetinghouse. The magistrate sent him to jail, where he was kept until court; but the court, upon knowing the circumstances, discharged him. Elder James Ireland was also imprisoned in Culpeper jail, and in other respects treated very ill; but at the time of his imprisonment Mr. Ireland was a Separate Baptist, though he afterwards joined the Regulars. The reason why the Regular Baptists were not as much persecuted as the Separates was that they had at an early date applied to the General Court and obtained licenses for particular places, under the toleration law of England; but few of their enemies knew the extent of these licenses, most supposing that they were by them authorized to preach anywhere in the county. One other reason for their moderate persecution perhaps was that the Regulars were not thought so enthusiastic as the Separates; and having Mr. Thomas, a learned man, in their society, they appeared much more respectable in the eyes of the enemies of truth.

All their persecutions, combined with their other exertions, could not materially retard the progress of the Gospel. The work went on. New churches were constituted and young preachers were raised up. Of these none were more distinguished than Richard Major, although he had passed the meridian of life before he embarked in the ministry. He seems to have made such good use of his time that he did more in the vineyard than many who had toiled all the day. Daniel and William Fristoe, Jeremiah Moore and others were early fruits of Elder Thomas's ministry. These young heralds, uniting their endeavors with those of the more experienced, greatly accelerated the progress of the Gospel. The Separates also, in the more southern parts of the State were carrying on a similar work. These fires met in Orange County, in the year 1767, as we have already related in another place. Jealousies arising between them, from some cause, produced the unhappy divisions which continued so long to disturb their peace. The breach was never very wide between them; not so wide but they often met in conferences as fellow-sufferers, and united their counsels to contrive plans for their mutual emancipation from ecclesiastical tyranny. Before the year 1770, the Regular Baptists were spread over the whole country in the Northern Neck above Fredericksburg. Between 1770 and 1780 their cords still continued to be lengthened. Mr. Lunsford, a young but extraordinary preacher, carried the tidings of peace downwards and planted the Redeemer's standard in those counties of the Northern Neck which are below Fredericksburg. Messrs. Corbley, Sutton, and Barnet* had moved over the Alleghany, and had raised up several churches in the northwestern counties as early as 1775. Mr. John Alderson had gone in 1777 to Greenbrier, and in a few years raised up a people of God in that region. Besides these there were some others who moved more southward, and raised up a few churches. During the time of the great declension in Virginia the Regulars were under the cloud as well as their brethren the Separates, and they also participated in the great revival. In the year 1783 only twenty-three were baptized in the whole of the churches in the Ketocton Association, whereas in 1789, after the commencement of the great revival, the returns from the different churches amounted to three hundred and fifty-nine. Since the great revival the Baptist cause has considerably declined in most parts of the Ketocton Association. Mr. Fristoe, in his history of this Association, observes that "very few young ministers have been raised up of late, and that the number of members has much decreased." The decrease is certainly not universal; there are some flourishing churches within the district. As the Baptists have decreased, the Methodists in many places have increased. It is not so easy to account for this change. Does it arise from the Arminian doctrine being more palatable to the self-righteous heart of man? Or, have they been more industrious in propagating their doctrines? Or, have they succeeded, as in some other places, in driving the Baptist preachers, imperceptibly, to dwell too much upon high Calvinistic points, to the neglect of the more simple but more important principles of Christianity? If we were to calculate principles according to the weight of talents by which they are supported, Baptist principles ought to prevail within the Ketocton Association as much as in any section of Virginia, if not more. The talents of the leading preachers in those parts stand in the first row. After all is said the adversity or prosperity of religion in any place is often wrapped in mystery too dark to be penetrated by mortal vision. The ways of God are past finding out. It is not impossible before this generation passes away that the Son of Man may come in power and demonstration of His Spirit for the salvation of thousands, and quickly place His people above all competition.

Having thus given a general account of the rise and progress of the Regular Baptists, we shall now proceed to furnish details respecting their proceedings in Associations and churches.

Name of churches	Year	Number at Constitution	Present Number	By Whom Planted	Former Pastors	Current Pastors	TABLE OF THE KETOC
Ketocton	1766		29	J. Garrard	J. Garrard, J. Marks, R. Major	W. Gilmore	Loudoun
Little River	1769	81	75	D. Thomas	J. Hickerson, J. Thomas	R. Latham	Loudoun
New Valley	1767	30	30	J. Thomas	W. Thrift	W. Gilmore	Loudoun
Goose Creek	1775	37	76			None	Loudoun
Leesburg	1803	27	40	W. Thrift	W. Thrift	None	Loudoun
Ebenezer	1804	19	49	W. Fristoe	W. Fristoe	W. Fristoe	Loudoun
North Fork	1787	30	57		A. Weeks	W. Gilmore	Loudoun
Frying Pan	1803	25	47	J Moore	J. Moore	J. Moore	Fairfax
Bull Run	1790	67	45	R. Major	R. Major	J. Moore	Fairfax
Difficult	1775	126	65	R. Major	R. Major, T. Bridges	None	Fairfax
Popeahead	1775	75			J. Moore		Fairfax
Occoquon	1775	121		R. Major	R. Major		Fairfax
Chappawamsick	1776	57	69	D. Thomas	D. Thomas	P. Spiller	Prince William
White Oak	1767		100	D. Thomas	W. Fristoe	W. Grinstead	Stafford
Hartwood	1791	76	95	W. Fristoe	A. Leach	H. Pitman	Stafford
Broad Run	1771	75	99		W. Fristoe, J. Hickerson	R. Abel	Stafford
	1791		63	D. Thomas	D. Thomas	W. Fristoe	Fauquier

Name of churches	Year	Number at Constitution	Present Number	By Whom Planted	Former Pastors	Current Pastors	Counties
Thumb Run	1772	22	104	W. Fristoe		R. Latham	Fauquier
Brent Town	1773	95	36	D. Fristoe	D. Fristoe	None	Fauquier
Upper Carter's Run	1784	50	23	J. Munroe	J. Munroe	None	Fauquier
Long Branch	1786	25	58	J. Munroe	J. Munroe	W. Grinstead	Fauquier
Back Lick	1782	45	97	H. Hagan	H. Hagan J. Moore	None	Fauquier Fairfax
Hedgeman's River	1791	100	100	J. Hickerson	J. Hickerson	None	Fairfax Culpeper
South River	1783	21	20	J. Ireland	J. Ireland J. Price	W. Northern S. O'Hendren	Shenandoah
Water Lick	1787	29	52	J. Price J. Ireland	J. Ireland W. Marshall		Shenandoah
Happy Creek	1783	64	72	R. Major W. Marshall	J. Price J. Taylor J. Ireland	B. Dawson	Frederick
Bethel	1808	17	58	J. Ireland	S. O'Hendron	S. O'Hendren	Frederick
Buck Marsh	1772	56	297	W & D Fristoe	J. Garrard R. Major J. Ireland C. Collins	W. Fristoe	Frederick
Zoar	1799	19	44	C. Collins	C. Collins	F. Moore	Jefferson
Mill Creek	1766		39	H. Loveall, Mr. Miller	H. Loveall S. Heton J. Garrard D. Thomas	J. Hutchinson	Berkeley
Timber Ridge	1809	7	7	J. Hutchison	J. Hutchinson	J. Hutchinson	Berkeley
North River	1787	26	27	B. Stone	B. Stone	J. Munroe	Hampshire
Crooked Run	1790	44	50		B. Stone	J. Munroe	Hampshire
Patterson's Creek	1808	16	17	J. Munroe	J. Munroe	J. Munroe	Hampshire
Nanjemoy	1793	63	50	A. Leach	A. Leach	A. Leach	State of Mary-

CHAPTER TWENTY-SIX:
The Proceedings of the Ketocton Association from their First Constitution until This Date.

It has been already shown that the first Regular Baptist churches in Virginia were united to the Philadelphia Association, but held yearly meetings among themselves, in which many things were attended to, such as are commonly done at Associations, and by which they were ripened for independence. In 1765 they were dismissed from the Philadelphia Association, and on the 19th of August, 1766, they met by their delegates at Ketocton, in Loudoun. Their first meeting being at Ketocton, the Association took that name. There were only four churches of this order in Virginia, all of which were represented by their delegates, as follows:

Ketocton—John Marks, John Loyd.
Smith and Lynville's Creek—John Alderson.
Mill Creek—John Garrard, Isaac Sutton.
Broad Run—David Thomas, Joseph Metcalf.

The minutes of this Association say nothing of their appointment of moderator or clerk, nor of their numbers, nor of their regulations of any kind, except a resolution to send to the Philadelphia Association for instructions with regard to this Association, by which they probably meant such rules and regulations as had been, or should be, advised by the mother Association. An affectionate and exhortatory letter was connected with the minutes.

The business transacted in the Association is so analogous to that of the other Associations already commented on that it is quite unnecessary to detail. We shall, therefore, in a kind of table represent the times and places, &c., of holding the Associations, and then make some general remarks upon the whole.

The first meeting of the Ketocton Association included the third Sunday in August as one of the days on which they were together. This has continued ever since. The day of assembling has been changed from Saturday to Friday, and from Friday to Thursday, which last has continued for many years. Thursday and Friday are devoted to the business of the Association, Saturday and Sunday to preaching and public ministrations. Until 1770, neither the number baptized nor the totals are minuted. In a few subsequent years, also, they are omitted.

In 1789, the Ketocton Association was divided into two by a line running from the Potomac a south course. The district above this line retained the name Ketocton; the other was called Chappawamsick. The districts met separately until 1792, when they again united. Some attempts at a division have again been made, but have not succeeded.

For more than twenty years after the Association was organized the custom of laying on hands upon all persons immediately after they were baptized was invariably practiced in this Association. It was an article in the confession of faith, and the want of it was deemed by many a bar to communion. After the great revival, first the necessity and then the propriety of it began to be questioned until it was finally disused, and in the revisal of the confession of faith that article was expunged.

Table of the Times and Places of the Meetings of the Ketocton Association

Year	Place	Baptized	Total	Number of churches
1766	Ketocton			4
1767	Mill Creek			6
1768	Smith's Creek			6
1769	Broad Run			8
1770	Chappawamsick	209	624	10
1771	New Valley	275	912	13
1772	Mountain Creek			17
1773	Little River	270	1050	
1774	Brent Town			23
1775	Buck Marsh	142	1349	29
177+	Mount Poney	82	1341	
1777	Popeshead	59	1322	15
1778	Chappawamsick	14	836	17
1779	Broad Run	41	1059	19
1780	Bull Run	57	1154	17
1781	Seneca	58	1037	20

1782	Mill Creek	23	1035	21
1783	Ketocton	38	1007	22
1784	Brent Town	33	1041	23
1785	Water Lick	31	948	14
1786	Goose Creek	21	624	26
1787	Chappwamsick	79	995	28
1788	Buck Marsh	168	1141	26
1789	Broad Run	359	1372	10
1789	(Oct) Water Lick	12	486	14
1790	Goose Creek	21	624	15
1791	Opeckon	55	667	29
1792	Long Branch	294	2005	34
1793	Water Lick	138	2187	31
1794	Little River	32	2017	31
1795	Goose Creek	39	1898	33
1796	Thumb Run	38	1882	32
1797	Frying Pan	48	1820	32
1798	Broad Run	90	1846	31
1799	Grove	63	1786	32
1800	Back Lick	35	1719	31
1801	Happy Creek	102	1780	30
1802	Little River	216	1901	31
1803	Buck Marsh	355	1853	31
1804	Broad Run	143	1831	21
1805	Thumb Run	94	1598	25
1806	Frying Pan	126	2003	31
1807	Opeckon	64		
1808	Ebenezer	183	2004	34
1809	New Valley	153	2036	31

In 1791, a case was brought before the Association which produced considerable agitation. James Hutchinson, who was born in New Jersey, but raised in Loudoun County, Virginia, had gone to Georgia, and there first became a Methodist and then a Baptist preacher. Previous to his joining the Baptists he had been baptized by a Methodist preacher. When he offered to join the Baptists of Georgia it was made a question whether his baptism, being performed by an unbaptized person, was valid. The Georgia Baptists decided that it was valid.

In the year above mentioned, Mr. Hutchinson came to Virginia to see his relations in Loudoun County. While he was there his preaching became effectual to the conversion of many. Mr.

Hutchinson baptized them. These things stirred up the question in the Ketocton Association whether the baptism of Hutchinson and his new disciples was valid. The decision here was just the reverse of the decision in Georgia. They determined not to receive either him or those baptized by him, unless they would submit to be re-baptized. After some time they consented and the ordinance was readministered. Their proceeding on this occasion was more strict than that of any other Association upon the same subject. The question has been before most of the Associations at one time or other, and in every other instance they either deemed it unnecessary to rebaptize or left it to the conscience of the party to be rebaptized or not. The arguments were: That the most important prerequisite to baptism was faith in the subject; that, although it was expedient to have a fixed rule for qualifying persons for the administration of the ordinances, yet the want of such qualifications in the administrator ought not to be viewed as having sufficient weight to invalidate the baptism. On the other hand, it was argued: That if such baptism was sanctioned everything like ordination might be dispensed with; that ordination was not only expedient, but an institution of the Bible, and, therefore, indispensable; that such proceedings, if allowed, might go to great lengths, and, ultimately, produce confusion.

About the same time the Association was consulted as to the propriety of a church's requiring of each of her members to contribute to the expenses of the church according to their property. The Association determined that a regulation of that kind in a church was lawful, and that persons that would not submit to it deserved to be excluded from the privileges of the church. It was easy for the church to ask, and for the Association to give her advice; the correctness of which cannot be doubted upon right principles. But it was not quite so easy to execute. The attempt was made in some of the churches, but in consequence of the violent opposition it met with, they desisted from it.

In 1787, the lawfulness of hereditary slavery was debated in this Association. They determined that hereditary slavery was a breach of the divine law. They then appointed a committee to bring in a plan of gradual emancipation, which was accordingly done. They were treading upon delicate ground. It excited considerable tumult in the churches, and accordingly in their letters to the next Association they remonstrated so decidedly that the Association resolved to take no further steps in the business.

The Association took up the subject of the General Meeting of Correspondence at different periods, but in every instance decided against encouraging it. There are, however, within the limits of the district a very respectable party who are favorable to the institution of the General Meeting; and it is hoped that at no very distant day the whole Association will discover how requisite such a meeting is towards preserving peace and uniformity among a great people.

The office of moderator has been discharged by Messrs. Fristoe, Moore, and Munroe, alternately, each of whom seems to possess the qualifications requisite to fill the chair with dignity and skill.

Their standing clerk for many years has been Mr. Thomas Buck. It is not presumable they will want any other as long as he is willing and able to act.

CHAPTER TWENTY-SEVEN:
Historical Sketches of the Churches in the Ketocton Association

Ketocton

Of the origin of this mother church some account has already been given in the general history of the Regular Baptists. After Mr. Garrard had removed to Mill Creek, the care of the church fell to Elder John Marks. From the time that their numbers first appear on the minutes until the present day there has been very little variation, from which we infer that their course has been even and smooth.

Elder J. Marks (mentioned above) moved from Pennsylvania into Virginia either with Mr. Garrard or about the same time. He was rather at an advanced stage of life when he came, but settling in a healthy country, and being very temperate and regular in his life, he lived to be very old. He died about the year 1786, having from first to last maintained a spotless reputation for piety and steadiness. As a preacher he was sound and sensible, yet cold and phlegmatic. Being a poor man and obliged to labor for his support, his ministerial services were confined within a small circle. To this circumstance, added to his cold and dry method, may be ascribed his not being more successful. For some years this mother church was without any regular pastor. Mr. William Gilmore, a warm and active preacher from Maryland, having lately settled within the limits of a neighboring church, has consented to attend them stately.

Little River

This was some of the early fruits of Rev. D. Thomas's ministry in Virginia. In this work, however, he was powerfully aided by Rev. Richard Major, their first pastor; for although the first seed were sown by Mr. Thomas, yet Mr. Major watered and nourished the plants until he brought them to perfection. So rapidly did the Gospel spread in this church that just two years after they were constituted they were the most numerous church in the Association, having two hundred and seventy-two members. Her branches, however, extended into the neighboring parts. When any of these branches became sufficiently numerous they were constituted into new churches, by which the mother church was reduced in numbers. During Mr. Major's life they were a happy and united people, greatly attached to their minister. After his death they were without any regular pastor for some years. Lately they have chosen Rev. Robert Latham as their pastor, who is a man of gifts, and who *neglects not the gifts that are in him.*

New Valley

This church was formed partly by emigrants from Pennsylvania and partly by converts in Virginia. Their first pastor moved from Great Valley in Pennsylvania, and, settling here, took the care of this church. He was not much distinguished, and the church seems to have trodden in his steps as to her religious prosperity. She was represented by her pastor in the Associations until 1778. After that time her name appears no more upon the minutes until 1793, and then she has only thirteen members. For eight or ten years after this they seem still to have been a declining people; but for four or five years past they appear to have been looking up. Mr. Gilmore's labors here, as well as in most of the places where he preaches, seem to be attended by a divine blessing.

Goose Creek

This church exhibits proof of how much good may be done by active and intelligent private members, who, like Aquila and Priscilla, are willing to be *helpers in Christ Jesus.* It does not appear during the thirty-five years they have been acting as a church that they ever had any regular pastor, and yet there are few churches in the Association whose course has been more prosperous. The compiler thinks it worthy of note that in his frequent and diligent researches of the minutes of the Association he has not observed a single session in which this church has not been represented. He has not been informed of her internal order, but he infers from what he has learned that she is, at home as well as abroad, a dutiful and obedient daughter of Salem.

Leesburg and Ebenezer

These are young churches that have not been distinguished for anything very remarkable. Neither of them at present has any resident pastor. Ebenezer has, however, the stated services of William Fristoe. Leesburg is frequently visited by Jeremiah Moore. These old, faithful and laborious servants of the most high God, through the scarcity of preachers, are under the necessity of serving several congregations besides those in which they are residents.

North Fork

This church was once under the care of Elder Alderson Weeks,[1] a preacher of acceptance and usefulness. Of late, Elder William Gilmore has become their pastor, and under his ministry God has granted them a precious revival. Returns of twenty-six baptized were made to the last Association, and the work was still going on. Mr. Gilmore is spoken of as a young preacher of good talents, who is willing also to occupy them.

Alexandria,

This church, in the city of that name, though not a large, is a respectable church. They are the fruits of Elder Moore's ministerial labors, and with whom they are a very favorite people; while they, on their part, reciprocate his tender regard. What more glorious sight on earth than a pious and affectionate people receiving the tidings of peace and salvation from pious, animating and affectionate ministers? The Methodists have taken the lead of late years in Alexandria; indeed, in most of the large towns in Virginia they have greatly outstripped the other Christian sects. Whether their government, being more energetic than that of the Baptists, is on that account better adapted to the disorderly habits of a town; or whether their frequent change of preachers tends to gratify that taste which, like that of the Athenians, prompts them to tell or to hear some new thing; or whether, having influence with their preachers, they station their best ones in populous cities, which is not the case with Baptists, cannot be easily decided. The friends of the Baptists in some places hope that at no distant day the scene will be changed.

Frying Pan

This has been a larger church than it is at present. Many of the

---

[1] Mr. Weeks, the first pastor of this church, moved to Bedford, and there has the care of a church. We presume it is the same man.—*Author's note.*

members moving to other parts, and there being little or no revival
to fill up the vacancies, they have for some years had rather discouraging prospects.

Elder Jeremiah Moore, their present pastor, is about sixty-four
years of age. He was born June 7, 1746, in the county of Prince
William, of parents in the middle rank of life, and raised in the
Protestant Episcopal Church. At about seventeen years of age he
heard Rev. David Thomas preach, by which his thoughts were
turned upon sacred things. He had never given in to the daring
vices of the age, but was rather virtuously inclined, having from a
very early period had some legal notions of religion. His convictions were extremely pungent, and lasted a considerable length of
time. At last a revelation of the Redeemer's fullness to save the
greatest of sinners was made to his mind, and he rejoiced in hope
of his glory. His first profession of grace was in the year 1772,
and he soon was baptized.

Mr. Moore is not only a preacher, but a writer. He published
some years since two or three treatises in defense of his principles,
in which very considerable ingenuity is displayed. His call to the
ministry has something worthy of note. His mind being previously
much agitated between his impressions to preach and his apprehensions of unworthiness, God decided his doubts by impressing
upon his mind in a distinguished manner these words: "Neglect
not the gift that is in thee"; followed quickly by these: "Study to
show thyself approved, a workman that needeth not to be
ashamed." After this he commenced preaching, fully persuaded,
weak as he felt himself, that God had called him. Persecution and
affliction are said to be proof of a minister's call. Mr. Moore soon
had this proof. In 1773, while he was preaching in the bounds of
the church called Difficult, a magistrate, attended by the rector of
the parish, had him arrested by a constable and ordered to prison.
His mittimus[1] was written in these remarkable words: "I send you
herewith the body of Jeremiah Moore, who is a preacher of the
Gospel of Jesus Christ, and also a stroller," &c. This was somewhat similar to Pilate's inscribing over the cross of Christ, "Jesus
of Nazareth, King of the Jews." Mr. Moore escaped this imprisonment by obtaining legal license for places of preaching.

---

[1] Court order instructing the police to arrest someone.

At another time a lawless mob, headed by two magistrates, seized Mr. Moore and another preacher who was with him, and carried them off to duck them. After they had ducked Mr. Moore's companion, they discharged them both. These, added to the scoffs and ignominious reproaches unjustly thrown upon him, were a part of his early sufferings in his Master's service. It is now little less than forty years since he began to preach, during all which time he has labored with increasing diligence.[1]

In point of talents Mr. Moore certainly stands in the front row of Virginia preachers. His person and voice are extremely advantageous; his style is strong and energetic, and, indeed, elegant; especially as he had not the advantages of a refined education; his ideas are brilliant, and really flow upon him so abundantly that by some of his friends it has been thought rather a hurt, as it prevented him from making so clear an arrangement as he might otherwise do. He is well versed in the Scriptures, and without doubt often gives lucid explanations of mysterious texts. His system is high Calvinism, which he preaches with great ingenuity, and, indeed, some of his warmest friends are of opinion that his talents and temper tending that way have sometimes prompted him to enter unseasonably upon the mysterious points in that system, and thereby to deal out to weak stomachs meats too strong for their digestion. His talents for pulpit satire is probably equal to any man's in Virginia. This he is thought sometimes to throw out rather too lavishly upon his opponents. Solomon says: "Though you bray a fool in a mortar, yet will not his foolishness depart from him." If that be correct, then it is better sometimes not to answer a fool according to his folly.

Finally, admitting these inaccuracies, yet it is doubtful whether any other preacher in Virginia has run a more honorable course than Mr. Moore—honorable to his God, honorable to himself and honorable to his people. His age foretells that the crown of glory will not await him much longer.

---

[1] In 1795, Mr. Moore preached at a General Committee, In Louisa, where the compiler heard him observe that he had traveled and preached distances sufficient to reach twice round the world. He has lost no time since that.— *Author's note.*

Bull Run

This has been a more numerous church than at present. When the Gospel was carried here by the admirable and amiable Richard Major a great revival of religion arose, so that in a little time a church was constituted having 126 members. From the constitution of new churches, &c., their number had become somewhat reduced, until about 1792 they had the smiles of Heaven and large additions were made. Not many less than a hundred were baptized, by which this church rose to higher prosperity than she had ever previously enjoyed. After the loss of Mr. Major they employed Thomas Bridges as their pastor. His conduct while among them was approved of as far as it was known, insomuch that when he left them they gave him a letter of commendation. It was after he left them that his nefarious practices were made manifest.[1]

Difficult and Popeshead

These were once large and increasing churches, being the mothers of many pious and useful members, many of whom moved off to the western country. See the note on the Ketocton table.

Occoquon

This is the only church wholly in Prince William County. She was raised under the ministry of David Thomas, and had him as the pastor for some time. Their present pastor is Elder Philip Spiller, a preacher who confines his labors chiefly to his own vicinity. His church has rather increased of late years.

Chappawamsick

This church has been much distinguished among her sister churches in the Ketocton Association. From her have been constituted several of the neighboring churches, and in her were raised some of the most eminent ministers of the Gospel that have ever appeared in the Association. William and Daniel Fristoe, Jeremiah Moore, and William Grinstead are all sons of Chappawamsick.

---

[1] Of late the compiler has had an opportunity of frequently seeing Bridges in the penitentiary. He professes to have repented and to hope that he has obtained pardon of God for all his crimes. His keepers and fellow-prisoners say that he has greatly reformed.—*Author's note.*

When Mr. Thomas first began to preach in these parts, he met with violent opposition. Public worship was sometimes prevented by the enemies of religion. To please God is to offend the devil. Satan felt his throne shake, and was determined to prop it with the pillars of darkness. Persecutions, scoffs, reproaches, false reports, &c., were tried, but all in vain. They fell before the Gospel as the walls of Jericho fell before the blowing of the rams' horns. Mr. Thomas sowed the first seed, which were watered by his ministerial sons, William and Daniel Fristoe, and in a few years by Mr. Moore also. So rapidly did the Word increase among them that in 1770, three years after the constitution, they had one hundred and seventy-six members; and the following year, after dismissing thirty-six members to form the Potomac church, they had remaining two hundred and twelve. The next year, dismissing ninety-seven at once to form Brent Town church, they were reduced to 116. From this period Chappawamsick gradually declined for many years. William Fristoe had fallen into Potomac and Daniel into Brent Town, so that the mother church was rather destitute. About 1786, William Fristoe returned and continued among them for many years. In the great revival about 1791 and 1792 this church arose from the dust and put on her garments of praise. Her number, from being very small, increased to nearly a hundred. After the revival subsided another winter succeeded. Times grew so discouraging that Mr. Fristoe had serious fears that God had removed the candlestick, and that He would no more be gracious to the people of this vicinity. With these impressions he moved some distance up the country. This took place about 1801 or 1802. A few years previous to Mr. Fristoe's removal, Mr. William Grinstead had been baptized. Mr. Fristoe's dejected feelings were caught by Mr. Grinstead. He was filled with anxiety. At length he felt impressions to look out for a remedy. He himself began to exhort, and from that to preach. God smiled, his labors were blessed, and more than sixty added to the church. "God works in a mysterious way." Had Mr. Fristoe continued, Mr. Grinstead, according to human views, might not have become a preacher. Under Elder Grinstead's ministry, they have been a happy people. Mr. Grinstead is a popular preacher, of pleasing manners, and extensive gifts.

Elder William Fristoe, though a considerable distance off, is still a member of Chappawamsick. He was born about 1748, in the county of Stafford. At a very early period of life he heard the Gospel from the mouth of David Thomas. He became seriously impressed, and strove to do many things in a legal way to obtain divine favor. When every refuge failed, he cast his care upon Christ, and found in Him a rich supply of pardoning, saving love. Although but a mere youth, he felt impressions to preach; and accordingly, at about nineteen years of age, he began to appear in public for that sacred purpose. He demeaned himself with so much gravity and prudence that no man could despise his youth. As he grew older he extended his labors to more distant parts. Wherever he went, his preaching was more or less effectual in the salvation of sinners. Some of the most eminent preachers in Virginia owned him as their spiritual father. Lunsford, Mason, Hickerson, with several others, received the tidings of peace from his lips. In 1774, when about twenty-six years of age, he was chosen moderator to the Association, although all the older preachers were present. From that time he often discharged the duties of that office. His zeal, like a lamp fed by inexhaustible stores of oil, has never been extinguished; indeed, has seldom burnt dim. Forty-three years of weariness and painfulness have not yet made him weary in well-doing. His infirmities of body, for many years, have been constant; yet, despite all, he travels almost incessantly, and deals out the food of life to the hungry flocks. He attends three or four different congregations statedly; and these at a considerable distance from each other.

In the pulpit, though not versed in the learning of the schools, he displays abilities which many doctors of divinity have not attained. His language, though plain, is strong and nervous; his manner is solemn, as one having authority; he is a strong Calvinist in his principles, and preaches them fully as much as is proper. Mr. Fristoe's age and infirmities indicate that he will be called ere long to receive his reward.

Mr. Fristoe, by the appointment, or rather at the request of the Ketocton Association, undertook to write her history. His book came out in the year 1809.

White Oak

This church appears first on the minutes of the Association in the year 1791, having been taken off from Hartwood, and constituted under the care of Andrew Leach. He continued pastor for many years, during which they had many trials as well as comforts. A few years past he removed to Nanjemoy, in Maryland. Since his removal they have obtained the ministerial attention of Elder Hipkins Pitman, a resident within the bounds of the Goshen Association; in consequence of which they were dismissed in 1809 to join the Goshen. They have had a small revival of late.

Hartwood

This church was formerly called Potomac. They were under the care of Elder William Fristoe. Mr. Fristoe remarks in his history of the Ketocton Association that "the weakness of her members in common was such that she was scarcely ever able to direct her own discipline, yet out of her arose a number of useful, and some very eminent gifts, viz., Lunsford, Mason, Hickerson, and several others that are less known abroad." Mr. Fristoe was their minister for several years, during which time the above preachers were raised up. After he ceased to act as pastor they obtained the ministerial services of Elder John Hickerson. Since his death Ephraim Abel attends them in the character of pastor.

In this church arose James Garrard, late Governor of Kentucky. While in Virginia he was distinguished by his fellow-citizens, and elected to the Assembly and military appointments. After he moved to Kentucky he began to preach, and was thought to possess talents for the pulpit. He continued to preach until he was made Governor. For the honors of men he resigned the office of God. He relinquished the clerical robe for the more splendid mantle of human power. The prophet says to Asa: "If ye forsake God, He will forsake you." It is not strange that Colonel Garrard, after such a course, should fall into many foolish and hurtful snares. While Governor he had for his secretary H. Toulmin, said to be a trans-Atlantic Socinian preacher, but a man of talents. Through this man, report says, Governor Garrard fell into the Arian or Socinian scheme. Through the Governor many others were corrupted, until a serious and distressing schism took place. So it remains at this time.

Let it be tried a thousand times, and in nine hundred and ninety-nine cases it will be found that preachers who aim at worldly honors will be completely ruined or greatly depreciated as preachers.

It is due to Governor Garrard to say that his conduct has been orderly and, indeed, gentlemanly, and that he has honored every other character which he has ever assumed, except the one which, of all others, he ought to have valued.

Broad Run

The origin of this church is treated of in our general history of the Regular Baptists. Since that time their course has been regular and steady. They have not for many years had any resident pastor, yet they were attended stately for a length of time by Elder William Fristoe. They are blessed with a number of valuable private members, whose actions say that their right hand shall forget her cunning before they forget Jerusalem. They are not so numerous as in the days of their youth.

Thumb Run

This church was planted by the labors of Mr. William Fristoe, who continued to attend them monthly for a long time, although he lived at the distance of forty miles. For many years the church dwindled, until they were almost reduced to nothing; but being revived in a small degree about 1802, they grew to about fifty members. A few years past they had another comfortable revival, by which they have risen to their present state. It does not appear that they have ever had any regular pastor, but have been visited by the preachers of the adjacent churches. They have some zealous and active private members. The labors of Mr. Latham, who is at present their occasional pastor, have been blessed among them.

Brent Town

This church was stricken off from Chappawamsick under the pastoral care of the indefatigable Daniel Fristoe. They were a very happy and united people during the time of Mr. Fristoe's continuance among them. By his death they sustained an almost irreparable loss. They have since passed through many perplexing scenes at different times, and have also enjoyed some heavenly seasons. Their state may be said to have been rather a declining one.

Upper Carter's Run

This was once a tolerably prosperous church, but by the removal of her pastor, with some other causes, she declined, until she has disappeared from the minutes of the Association.

Long Branch

This church was formerly under the care of Elder John Munroe. Their course has not been marked by anything singular. Elder William Grinstead is their present minister, though living at some distance from them.

Back Lick

This was first called Accotink, but assumed her present name about 1792. She was made up of members taken off from Popeshead and Difficult churches. Her first minister was Henry Hagan, a preacher of some distinction. He died about 1793. Mr. Moore then preached for them for some time. Of late they have had no stated ministry. They have had at different times some pleasant revivals, and may be said to be a church of very respectable standing.

Hedgeman's River

This church lies upon the borders of Fauquier and Culpeper. The members of which, when she was first composed, were dismissed from Hartwood for that purpose, the year of 1791. They had Rev. John Hickerson for their preacher from the time of their constitution until he died. Since his death they have had no stated preacher. They have been a flourishing church.

Elder John Hickerson was born in Fauquier. His father, Nathaniel Hickerson, is still living. John professed to know the joyful sound when quite a young man. The following is a short representation of him given by Rev. Jeremiah Moore, who was his intimate friend: "Brother Hickerson was eminent for piety, zeal, and laboriousness in the work of the ministry. He never lost sight of the precious doctrines of rich and sovereign grace. Few, very few, have made equal progress in divine knowledge, who stood on the same ground with him." He died suddenly of cramp in the stomach at Leesburg. Virginia, on Saturday, the 28th of January, 1809.

His remains were conveyed to his mournful family and interred on Monday following. The following verses were composed by

Mr. Moore in honor of his memory:

Hark, hark! what awful tidings roar!
What strains of grief we hear!
The mighty herald is no more,
And Zion drops the tear.

In mournful accents she complains.
Ah! must the mighty fall!
And death the tyrant ever reign,
The grave consume us all?

Must prophets and apostles die,
And saints forever weep;
Must useful gifts and virtue die,
In death's eternal sleep?

No! Faith forbids these mournful sighs,
And dries the flowing tear;
Sees saints from sleeping tombs arise
And the Great Judge appear.

Then shall the herald quit the tomb,
With shouts to sovereign grace;
The day of full reward is come
And saints must take their place.

At Christ's right hand his bride appears,
From sin and death released;
Her eyes are washed from grief and tears,
Her soul is filled with peace.

Eternally his saints shall sing
His praise in lofty strains.
And Heaven with hallelujahs ring,
"The Lord the Saviour reigns."

South River

This has always been a small church, but has had some very worthy and respectable members. William Northern, who at present discharges the duties of pastor, has not been many years in the ministry. The pious own him as a messenger of peace.

Water Lick

This was, in a considerable degree, the fruit of the ministry of Rev. John Price; and he was their first pastor. After Mr. Price moved to Kentucky, they had the services of Rev. James Ireland, until his death. Since Mr. Ireland's death, God has raised up for this and some of the adjacent churches the active and useful Samuel O'Hendren. This church has passed through a course hitherto not very prosperous nor very adverse.

Rev. John Price, their first pastor, is a man of considerable gifts. He acted for many years as clerk to the Ketocton Association; and was, while in Virginia, considered a man of weight in religious concerns. In Kentucky likewise, he has been distinguished as a man of zeal and parts. By some of his acquaintances, however, it has been thought that his zeal partook too much of the nature of party spirit. In the disputes about hereditary slavery Mr. Price took a very active part in favor of hereditary slavery. In the late unhappy divisions in that country respecting the affair of Jacob Creath and others, Mr. Price is on the side of the minority, who seem disposed to push things to extremes. In disputes as inveterate as this has been, it is out of the question, in the estimation of men influenced by pious feelings, whether the merits of the case be on this side or that. Men prompted by disinterested motives, for the love of God, will say to all parties, "Are ye not carnal?" It is impossible in disputes carried on as this has been but that both sides must be wrong. It is charitable to hope that Mr. Price and those respectable characters engaged with him will in their last days see better times whenever love shall regain its ascendency, and they shall cease to bite and devour one another.

Thomas Buck, clerk to the Association, is a member of this church. He, though not a preacher in words, is a preacher in works. He is a man of wealth.

Happy Creek

This church was first called Lower South River, and has long been a church of good standing. Although never numerous, there have always been members in her communion who were an honor to the cause which they professed.

Mr. Ireland was their first pastor. He resigned, and after others had acted and moved off he again became their preacher until his death. Mr. Marshall, the second pastor, was among the first fruits of the ministry of the Separate Baptist preachers in Fauquier, about Carter's Run. He soon became a very zealous and successful preacher. From Carter's Run he went to Battle Run and preached to much purpose. From thence he traveled over the Blue Ridge, and preached in his zealous way upon South River, where was a considerable and rather singular stir. (It is said that those religiously exercised would bark as dogs. This exercise is said not to have been uncommon when *the jerks* prevailed in Kentucky.) Mr. Marshall being a man of more warmth than wisdom, more grace than gifts, did not obtain the pastoral care of a church at first. After some difficulties he was at last chosen pastor of South River, now called Happy Creek. But, moving to Kentucky about 1782, he was succeeded in the care of the church by John Taylor, one of her own sons. Mr. Taylor also, about 1783, moved to Kentucky, and has been there, as he was in Virginia, a preacher of weight, wisdom and usefulness.

Benjamin Dawson, their present pastor, a few years past moved into the upper end of Fauquier, and although not within the limits of Happy Creek, yet being convenient he was called as their preacher. He appears to be highly estimated by his fellow-laborers in the Association and by his acquaintance generally. He is certainly a man of gifts and of very pleasant manners.

Bethel

This is a young church taken off, as to the first members, from Buck Marsh, but has since increased rapidly.

Samuel O'Hendren, their pastor, is a young preacher in high estimation wherever he is known. As thriving trees show in spring by their blossoms that ripe fruit in plenty may by and by be gathered, so Mr. O'Hendren's present exhibitions indicate some precious and plenteous ingatherings at a future day. May neither frosts nor blasts corrupt or destroy the ripening fruit!

Buck Marsh

This has long been far the most numerous church in the Ketocton Association. This church was planted by the labors of Daniel and William Fristoe and others. After their constitution they were joined by a considerable number of members who were dismissed from Mill Creek. The distance at which the two Mr. Fristoes lived rendered it inconvenient for them to act as stated pastors; they, therefore, procured the attendance of Rev. John Garrard. After Mr. Garrard's death Mr. Ireland became their pastor, which took place about 1788. He continued their faithful and successful pastor until his death, in 1806. Mr. Collins, the pastor of Zoar, a neighboring church, then became their stated minister. He also died the year 1808. Of late Mr. Fristoe gives them statedly his ministerial labors in much weakness and in much wisdom, viz., bodily weakness and spiritual wisdom, the result of above forty years' experience.

Zoar

This church was first so called because "she was a little one." Although somewhat grown, they are still but a small people.

Mr. Christopher Collins, their first pastor, was a man of strong mind, greatly improved by study and literary pursuits. He moved from Westmoreland to Jefferson some years after he was baptized, but before he began to preach. The great dearth of good things in his new habitation stirred up his spirit to appear in the pulpit. Being advanced in life before he became a preacher, his talents did not appear to advantage. As a preacher, he was rather dry and tedious; yet what he said was sensible, and his labors were owned of God for good. He kept a kind of diary of his religious movements, by reference to which he could tell every text and the heads of every discourse he ever delivered or heard delivered. In his conduct he was very remarkable for his singular correctness. He died regretted by all descriptions of persons.

Mr. Francis Moore, their present pastor, has been laboring in the vineyard but a few years. He commenced after the death of Mr. Collins, and was soon recognized by the church as their pastor. He is the son of Jeremiah Moore, mentioned above, and is thought to have drunk from the same fountain. His ministry is thought already to have been productive of good, and is said to promise much and extensive good.

Mill Creek.

This has been shown to be the oldest church in the Ketocton Association. Mr. Garrard continued to be their pastor until his death. After some years, viz., about 1788, they invited and obtained the services of Rev. David Thomas. The church had become much smaller before Mr. Thomas became their pastor. For a season they rejoiced in his ministry; but some of the members becoming wise in their own conceit, took it into their fancy that Mr. Thomas preached false doctrine. It would be a waste of time and paper to state the ground of dispute. It was, in fact, a dispute almost about nothing. But, behold, "how great a matter a little fire kindleth." Out of this they made out to stir up a contention that lasted several years, caused a schism in the church, and interrupted the harmony of the Association for several sessions. The party who objected to Mr. Thomas's doctrine, and who were excommunicated by the majority, formed , something like an independent church, offered to join the Philadelphia Association, got themselves a preacher, baptized several persons, and really caused no little disturbance. In 1800, however, the breach was healed in great measure. Most, if not all, that had been excluded were reinstated, and those that had been baptized by unauthorized persons were rebaptized. In the meantime.

Mr. Thomas, discouraged by these inauspicious circumstances, added to some other cause, moved to Kentucky, where he is now living, but is almost blind. After their unhappy disputes were settled, the church invited Mr. John Hutchinson, their present pastor, to come and live among them and take the pastoral care. Since Mr. Hutchinson has resided among them they have moved on in a more orderly and peaceable way. Mr. Hutchinson is respected as a preacher of gifts, sound in the faith and successful in doing good.

Timber Ridge

This is quite a new church, raised by the labors of Mr. Hutchinson.

North River, Crooked Run, and Patterson's Creek

These are new churches, concerning which nothing interesting is known, except that they are preached to by Elder John Munroe, a practitioner of medicine. The two last of these are new churches raised up under his labors.

Dr. Munroe has long been engaged in the heavenly business of dispensing the Gospel. In the pulpit he is a man of solemn dignity, warm address, and speaks as one having authority. He frequently takes up contested subjects, and his opponents sometimes complain that at such seasons he administers very strong corrosives. The Doctor, however, independent of this, preaches the Gospel of peace in power and demonstration of the Spirit. He is now getting old, and has professed divine things from early life, yet has maintained from first to last an unblamable conversation. As a physician he has been in extensive practice, and generally viewed as a man of skill.

Nanjbmoy

This church lies in the State of Maryland, but having been raised by the labors of preachers within the Ketocton Association, they have hitherto continued among them.

TABLE OF GREENBRIER ASSOCIATION

Name of churches	Year	Number at Constitution	Present Number	By Whom Planted	Former Pastors	Current Pastors	Counties
Greenbrier	1781	12		J. Alderson	J. Alderson	J. Alderson	Greenbrier
Big Levels	1796	14	58	J. Alderson J. Osburne	J. Osburne	J. Osburne	Greenbrier
Taze's Valley	1805	27	45	J. Alderson J. Lee	J. Lee	J. Lee	Kenhawa
Mud River	1807	10	20	J. Alderson J. Lee	J. Lee	J. Lee	Kenhawa
Kenhawa	1796	12	33	J. Alderson J. Johnston	J. Johnston	None	Kenhawa
Cole River	1807	45	35	J. Alderson J. Johnston	J. Johnston	J. Lee	Kenhawa
Peter's Creek	1803	32	25	J. Alderson J. Osburne E. Hughes	E. Hughes	E. Hughes	Kenhawa
Indian Creek	1792	28	61	J. Alderson	M. Lacy J. Alderson	J. Ellison	Monroe
Blue Stone	1804	12		J. Alderson Mr. Stanley	Mr. Stanley	None	Giles

CHAPTER TWENTY-EIGHT:
History of Greenbrier Association, Including the Sketches of Churches.

Besides the churches west of the Alleghany in Greenbrier and the adjacent parts, there were some likewise, formed more southward, on New River, &c. These last associated with the Strawberry; but being very inconvenient, they were organized in 1793 as a separate Association under the name of New River Association. The churches in and about Greenbrier associated with the Ketocton; but now, finding it more convenient to unite with the New River, they petitioned the Ketocton and obtained a dismission from them, and in 1795 became members of New River, which then consisted of ten churches. The New River Association was in the habit of holding what they called conference meetings, in which several churches united in communion, &c. The Greenbrier churches also met occasionally in what they termed society meetings, in which they proceeded almost in the same manner as an Association. They received letters and delegates, attended to the requests of churches, gave their advice and sent a circular letter from each meeting, &c., &c.

The society meetings, it seems, had a happy tendency towards ripening them for a separate Association, which their inconvenient situation, as it respected the other part of the New River District, seemed to demand. After associating about six years with the New River Association, they petitioned and obtained leave to form a separate constitution. Mr. Osburne mentions this subject in the following words:

The reason which induced us to become an Association was convenience. The New River District, being at such a distance from us, made it inconvenient to attend. Brethren Alderson, Johnston and myself were delegated to attend the Association, and while we were there a motion was made by some person that we should become an associate body by ourselves. The next year we accordingly petitioned to that effect, and had our petition granted. This measure threw my mind into a great exercise in respect to supporting the digni-

ty of an Association, seeing at that time we had but four churches and three ordained ministers. When the time came for our society meeting, in which we were to consult whether we were to become an Association or not, my mind was so overpowered with a sense of the greatness of the undertaking that I was determined to oppose its constitution; but Brother Alderson being appointed to preach the introductory sermon, accordingly preached. In his sermon he showed that God did not choose the Jews because they were numerous, but because they were few in number, in order to show His power and make Himself a glorious name. This discovery had its proper effect. I plainly saw that God could, of a handful of weak and despised outcasts, make a great people. Although pressed on every side, He will cause them to grow and thrive. Thus, while we were but a weak and feeble band, we were constituted, in 1807. At that time we were but four churches; now we are nine, with a hope that we shall still continue to increase.

They have continued to meet regularly since their constitution. The business of the Associations has been conducted prudently; and at them the preaching and other public exercises have been often very powerful and generally happy. Not having any of their minutes, details of the proceedings of the Associations cannot be given. The Association meets annually the Friday before the second Sunday in September, and continues three days. Mr. John Alderson has generally acted as moderator, sometimes Mr. Josiah Osburne; and Mr. Crutchfield of late years as clerk; before him Mr. Osburne was clerk. We shall now proceed to the sketches of the churches, beginning with:

Greenbrier

By giving a historical relation of this church in particular, the reader will be informed of the first rise of the Baptists in these parts, seeing this is the oldest church in the district, and is, in a sense, the mother of the rest. They have been from first to last a prosperous people; yet, like all others, have had their ebbs and floods. By attending to Mr. Alderson's memoir we shall see their rise and progress.

Mr. Alderson was born in the State of New Jersey, and was the son of Rev. John Alderson, a Baptist minister of considerable distinction. His father had the pastoral care of Lynville's Creek church, in Rockingham County, where his son first entered upon the ministry.

Mr. Alderson, in his communications to the editor, gives the following account of his early life:

"My father being much from home, and I being the oldest son, much dependence was placed on me to take care of the farm, so that I had very little opportunity to learn. The chief of the books that I read were the Bible and the Baptist catechism, which last I got by heart, and not only said it over at school but also in the public congregations on Sundays after sermon. By these means I was kept from all gross immoralities. By an expression dropped from my father, after I had recovered from a very severe spell of sickness, my mind was very solemnly impressed, which I have never lost to this day. After passing through a painful and tedious law work, in which I would set resolutions and then break them, I became at last deeply concerned. I sought the Lord with my whole heart, and at last obtained comfort, great comfort, by the application of these words, 'Ye are built upon the foundation of the apostles and prophets, Jesus Christ himself being the chief cornerstone.' After many trials and doubts as to my conversion, I began at last to be exercised about preaching. I, at first, thought it impossible that so weak a creature as I could be called to preach; but being persuaded at last by many divine tokens that it was the will of God, I entered upon the solemn work.

October, 1775, which was after the removal of his father, he was established as pastor of Lynville's Creek church. A short time after this he visited Greenbrier, and finding a wild, uncultivated place, in which Christ and His cross were seldom, if ever, preached, his bowels yearned toward the people. He proclaimed among them the pure Gospel. It produced some gracious consequences. Sometime after his return home he was particularly sent for to revisit Greenbrier. He went, and found one person, at least, ripe for baptism, whom he received (being aided by two of his members who had removed to that country) and baptized.

At another visit, sometime after, he baptized two others. On this visit he began to meet with opposition. Some of the people held the Baptists in very great contempt. He continued his ministrations in Greenbrier, and continued them with success. God was with him and prospered him. The desert has blossomed as a rose.

Mr. Alderson moved to Greenbrier to live in the year 1777, and has ever since continued among them in the same place where he first settled. About this time the Indian war broke out, and the inhabitants of Greenbrier, &c., were obliged to shut themselves up in forts. This continued four years, and was a great hindrance to the progress of the Gospel. Mr. Alderson, notwithstanding, continued his ministerial labors. After having preached to the inhabitants of one fort, protected by a small guard, he would travel through woods and wilds until he reached another. In some of the forts he was gladly received and attentively heard. In others he was sometimes much opposed. One fort proposed to shut their gates against him, but he finally obtained admittance. At times he was threatened with very rough treatment, but these threats were never executed. He continued his labors through these various discouragements. Neither cold, nor heat, nor storms, nor perils from savages, nor perils from his own countrymen, nor perils from destructive beasts, nor inward temptations, nor outward afflictions, retarded his labors. He that was for him was more than all that could be against him. Seven long years did Mr. Alderson continue his work, during which he never heard nor saw a Baptist preacher except himself. As many as two or three licensed itinerant Presbyterian preachers passed through the settlement at that time. These preached the doctrine of free grace, and were acceptable to Mr. Alderson and his handful of members.

Having gathered as many as twelve members, all of whom, with their preacher, considered themselves as an arm of Lynville's Creek church, they petitioned the Ketocton Association for help that they might be organized into a church. One chief view which they had in applying to the Association was a hope that some other preachers might be sent among them. For, some of the opposers said they were entirely a new people, and that there were none others in the world. In these hopes they were disappointed. The Association replied that if they wished to be constituted they had the power in their own hands. Accordingly, on the 24th of November, 1781, they, by mutual consent, formed themselves into a Gospel church called Greenbrier. They had a written church covenant, which they placed in the front of their church-book. Mr. Alderson, of course, was their pastor.

The next spring they appointed a communion, or, in other words, the administration of the Lord's supper. Numbers came forward and requested the privilege of communing with them, to whom the church replied, as might be expected, that none were admitted to the communion except they were previously baptized upon a profession of vital faith, and had yielded themselves as members of the church. When they heard this many of them changed their tone and became enemies.

In 1786 the work of God broke out on the right hand and on the left through different parts of the country, and continued until 1790. In describing this revival our informant, the Rev. Josiah Osburne, makes use of the following language:

> *In this revival a number of members were added, and the mouths of gainsayers were stopped. The people's mouths, ears, hearts and doors were all open to receive the Word. Now the time of the singing of birds was come, and the voice of the turtle was heard in our land; which caused the heart of the old mourning preacher to rejoice in his God and to say with the prophet, 'Zion's cords are lengthened and her stakes are strengthened.' Thus where darkness reigned and the savage yell was heard, the unwilling captive, led in chains through the wilderness to a land of sorrow and worse than Egyptian darkness to linger in sorrow and pain the wretched remains of life, the Lord opened a wide and effectual door for the preaching of Jesus, by which numbers felt the virtue of His blood and were brought home to God.*

In the midst of these goodly times the Methodists made their appearance and raised no small opposition about doctrines.

> *They,* says our informant, *took Brother Alderson's track, made his preaching places theirs. Numbers under conviction and in a hopeful way joined them, and, although alarmed by the preaching of the Baptists, turned to be their persecutors.*

The revival being over, a declension ensued. The love of many waxed cold, and several were excluded. Mr. Alderson now deplored the state of Zion; but God heard his groans.

Indian Creek church, hitherto an arm of Greenbrier, was constituted in the year 1792, under the care of Mark Richards, a preacher who had been raised up in the revival. In the constitution of this church, Mr. Alderson obtained the aid of Mr. Johnston, who was the first Baptist preacher that ever visited those parts after Mr. Alderson's removal thither. Mr. Johnston finally became a resident. After the year 1792 times became better, and they had a gradual revival. In 1794, Elder Josiah Osburne moved from Hardy County and settled in Greenbrier. He was a great accession to Mr. Alderson who thus speaks of him: "Brother Osburne, then a licensed preacher, moved from Lost River, Hardy County, and settled on the Big Levels of Greenbrier, where there was one arm of our church. Thanks to the Lord, we have stood together ever since."

Mr. Alderson is now a very old man, yet labors as much as ever, if not more. He has given up the world, as to its cares, and is only waiting for the crown of life.

Big Levels

This church was raised under the ministry of Elder Josiah Osburne, except as to a few who had been baptized by Elder Alderson, previous to the removal of Elder Osburne into that country. It has always prospered moderately, and has enjoyed harmony and peace. An incident has been told Elder Osburne respecting this church, which appears worthy of notice. A man by the name of Newel was severely afflicted with convulsive fits. He had them so violently that his life was despaired of. He became a Christian, and was baptized, since which he has never had a fit within the knowledge of any person. How is this to be accounted for? The unthinking will say that it is happenstance. The philosophers without faith will say that it is owed to the same natural cause, perhaps the baptizing effected the cure, seeing cold baths are sometimes beneficial in some cases. But a spiritual believer will see in it an unseen hand, capable of working with or without natural causes.

Elder Josiah Osburne, pastor of the above church, was born March 5, 1750, and raised a Presbyterian. His education was almost nothing, being scarcely able to read when he grew up to manhood. Having received religious instruction from his parents, he had early excuses about religion, but all together in a legal way. He continued outward appearances, until he left his father's house, then gave up all pretensions to seriousness and became openly vicious until he was twenty-eight years of age. He then heard a Baptist minister preach; the word came home to his heart and he felt himself under the care of God's broken law. His convictions became so strong that he despaired mercy. His despair, however, was not of long continuance in the due season. God revealed His arm and showed that He could justify sinners without the deeds of the law. He rejoiced in the discovery with unspeakable joy. His impressions now led him to wish to do something for his redeemer who had done so much for him, but he felt himself incapable. He drove for divine instruction and God applied forcibly to his mind this text: "I have chosen these things that are not to bring to naught things that are." He then yielded and began to preach, yet under very great embarrassments. When a meeting be appointed, he thought that he would attend that, and would then decline for the future. Having obtained hope, he has continued from that day to this. Preaching the gospel of the kingdom, Mr. Osburne's labors in the ministry have been exceedingly blessed in the country where he resides.

As a preacher, he stands equal, if not superior, to any in that country. He has a singular turn for touching the feelings so that in associations and great meetings it is generally laid upon him to close the meeting. In such cases, God has often owned his exhortations &c. to valuable purposes.

A few years passed, he was drawn into a debate about believers' baptism by some of the pedobaptists. In consequence of this, his mind was imperceptibly led to think much on this subject, and finally to commit his thoughts to writing. This he did in such an able manner that his friends to whom he showed it insisted on printing it. He contended and came out under the title of David and Goliath. By many this is considered one of the best treatises on baptism that has ever been published.

Taze Valley and Mud River

Nothing has occurred to either of these churches worth noticing. They lie in the lower end of Kenhawa country, contiguous to the Kentucky line.

Kenhawa

The church flourished greatly while it was under the care of Elder Johnston, insomuch that in a few years two other churches were constituted from it. But the removal of their minister, who went to Kentucky, proved a heavy misfortune. They experienced great declension, and have ever since been without a pastor.

Cole River

She had, at the time of her constitution, a considerable revival within her limits. But her minister, Elder Johnston, removing to Kentucky in a short time, they declined in some degree. Elder Lee is their preacher at present.

Peter's Creek

This church was in a revived state when constituted, but now is the reverse. It was literally, when constituted, a church in the wilderness.

Indian Creek

This church was taken from Greenbrier, as has been shown. When constituted, Mark Lacy was pastor. At first, for a small space of time, the church flourished. But Lacy, after a short period, began to conduct himself in a way unbecoming his station, which finally ended in his exclusion. In consequence of this, the church drooped, and were on the point of dissolving their constitution, when in the year 1797, Mr. Alderson undertook to supply them. Being a favorite son of Heaven, through his labors the church again revived; and God raised, within her borders, what may be termed one of the best gifts that a church can receive, a faithful minister. James Ellison was ordained to the pastoral care of this church, in the year 1808.

Blue Stone

There is nothing remarkable respecting this church. They are very destitute of ministerial supply.

TABLE OF UNION ASSOCIATION

Name of churches	Year	Number at Constitution	Present Number	By Whom Planted	Former Pastors	Current Pastors	Counties
Simpson's Creek	1771	5	45	J. Sutton	J. Sutton	J.H. Goss	Harrison
Buchannon	1786	5	17	J.W. Loveberry	J. Loveberry J. Cazod	J. Carney	Harrison
Good Hope	1806	12	12		J. Waldo	J. Waldo	Harrison
Olive Branch	0803	9	23			P. Wells	Harrison
West Fork						J. Hickman	Harrison
Salem	1801	9	14		J. Denham J. Morris	J.H. Gross	Harrison
Union	1802	5	20			P. Wells	Harrison
Valley	1806	10	22			P. Wells S. Hariss	Randolph
Little Bethel	1795	5	27			P. Wells	Randolph
Pritchel's Creek	1786	8	28		J. Denham	J. Hickman	Monongalia
Pawpaw	1803	7	14			T. Martin	Monongalia
Sandy Creek	1798	15	21			J. Smith	Monongalia
Gethsemane	1803	10	7			None	Monongalia

CHAPTER TWENTY-NINE:
History of the Union Association, Including the Sketches of Churches.

The churches of which this Association is composed were in connection with the Red Stone until 1804, when they were dismissed to form an independent Association, having nine churches. They meet once a year, viz., the Friday before the last Sunday in August, and continue three days. Of their proceedings in the Association nothing is known. We can offer a few remarks respecting the churches, &c.

Simpson's Creek

At the time that this church was constituted the country where the members resided was but newly settled. They passed through many difficulties at first, but finally rose above them all.

Their first pastor, Mr. Sutton, was considered a man of talents, piety and usefulness. Elder Goss, their present pastor, moved a few years past from Albemarle, having previous to that traveled and preached very considerably. It is presumable he is equally industrious in his new habitation, and probably more successful.

Buchannon

This church, at first very small, was revived soon after their constitution and became large and respectable; but by the constitution of other churches they are now reduced to seventeen.

Olive Branch

They enjoyed a comfortable revival soon after they were constituted. But churches, like individuals, when they think they stand, should take heed lest they fall. There has been a great declension in this church of late.

West Fork

Under the labors of Elder Hickman, this church has rather flourished than otherwise.

Salem

They have rather prospered. From 1801 until 1805 Elder John

Denham was pastor; from 1805 until 1809, Isaac Morriss. They now have the ministerial services of Mr. Goss.

Valley

This church has no regular pastor, but is statedly supplied by Elders Wells and Hariss. They are a thriving people.

Little Bethel

This church is also supplied by Mr. Wells. And although in the midst of mountains and a wilderness country, they enjoy the sweet sunshine of divine mercy.

Pritchel's Creek

This church, though small at first, increased in 1805 to fifty members, but by the dismission of members, &c., is now reduced to twenty-eight.

Sandy Creek.

"This church," says Mr. Alderson (who furnished all our accounts respecting this Association), "has gone through various scenes as to revivals and declensions, as most of the churches on the western waters have. We all have to stand against a torrent of opposition, from different quarters, especially the Arminians."

Gethsemane

This church is at present rather declining. They have no stated ministry, but catch the Gospel as it is occasionally brought by traveling preachers.

Good Hope, Union, Pawpaw

Of the above churches, concerning which nothing is said, nothing is known by the compiler, except the items found in the table. We should have been highly gratified to say something respecting the ministers of the Gospel in this Association, but for the want of acquaintance cannot.

TABLE OF RED STONE ASSOCIATION

Name of churches	Year	Number at Constitution	Present Number	By Whom Planted	Former Pastors	Current Pastors	Counties
Little Bethel	1801	11	50		J. Patterson	J. Patterson	Monongalia
Forks of Cheat	1795	12	47		J. Corbley	None	Monongalia
Mount Tabor	1788	9	47			J.W. Patterson	Monongalia
Mount Olivet	1801	10	18			None	Monongalia
Antioch	1806	9	18			J.W. Patterson	Monongalia
Short Creek	1802	12	104		E. Martin	E. Martin	Ohio
Cross Creek	1802	13	60		J. Pritchard	J. Pritchard	Brooke

CHAPTER THIRTY:
History of the Red Stone Association, Including the Sketches of Churches.

Red Stone Association was organized October, 1776. It is not known how many churches were in the Association at the time of the constitution, as it is probable there were some dismissed from different Associations for that purpose. The Ketocton Association, in her session for 1775, dismissed the four following, viz.: Laurel Hill, Isaac Sutton, pastor, thirty-seven members; Ten-Mile Creek, James Sutton, eighteen members; Patterson Creek, Joseph Barnet, pastor, six members; Goshen, John Corbley, pastor, sixty members—making in all one hundred and twenty-one members, and four preachers. The Red Stone District is partly in Pennsylvania and partly in Virginia.[1] The number of churches in Pennsylvania is not known. The proceedings of the Association are not known in any degree. The state of the churches, beyond what is represented by the table, is very little known. Such as is known shall be here given.

Little Bethel

Soon after their constitution this church had a pleasant revival, and arose from eleven to fifty. They receive and feed upon the bread of life, dealt out to them statedly by their beloved minister, John Patterson.

Forks of Cheat

This church was first organized under the attention of Rev. John Corbley. They have been rather a thriving people, especially during the time of Mr. Corbley.

Mount Tabor

They had about the year 1802 a precious revival, when their numbers increased to upwards of sixty. Since that pleasant season they have rather declined.

---

[1] It is also said there are some churches in the Ohio State belonging to Red Stone Association.—*Author's note.*

Short Creek

They began with the small number of twelve, and have increased through the riches of grace, to one hundred and fifty. Elder Enoch Martin, their pastor, at the command of God, has cast the net on the right side, and gathered it full.

Cross Creek

This is also a thriving church. Elder John Richard, their minister, has the happiness, most to be desired by a faithful preacher of the Gospel, viz., the success of his labors.

Mount Olivet, Antioch

Nothing more than what is seen in the table is known of the churches passed over.

The term *Regular Baptists* is kept up in Red Stone Association, in contradistinction to the Seventh Day Baptists, who are numerous in some parts of the district

There are also some who were deluded by the impostor Samuel Counsel, mentioned in our account of the Accomac Association.

The number of members in all the Red Stone Association, a few years past, was 1,335, among whom were thirteen or fourteen ordained preachers, besides licensed ones. Some of the preachers in the Red Stone Association are said to be men of great abilities.

TABLE OF PORTSMOUTH ASSOCIATION

Name of churches	Year	Number at Constitution	Present Number	By Whom Planted	Former Pastors	Current Pastors	Counties
Pungo	1762	45	86	Chas. Daniel John Burgess	J. Gamewell G. Plummer	J. Lawrence	Princess Anne
Blackwater	1784		69	G. Plummer T. Armistead	W.Sorey	W. Sorey	Princess Anne
London Bridge	1784	55	193	Daniel Gould W. Morris	W. Morris	J. Ritter	Princess Anne
Norfolk	1804		290		W. Goodall		Norfolk
Portsmouth	1789		68	T. Armistead E. Baker	T. Armistead D. Biggs		Norfolk
Upper Bridge	1782	9	56		E. Mintz T. Etheridge J. Grigg	D. Casey	Norfolk
Shoulder's Hill	1785		217	D. Barrow E. Mintz	E.Mintz J. Ritter	T. Bunting	Nansemond
Western Branch	1779	8	49		E. Mintz	T. Bunting	Nansemond
South Quay	1785	24	96	D. Barrow	D. Barrow	J. Bowers	Southampton
Black Creek	1786	70	103	J. DuPuy D. Barrow	D. Barrow	W. Browne	Southampton
Meherrin	1788		139	J. McGlamre	J. McGlamre	W. Browne	Southampton
Tucker's Swamp	1807	15	26	J. Crumpler J. Bowers	H. Jones	H. Jones	Southampton
Seacock	1787	18	55	E. Baker		W. Browne	Sussex
Raccoon Swamp	1772	87	168	J. McGamre	J. McGamre	W. Browne	Sussex
High Hills of Nottoway	1787		34		W. Browne	W. Chambliss	Sussex
Sappony	1778	6	59	J. Walker	J. Bowers J. Bell		Sussex
Mill Swamp	1774	11	200	J. McGlamre	D. Barrow	W. Browne	Isle of Wight
Otter Dams	1791		81		B. Boothe	B. Boothe	Surry
Rowanty	1775		22		J. Lee		Dinwiddie
Davenport's			165	J. Lee	J. Lee, J. Wright		Prince George

CHAPTER THIRTY-ONE:
History of the Portsmouth Association from the First Settlement of Baptists within Her Limits.

It has already been shown that the first Baptists who made their appearance in Virginia settled in the southeast part of the State; of these it is now proper to treat.

The accounts of their origin are somewhat different. In certain memoranda furnished by Mr. Leland it is stated that "the first society of Baptists that was ever in Virginia that we have any account of was in Isle of Wight, at a place called Burley, about 1727. This society was composed of emigrants from England, who had Rev. Richard Nordin for their pastor. He soon returned to England, and was succeeded by Messrs. Casper Mintz and Richard Jones. The church was formed upon the Arminian plan and is now extinct." Mr. Leland's manuscript was for some time in possession of Mr. Backus, of New England, who inserted the following note:

A letter is now before me, written from Virginia to Elder Eyres, of New Port, January 28, 1742, by John Hamerstley, where it appears that in consequence of letters from Virginia, Robert Nordin and Thomas White were ordained in London in May, 1714, and soon sailed for Virginia; but White died by the way, and Nordin arrived in Virginia and gathered a Baptist church in Prince George County, and held meetings there and in other places until he died, December 1, 1725, in a good old age. And on April 30, 1727, the church ordained Richard Jones, their elder, who continued to be their minister. In 1742 the church had about forty members.

Isaac Backus.
May 31, 1808

Mr. Backus further notes: "William Sojourner went from that church and gathered a church in North Carolina about 1740." Mr.

Leland, observing Mr. Backus's note, says in a letter to the editor: "You will see in my manuscript Elder Backus's note. I collected my account from Mr. Morgan's materials. Mr. Backus got his information from an old letter sent to Elder Eyres. If there was a Robert Nordin in Prince George and a Richard Nordin in Isle of Wight, the difficulty ceases. But if there was but one Nordin who emigrated from England to America, one of the accounts must be wrong. Perhaps Burkit's history will solve the doubt."

Burkit and Read's history says nothing about it; nor is it probable there can be any further information obtained at this day. It appears, however, to the editor, more than probable that Mr. Backus is substantially correct, for the following reasons: Mr. Backus had a document before him, written as early as 1742, about twenty-eight years subsequent to the earliest time mentioned; so that, without supposing the writer to be more than forty or fifty years of age, he might have been an immediate witness of the facts related; and, indeed, from his exactness as to dates, both in London and America, it is quite likely that he was himself one of the first emigrants that composed the church. At any rate, he writes as one who possesses an intimate acquaintance with the subject from first to last. The difference between the two statements may be accounted for by considering that Mr. Edwards did not procure his information until about forty years after the date of the letter mentioned above, and that at that period a great deal of it must have been traditional, and consequently much more liable to be incorrect. This may explain the difference of names and dates. As to the difference of counties, it is not improbable that Isle of Wight and Prince George might have been at that time all one county.

From these considerations, it appears Mr. Backus's note must be accurate, and that Baptists and Baptist principles have been in Virginia very little, if any, less than one hundred years.

Let us now pursue the narrative, as we have it laid down in Mr. Leland's memoranda, and in the history of the Kehukee Association.

We find this church in the year 1742 tolerably prosperous under the care of Rev. Richard Jones, who, it appears, from both statements, was installed as pastor in 1727. How long Mr. Jones continued after this date is not known. The church itself is now extinct. The last account of her existence was in December, 1756, at which time there was a division among them. Some died, and some moved to North Carolina, &c., so that it is not improbable that her dissolution took place not long after. Those that moved to North Carolina were much more successful. In the course of ten years after this they were increased to sixteen churches. The Kehukee history relates that "under the ministry of Messrs. Paul Palmer and Joseph Parker the most of the original churches were planted." It is not said whether they were emigrants from England or native Americans. The most probable conjecture is that they were some of the first fruits of the labors of Mr. Sojourner, mentioned in Mr. Backus's note. And indeed there can be but little doubt that Mr. Nordin and Mr. Jones, the first of whom lived here eleven years, and the second at least sixteen, extended their ministry farther than the immediate church to which they acted as pastor. Palmer and Parker were both Arminians, and so were the churches and preachers raised under their ministry; from which circumstance, together with some original papers still extant, it seems almost certain that the first emigrants were what in England are called General Baptists.

Their manner of gathering churches was very loose indeed, or at least was very adverse to the method now prevalent among the Baptists in Virginia. They required no experience of grace or account of their conversion, but baptized all who asked it and professed to believe in the doctrine of baptism by immersion.[1] It does not appear that they ever held Associations or meetings by that name, but instead of these they had yearly meetings, at which they transacted business of a general nature, or such as respected the welfare of all their churches.

Sometime previous to the year 1765[2] Rev. Messrs. Van Horn and Miller, residents of New Jersey, were sent from the Philadelphia Association to visit the churches and to set things in order among them. By some they were viewed with jealousy and dis-

---

[1] It is probable they required a promise on the part of the candidate to reform his life, and in general to be religious, which it is said is all that is required by many of the ministers of the General Baptists in England.— *Author's note.*

[2] The editor could not find from the Kekukee history, or from any documents before him, the precise year in which they came.—*Author's note.*

trust, being styled New- lights, but by most of the churches they were cordially received. Their labor was not in vain. They effected much, very much indeed. By their preaching and conversation many precious souls were raised from the sleep of death. The spirits of such as had ever tasted that the Lord was gracious were much refreshed. The honor of religion, as professed by the Baptists, was exceedingly enlarged. Their speech and preaching were not with enticing words of man's wisdom, but in demonstration of the Spirit and of power. Many of the members of the churches were convinced of the incorrectness of the Arminian doctrine and relinquished it. And where these were sufficiently numerous and otherwise qualified they were newly organized and formed into new churches, according to the plan of the Philadelphia Association, or rather according to the Baptist confession of faith, published in London in 1689, in conformity with which it seems the Philadelphia and Charleston Associations were organized. What these reverend fathers left unfinished was afterwards completed by their sons in the ministry. The Arminian doctrine and discipline soon disappeared, and the churches all became Regular Baptists. It is not intended to be understood that this revolution met with no opposition. This was not to be looked for. Messrs. Parker and Palmer, it has been said, were the fathers of these churches. Mr. Palmer was dead; Mr. Parker was living, and with two other preachers, viz., William Parker and Winfield, continued still to pursue their former method. But being deserted by so large a majority, their party finally dwindled to nothing.

Nothing certainly appears by which it can be ascertained whether they corresponded with any other Baptists in America previous to the above reformation. There are some circumstances, however, which make it probable that they did:

First. The letter written by Mr. Hamerstley to Mr. Eyres, mentioned in Mr. Backus's note, renders it probable that some previous intercourse had subsisted between the Baptists in Virginia and those of New England.

Secondly. It would appear hardly reasonable that the Philadelphia Association would send messengers to any place or people with whom they had no correspondence.

Lastly. It is presumable from the correspondence with the Charleston Association, which immediately took place after the

Kehukee Association was formed, that there had been some former acquaintance.

The churches thus newly organized formed themselves into an Association. Their first session was held in the year 1765, at a place called Kehukee, and for this reason their Association was called by that name. They immediately established a correspondence with the Charleston Association. The ministers belonging to the Kehukee Association at first, or, however, the principal ones, were Jonathan Thomas, John Thomas, John Moore, John Burgess, William Burgess, Charles Daniel, William Walker, John McGlamre, James Abbington, Thomas Pope, and Henry Abbot. Of these only two, viz., John McGlamre and James Abbington, were baptized after the introduction of Calvinistic principles.

About the time of the constitution of Kehukee, the Separate Baptists became very numerous in the upper parts of North Carolina and Virginia, and had formed themselves into an Association. The Kehukee Association being desirous to form a closer connection with people whose zeal and piety they so much revered, about the year 1772, sent Elders McGlamre and Thomas as deputies to the Separate Baptist Association, which was held at Waller's meetinghouse, in Spotsylvania County. The deputies were kindly received, and the Separate Association also deputed two of their ministers, viz., E. Craig and David Thompson, to visit the Kehukee the next August, at their Association to be held at the Kehukee meetinghouse, Halifax County, North Carolina. They attended; the subject was taken up, and the Separates stated the following objections to a communion with them: First, that they were not sufficiently strict in receiving church members; secondly, they were, as they alleged, too superfluous in their dress, contending that excessive dress ought to be made a matter of church discipline; thirdly, that their principles and practices were at variance, because, although they believed that faith in Christ Jesus was essential to baptism, yet they retained many members in their churches who acknowledged themselves to have been baptized in a state of unbelief. This last was declared to be the main bar to a complete union. Their objection upon this ground was the more effectual, because it had been a matter of considerable embarrassment to a great number of the Kehukee ministers, who had many thoughts of attempting a reformation. This occurrence furnished them with more favorable ground to make a beginning, which was accordingly done in the year 1774.

Mr. Burkit's church first held a conference and publicly proclaimed that they would commune with none who confessed they were baptized before conversion, alleging that adult persons had no better claim to baptism while they were in a state of impenitence and unbelief than infants had. Mr. Burkit's church was followed by several others. But when the next Association met, which was that year, viz., 1775, held at Moore's meetinghouse in October, the reformers met with severe opposition. The correctness of their proceedings was much questioned. Much dissension arose. One party blamed the other for doing too much, who in their turn were equally blamed by their opponents for not doing enough. Not inclined to associate together, each party claimed the right of being called the Association; the reformers, because what they had done was exactly congenial to the original plan upon which the Association was organized; and the other party, being most numerous, insisting that a majority ought to retain the power, and consequently the name of the Association. They moreover argued that whatever might be their principles, it was well known at the time of the constitution of the Association that this evil existed in greater force than it did at that time, seeing none had been baptized in known unbelief since the constitution; that therefore it was virtually if not pointedly agreed that such as were then in orderly standing might retain their membership, lest more mischief might ensue by being too rigorous than by submitting to small inconveniences for the sake of peace; that the Association having been in existence for eight or nine years, during all of which time they had suffered the inconvenience, it was now rather strange that they, at this late period, should attempt a revolution so likely to disturb the peace and harmony of the churches. To all these arguments it was answered that to them it was a matter of conscience, which they could not relinquish without wounding their own souls. As neither side would give way, things came to extremities. Each party organized a distinct assembly or Association. The reformers kept possession of the meetinghouse, whilst the opposite party retired, first to the woods, and on the second day procured a private house in the neighborhood. All attempts at reconciliation proved ineffectual during this session. Each party transacted their own business, of which, however, very little was done. These party broils were exceedingly afflicting to the pious on both sides. It would appear from the arguments on the old side that many of them did not deny the principles of this reformation so much as its necessity, seeing it would unavoidably produce much confusion, and if let alone the evil would, of course, in time vanish. Those who had undertaken to effect the reformation persevered, and finally accomplished their wishes.[1]

In August, 1777, they held their first undisputed Association at Elder Bell's meetinghouse, in Sussex County, Virginia. They found, on assembling, that their strength had very much increased. Ten churches had sent letters and delegates; of which it appeared that six were Regulars, or the old side, and four were Separates, who, finding their former obstacles removing, and being convenient, were incorporated with this Association. Of these ten churches, four were in Virginia and six in North Carolina. Their whole number of members consisted of 1,590, which was indeed very considerable for that early period. They agreed now upon an abstract of principles, which was afterwards printed and published. In doctrines and discipline it did not substantially differ from the confession of faith generally received among the Baptists. They agreed to hold two Associations annually, and appointed the next at Burkit's meetinghouse, the next May. The Kehukee Association continued to meet regularly, and to increase rapidly until the year 1790. At their October session for that year it was found that there were no less than sixty-one churches, having more than five thousand members. Several ineffectual attempts previous to this had been made to divide the district. The number of churches was now so large that a division was almost indispensable. They accordingly agreed to divide by the State line, leaving forty-two churches in North Carolina and nineteen in Virginia.

The Virginia churches met by their delegates for the first time, May, 1791, at Portsmouth, and on that account named their Association the Virginia Portsmouth Association. Their time of meeting has been from the first on the fourth Saturday in May, annually. Their business has been transacted in peace and prudence; the

---

[1] The Regular Association dwindled and finally came to nothing, partly by falling in with the Separates and partly by other causes.—*Author's note.*

number of churches has increased, but not so rapidly as in some other Associations.

While Elder McGlamre lived and attended the Associations, he generally acted as moderator. After his death, and when he was absent, the duties of moderator most commonly devolved upon Rev. David Barrow, until his removal to Kentucky. Since his removal Elders Browne, Bowers, Murrelle, &c., have occasionally acted.

Until the division of the Kehukee District, Mr. Burkit (joint author of Kehukee history) was the standing clerk. Since the division that office has fallen into the hands of different persons, at different times.

Elders William Browne, James Wright, &c., were in their turns placed in that office. Not having a regular file of the minutes of the Association, a detail of their proceedings cannot be exhibited. This, however, is the less necessary at this stage of our work, inasmuch as the business of so many others is already detailed that it is not presumable that there would be anything new or singular.

There are some very valuable and able preachers within the Portsmouth Association; but it is the opinion of some who are intimately acquainted that in point of ministerial talents they have rather depreciated. A sanguine believer can, nevertheless, anticipate a day when God shall send them judges as at the first, and counselors as at the beginning; when the watchmen now upon the walls, aided by a new band, shall proclaim to Zion, "Thy God reigneth."

Pungo

This church is among the oldest churches in Virginia. Whilst they have had their days of adversity, as well as their clays of prosperity, God has still preserved them a name among the families of Israel. Preachers, like servants, can give us much ease; they can also stir up much confusion. In 1766 their first pastor, George Plummer, was inaugurated. He, forsooth, must marry his wife's sister, and was, of course, suspended. In January, 1774, they made choice of Joshua Lawrence. For some years he stood in high estimation; but some charges being exhibited against him, though not satisfactorily proven, the church, with the assistance of helps, offered an appeal to his own conscience, proposing that he should acknowledge or deny the charges exhibited against him. This he refused, and was excluded. He then commenced preaching upon his own independence, and publicly and solemnly denied the charges, thereby showing more respect to the world than the church. He formed a party, who built him a meetinghouse. After some years, however, he was reinstated. Well might Paul say of ministers, "not self-willed."

Blackwater

This is an arm of Pungo. Nothing very remarkable has occurred here.

London Bridge

This has generally been a prosperous church. Their first pastor was William Morris, who, after serving them faithfully about seventeen or eighteen years, in 1802 took a dismission to Kentucky, the cemetery of Virginia Baptist preachers. This was matter of great grief to his affectionate people.

They next obtained the services of Jeremiah Ritter, who has ministered to them with considerable success. Of late years God has raised among them William P. Biddle, a young preacher of promising talents and very amiable deportment. How refreshing are these young and faithful ambassadors!

Norfolk

This church was taken off from Portsmouth. They have had their full share of calamities—calamities severe and sorrowful in deed and in truth. Before their constitution they were cursed with an errant impostor by the name of Frost. He came from Europe and pretended to be a preacher. He made much confusion, to settle which the church appointed certain persons to take him under leadings. Frost refused to hear them and attended an appointment of his to preach that evening. Just as he commenced preaching he dropped down in the pulpit and expired in about three hours. In 1802 one Mather, another European vagabond preacher, came to Norfolk and made no little confusion. He also soon died. In 1803 Benjamin Ashley, Peter Sugg, Henry Keeling, and James Mitchell were ordained to the ministry. When the church was constituted they had several preachers in their limits, none of whom, however, were called upon by the church to take the pastoral care. They inconsiderately invited a certain William Goodall to become their pastor. He was then a resident of Hampton. He proved the greatest stumbling-block of all. Goodall was a man of some talents as a preacher; but devoid of something more valuable than talents, he blackened the Baptists in Norfolk more than all his preaching could wipe off if he were to live an hundred years. He fell into the sin of polygamy and was put out from among them. Goodall's apostasy, with some other severe calamities that have since befallen them, has apparently almost ruined the Baptist cause in Norfolk; but if it be the cause of Christ it must rise again. The gates of hell may annoy but cannot prevail against the true church. They have still several ordained preachers among them, but no pastor. Elder Browne has of late undertaken to attend them once a month.

Portsmouth

This church was constituted under the pastoral care of Elder Thomas Armistead. His labors were much blessed, and the church grew and multiplied. About 1792, partly from bad health and partly from other causes, Mr. Armistead resigned his charge. After his resignation the church declined greatly. They employed Jacob Bishop, a black man of considerable talents, to preach for them. This, as might have been expected, could not answer in Virginia. Elder Thomas Etheridge and Jacob Grigg, in their turn, served them a small space of time. In 1802, Elder Davis Biggs moved into the vicinity of Portsmouth, and became their pastor. Under his watchful care the church has moved on in a much more tranquil manner.

Elder Armistead, the first pastor of this church, was a man of high family and rich connections. He served as an officer in the American army during the Revolutionary war. He was universally esteemed as an officer of the most unwavering courage. He was also a man of strong mind, and in all likelihood would have made a figure in the military line if he had not become a Baptist. This, by lessening his military ardor as well as rendering him somewhat unpopular in the army, probably prevented that distinction to which he might have been otherwise raised. Few men talked with more pleasure about military movements than Major Armistead.

After his resignation, as above, he was never again as useful. He became a merchant, moved from place to place, and preached whenever he found an opportunity. The Major never could completely shake off his high notions of honor and resentment, imbibed in the army. He was not infrequently engaged in making arrangements to settle affairs of honor. Invitations from others he would not refuse; he would sometimes offer them on his part. This, with some other matters of disorder, expelled the Major in 1803 from the Baptist community.

He still occasionally preached, but not with much, if any, success. In 1809 he was again restored to his membership and died shortly after. The Major was thought by many, in his best days, to injure his usefulness by not rightly dividing the word of truth. He dwelt too much upon the deep and mysterious doctrines of Calvinism— doctrines hard to be understood, and which therefore ought to be cautiously managed.

Elder Biggs, their late pastor, is a sound and ingenious preacher, and esteemed by his acquaintances as an exemplary man. He also has lately moved to the western country.

Upper Bridge

Nothing singular has occurred in this church.

Elder Jacob Grigg, former pastor of Upper Bridge, is an Englishman who received an education at the Bristol Baptist academy after he began to preach. When he finished his education he was sent by the missionary society into Africa. Having some disturbance there with the governor of the colony, he came to Norfolk, in Virginia. After preaching for the church there awhile, he came to Upper Bridge, and was there very useful. At length he moved to Kentucky, and was pastor to one of the most prosperous churches there. But in consequence of the disturbances about hereditary slavery, he again moved to Ohio, and finally to Richmond, Va., where he now resides. His high, and perhaps in some respects, untenable opinions of civil liberty, involved him in embarrassments both in Africa and Kentucky. Some of his friends are of opinion that age and experience have corrected these protuberances. His moral character has never been assailed. By all who know him he is esteemed pious and zealous. As a preacher, for deep investigation, for clear and lucid exhibition of divine truth, he is unsurpassed by any preacher in Virginia.

Shoulder's Hill

On the first preaching of the Baptists in these parts they met with violent opposition. A mob collected at one of their meetings and seized the preachers, Barrow and Mintz, and carried them to a water not far distant. There they dipped them several times, holding them under the water until they were nearly drowned, asking them *if they believed.* At length Mr. Barrow replied: *"I believe you mean to drown me."* After sporting with them thus, they let them go. Notwithstanding this opposition the Gospel progressed. The church, with some interruptions, has enjoyed peace and prosperity.

Western Branch

This is a small but increasing church. Mr. Bunting, their present pastor, is a native of the Eastern Shore, and is esteemed both in his new and old habitation a good man and sound preacher.

South Quay

Nothing of note has come to our knowledge as to this church.

Black Creek

This has generally been a happy and peaceful church. They sustained a great loss in the removal of Elder David Barrow in 1797, since which time, however, they have had the occasional ministrations of others, whose labors have been blessed.

Meherrin

This is a daughter of Raccoon Swamp, now under the care of Robert Murrelle, a pious and exemplary minister of the New Testament, and a leading man in the Association.

Tucker's Swamp

This is a small new church under the care of Henry Jones, a preacher of plain but useful gifts.

Seacock

Nothing remarkable has taken place here.

Raccoon Swamp

This has been a large and flourishing church. She has been the mother of many ministerial sons. James Bell, Zadoc Bell, Balaam Ezell, John Wall, Randall Nusam, and William Browne were raised here.

High Hills of Nottoway

Also a daughter of Raccoon Swamp, this church has nothing remarkable.

Sappony

This church fell first under the pastoral care of Mr. Rivers, a pious minister; but his life was short. James Bell was then inaugurated as pastor. He also lived but few years and died. Since his death they have had no regular pastor, but have been attended by Mr. Browne statedly. They have had some revivals.

Mill Swamp

Within the limits of this church there have been for many years some Freewill Baptists, as they were termed. Sometime previous to the year 1774 several of the Baptist preachers holding with free grace preached among them. Their labors proved successful and a church was constituted. They asked and obtained the pastoral services of David Barrow. From the time of the constitution until this time they have been remarked for their regularity in the preservation of discipline and order. God has been honored among them. Elder Barrow, their pastor, was called of God to occupy the pulpit at an early period of his life. Having a strong wish to advance the Redeemer's kingdom, he availed himself of every opportunity to improve his mind. He applied himself to reading, and sought instruction from every quarter within his reach. His progress was very considerable. His preaching and conversation were admired. Mr. Barrow had no notion of preaching barely for the sake of being admired. He sought the salvation of men—he sought it earnestly. Receiving from heaven the bread of life, he dealt out to each one his portion in due season. He traveled and preached far and wide. Jesus was with him and gave him many seals. His spotless character as a Christian greatly aided his pulpit labors. All who knew him at all knew he was a good man. In the time of the Revolutionary War, Mr. Barrow was a warm Whig. He exhorted his countrymen to face the enemy and shake off the yoke of British bondage. He set them the example. When dangers pressed, Mr. Barrow voluntarily shouldered his musket, joined the army and was found ready for the field of battle. His unexceptionable deportment rendered him very popular with all descriptions of men. After the Revolution he was persuaded to accept the office of magistrate, the duties of which he discharged with fidelity and ability for some years. Finding this office incompatible with the regular discharge of his ministerial duties, he threw it up, resolving not to be entangled with the affairs of this life.

He carried his opinions of liberty so far as to think it criminal to hold negroes in slavery. He therefore emancipated all he had. Although this measure proved his disinterested zeal to do right, it is questionable whether it was not in the end productive of more evil than good. While it embarrassed his affairs at home by lessening his resources for the maintenance of a large family, it rendered him suspicious among his acquaintances, and probably in both ways limited his usefulness. After he removed to Kentucky it was a source of much vexation. After a life of twenty-odd years' usefulness in Virginia he moved to Kentucky, where he quickly distinguished himself as a man of talents, piety and usefulness. He is still living.

Otter Dams

This is now under the care of Beverly Boothe. He is a preacher of gifts and respectable among his acquaintances.

Rowanty

This church was formerly under the care of Jesse Lee, a preacher of information. He died and they have since been destitute of a regular pastor.

Davenport's

This church has very few white members, but being in the vicinity of Petersburg, there are in that city a number of people of color who are members. These have built a meetinghouse and carry on their worship regularly through their preachers of color. Many of them are said to be very pious and respectable, whilst many others by their wretched conduct make the Baptist name a term of reproach.

———————

This is the latest Association which can now be taken up. Besides those already treated on, there is one other called Mayo, partly in Virginia and partly in North Carolina, concerning which the documents have unfortunately miscarried. They are now sent for particularly, and it is hoped may arrive in time to be annexed as a supplement

APPENDIX:

Including Biographical Sketches, Copies of Letters, Memorials, Addresses, and other Documents Bearing upon the Subject Matter of this History.

Elder William Webber

Elder William Webber is mentioned in numerous instances in this history. He was born August 15, 1747, and was baptized June, 1770, as one of the first fruits of Elder John Waller's ministry. He was early chosen as pastor of Dover church, and served them long and faithfully. On various occasions he was called to suffer imprisonment for preaching the Gospel without license, and many, it is believed, were savingly reached through the Word preached by him through the grated windows of jails. His talents as a preacher were not of a high order, but his manners were dignified and manly, gentle, affectionate and engaging; he was the soul of simplicity and frank sincerity, and greatly beloved by his members, and highly esteemed by all who knew him. For a number of years he acted as moderator of the General Association, as also of the General Committee. He died in great peace and triumph February 29, 1808.

Elder John Picket

Elder John Picket was born in King George County, Va., January 14, 1744. He was in early manhood a lover of pleasure and a dancing master. He was converted to Christ under Joseph Murphy's preaching in North Carolina in 1765. Returning to Fauquier County, at that time the home of his parents, in 1767, he began to exhort. Carter's Run church was originated in a large measure from his labors. He became pastor here May 12, 1773, the date of his ordination. He suffered imprisonment in the Fauquier jail, and preached to the crowds that gathered at the windows. He traveled extensively on tours of preaching, in which he was greatly blessed. Fifty were baptized at one time in the Shenandoah River as the fruits of his preaching. His zeal increased with his age, and in June, 1803, God called him to his reward.

Elder John Courtney

Elder John Courtney was a native of King and Queen County, where his parents and eldest brother were prominent members of the Episcopal Church. He is said to have rendered repeated religious service in the camp and the field during the Revolutionary War. At the close of the war he removed to Richmond and entered upon the pastoral care of the Baptist (the old First) church, and in this position he rendered valuable service for forty years. In the feebleness of his later years he was assisted by Elders John Brice, Andrew Broaddus, and Henry Keeling. He died December 18, 1824, and an appreciative sketch of his life, prepared by Henry Keeling and published in the *Evangelical Inquirer*, has been preserved in Taylor's *Virginia Baptist Ministers*.

Lewis Craig

Lewis Craig was an elder brother of Elijah and Joseph Craig, all of whom were prominent in the early struggles of the Baptists in Virginia and Kentucky. He was largely instrumental in the formation of Tuckahoe, Upper King and Queen, and Upper Essex churches in the former State, and of the first Gilbert's Creek and South Elkhorn churches in the latter. About 1792 he removed to what is now Bracken County, and has been termed the father of the Association of the same name. His noble endurance of persecutions in several places in Virginia, and his leadership of Craig's church from Spotsylvania, Va., to Gilbert's Creek, Ky., through the vast forests of 1781, invest his sturdy character with a picturesque and stirring interest. He died about A.D. 1824, in the eighty-seventh year of his age, leaving an honored memory as an earnest and powerful exhorter, a sweet-spirited companion, a heavenly minded Christian, and a minister of the Cross who had endured "hardness as a good soldier of Jesus Christ."

Lewis Lunsford

Lewis Lunsford, who was in an important sense the founder of the Baptist denomination in the Northern Neck of Virginia, was born in Stafford County about the year 1753; and there he was baptized while yet a youth by Elder William Fristoe. When not yet eighteen years of age he began to exhort, and large crowds flocked to hear "the Wonderful Boy," so remarkable were his talents and eloquence. About 1774 he made his appearance in Westmoreland, Richmond, Lancaster, and Northumberland counties, where for a time his preaching was interrupted by mob violence and legal proscriptions. These persecutions served, however, to increase his popularity, and in 1778 Morattico church was formed and he chosen as their pastor. His zeal and activity were unabated, and the success of his ministry truly remarkable. No other preacher in Virginia has probably received more conclusive testimonials to the eloquence and power of his sermons than Lunsford. Semple said of him: "In his best strains he was more like an angel than a man. His countenance, lighted up by an inward flame, seemed to shed beams of light wherever he turned. His voice, always harmonious, often seemed tuned by descending seraphs. His style and his manner were so sublime and so energetic that he was indeed an ambassador of the skies, sent down to command all men everywhere to repent."

He continued in the pastorate of Morattico church until his death, which occurred on October 26, 1793, in the prime of his manhood. From the meeting of the Dover Association at Glebe Landing church, in Middlesex, he went to preach at Bruington, where, having taken cold, he became rapidly ill, and died in the vicinity of Miller's, in Essex County, where also his remains were interred. Two funeral sermons by Elder Henry Toler were published and extensively circulated, and he was further commemorated with a marble monument placed by his churches over his grave.

Elder George Smith

Elder George Smith was born in Buckingham County, Va., March 15, 1747; married Judith Guerrant October 20, 1765; died on his farm on Elkhorn Creek, Franklin County, Ky., August 9, 1820. His strong anti-slavery principles made him generally unpopular among the Kentucky churches. He lived in Kentucky upon terms of the most endearing intimacy with his old Virginia yoke-fellow, William Hickman.

Elder George Stokes Smith

Elder George Stokes Smith was a younger half-brother to the above, and probably accompanied Lewis Craig and party to Kentucky in 1781. He was a constituent member of Gilbert's Creek church, and a messenger from that body to the Convention at South Elkhorn in 1785; aided in constituting Marble Creek church in 1787, and was a member of the political convention at Danville in 1792 which framed the constitution of Kentucky. He died in 1809 while pastor of Mt. Pleasant church, in Jessamine County.

Elder Lewis Chadoin

Elder Lewis Chadoin was a native of Chesterfield County, and served as a soldier in the Revolution. He afterwards resided in Goochland County. He was for nearly or quite sixty years an active preacher of the Gospel. He died January 4, 1845, aged ninety years and some months. His funeral sermon was preached by Elder Andrew Broaddus, and was in its eloquence and power a fitting tribute to a worthy and eminently useful life.

Elder Rane Chastain

Elder Rane Chastain was born in Powhatan County June 28, 1741. Most of his life was spent in Buckingham, where he served the church of that name for more than half a century. Cumberland, Providence, and Mulberry Grove churches also enjoyed at times his ministerial supervision. Like many other early preachers he was in straitened financial circumstances, and much of his life spent between the plow handles. Still, when dying in old age, he could say as his last utterance, "I have made full proof of my ministry."

Elder Henry Toler

Elder Henry Toler was a native of King and Queen County, where he grew to manhood. His conversion occurred under the preaching of Elder John Courtney. Becoming a member of Upper College church he was soon licensed to exhort, and, being led to the Northern Neck, he attracted the attention of Counselor Robert Carter, of Westmoreland, who had himself recently become a Baptist. By Mr. Carter's friendly assistance he was enabled to pursue a course of study with Dr. Samuel Jones, of Lower Dublin, Penn. His permanent ministry in the Northern Neck began in 1782 or 1783. In April, 1786, Nomini church was organized and he was chosen pastor. In this relation his labors were greatly blessed for more than twenty years. About the year 1810 he removed with his family to Fairfax County, whence after a brief residence he went to Kentucky and located at Versailles. He became pastor here, where he spent the remainder of his life, and died March, 1824. Few, if any, of the early Baptist pastors of Virginia were permitted to rejoice in more seals to their ministry than Henry Toler.

David Tinsley

David Tinsley was born in Culpeper County in 1749, and soon afterwards was brought by his parents to Amelia. He became a preacher in early manhood, and William Hickman (afterwards "Father Hickman," of Kentucky) was one of the first trophies of his ministry. Besides Totier in Albemarle, of which he was the first pastor, he served Powhatan church for five or six years. The hand of persecution immured him for four months and sixteen days in Chesterfield jail. Through the grated window of this prison he with others of his fellow-prisoners preached to the crowd without. One who was led to Christ by this preaching has testified: "All around the jail the crowded assembly would stand, some weeping and others rejoicing, as they received the word of truth." In 1782 Elder Tinsley entered upon a brief pastorate with Mathew's church, in the Dover Association. In 1785 he removed to Georgia, having sailed from Yorktown to Savannah. He settled with Abilene (then called Red Creek) church, in the vicinity of Augusta. He died at the age of fifty-two years, in October, 1801.

William Woods

William Woods was one of the constituent members of Albemarle church in 1773, and was ordained at the call of that body July 1, 1780. There is a record that at the solicitation of Thomas Jefferson he surrendered his credentials as a minister in order to run for the Legislature, to which he was chosen. His relations with the church do not appear to have ever continued long of a peaceful or orderly character. He was dismissed by letter, with his wife, in September, 1810, and removed to Kentucky, where he finished his course in 1819. The place of his ordination and scene of his principal labors in the ministry was about three-quarters of a mile from where the University of Virginia now stands.

Ambrose Dudley

Ambrose Dudley was born in Spotsylvania County in 1750; served as a captain in the army of the Revolution; preached a few years in Virginia, and in May, 1786, settled in the vicinity of Lexington, Ky. Here he became pastor of Bryant's and David's Fork churches. He was highly respected and honored, and became a leader in Elkhorn, and subsequently in Licking Association. For nearly forty years he pursued, in his adopted State, a popular and useful ministry, unspotted with worldly entanglements, and remarkable for fidelity to truth and duty as well as punctuality in meeting appointments. He died January 27, 1825, having passed his three-score years and ten. Among the numerous children left by Elder Dudley were Dr. Benjamin W. Dudley, an eminent surgeon, and Rev. Thomas P. Dudley, who succeeded to the pastorate of Bryant's church in 1825, and maintained it for nearly sixty years. Dr. Richard M. Dudley, the late president of Georgetown College, was a great-grandson of the subject of this sketch.

James Chiles

Jambs Chiles is said to have possessed "a sturdy set of limbs" and "a resolute spirit," which, prior to his conversion, he sometimes employed "in bruising his countrymen's faces." He was an early instrument in planting the Gospel in the region of Blue Run church, in Orange, and he was a pioneer laborer also in Albemarle. He removed to South Carolina at an early day, where he organized a large church. He is said to have had implicit faith in signs and visions—a weakness which was more than counterbalanced by his ardent zeal and large success. Going to the house of a woman upon a certain occasion, he informed her that God had said he must die there that day. Despite her remonstrance, he reaffirmed the certainty of the decree, and having so said, "he stretched himself upon the bed and yielded up the ghost."

Elijah Baker

Elijah Baker was born in Lunenburg County in 1742. He was converted to Christ under the preaching of Jeremiah Walker, or rather received from him his first serious religious impressions. In 1769 he was baptized by Elder Samuel Hariss, and at once began to exhort. His preaching in his native county was instrumental in gathering several churches. About 1773, his itinerant labors were extended to Henrico County, and thence down the peninsula between the James and York Rivers. In this region he was abundantly blessed in the establishment of churches. Having crossed thence into Gloucester, where he labored a short time, he next set sail, in the spring of 1776, for the Eastern Shore. In this new field, amidst much opposition and severe persecution, he founded no less than ten churches. He was brother to Leonard Baker, the pastor of Musterfield church, in Halifax County, to whom in his last sickness he addressed an affectionate letter, and who reached his bedside only in time to see him die. His death occurred November 6, 1798, at the residence of Dr. Lemon, where another pioneer Baptist preacher—Philip Hughes—also breathed his last.

William Murphey

William Murphy belonged by birth to the southern part of Virginia, and his earliest ministerial labors appear to have been in the region of Halifax and Pittsylvania. With his brother Joseph he traveled extensively, and though neither of them possessed educational advantages their ministry was popular and effective. Samuel Hariss was won to Christ through the ministry of William Murphy. The two brothers—William and Joseph—after an honorable career in Virginia, where they were widely known as "the Murphy boys," removed, the former to the West, and the latter to North Carolina, where he became a leading figure in the Yadkin Association. The home of the latter was Surry County, where he lived, highly respected and esteemed, to a very old age.

Elder John Williams

Elder John Williams was born in Hanover County in 1747, and probably soon afterwards was taken with his parents to Lunenburg County, which became his subsequent home. Here, about 1769, he served as sheriff. The year following he was baptized. In 1771 he accompanied Jeremiah Walker to the first meeting of the General Association at Blue Run meetinghouse. In November following he became pastor of Meherrin church. In 1785 he united with Sandy Creek church, in Charlotte, becoming also their pastor, and the next year he began to serve Blue Stone church, in Mecklenburg.

Meanwhile he was instrumental in organizing Allen's Creek church.

Elder Williams was marked for intellectual force, a broadly catholic spirit, methodical habits, laborious diligence in the ministry, and an ardent love for souls. He was a prompt and regular attendant upon the meetings of the General Association and the General Committee, and in the labors and plans of the denomination in behalf of religious liberty, education and the preservation of their history he was a most prominent and efficient actor. Not a few of the memorials and petitions in behalf of religious rights sent to the Assembly by the early Baptists were committed to his hand, if they were not also the products of his pen.

An accidental fall from a step in 1793 made him somewhat of a cripple for the remainder of his life. He would yet hobble on crutches into the pulpit, and there, seated in a chair, proclaim the Gospel that was so dear to his heart. He died from an attack of pleurisy April 30, 1795.

John McGalmre

John McGlamre removed to Halifax County, N.C., from one of the Northern States, where he was born June 7, 1730. In the thirty-fourth year of his age he became a subject of redeeming grace, and united with Kehukee church, of which he was soon called to be the pastor. He served here until 1772, making meanwhile numerous preaching tours into Virginia with encouraging success. He at length removed to Sussex County, where Raccoon Swamp church was formed through his instrumentality. Various other churches—Mill Swamp, Black Creek, Seacock, and High Hills— were brought into being largely through his labors. For twenty years or more he presided over the Kehukee Association as moderator, and a similar respect was shown him when the division occurred and he became a member of the Portsmouth Association. His death occurred December 13, 1799, within a few hours of that of "the Father of his Country."

Reuben Ford

Reuben Ford was probably a native of Goochland County, where his long and laborious ministry was chiefly spent. He was the principal agent in organizing Goochland church in 1771, from which Dover church sprang two years later. For more than thirty years he served Dover Association as clerk. To him, more than to any other of the early preachers in the days that "tried men's souls," was the duty committed of waiting on the General Assembly with petitions and memorials respecting religious rights. He lived to an advanced age, and towards the end of his life labored under great bodily infirmity. He manifestly was one to whom the inspired testimony applies: "The memory of the just is blessed."

The Warrant for Arrest of Elders Saunders and McClannahan

Culpeper, Sct.:

Whereas we have received information that Nathaniel Saunders and William McClannahan, stiling themselves Protestant dissenters, does teach and preach contrary to the laws and usages of the Kingdom of Great Britain, raising sedition and stirring up strife amongst His Majesties leige people.

Therefore in His Majestie's name we require you, Samuel Ferguson and John Lillard, to take Nathaniel Saunders and William McClannahan and their abettors and bring before some justice of the peace for the said county to be examined touching the charge, and we do hereby command all His Majestie's subjects to be aiding and assisting in the due execution thereof.

Given under our hands this 21st day of August, 1773.

John Slaughter,
George Wetiierall.

To the Sheriff or any Constable of this county, or to Samuel Ferguson and John Lillard.

Executed: Pr. Samuel Ferguson,
John Lillard.

Letter from Middlesex Jail by Elder John Waller

Urbanna Prison, Middlesex County,
August 12, 1771.

Dear Brother in the Lord:

At a meeting which was held at Brother McCan's, in this county, last Saturday, while Brother William Webber was addressing the congregation from James 2:18, there came running toward him, in a most furious rage, Captain James Montague, a magistrate of the county, followed by the parson of the parish and several others, who seemed greatly exasperated. The magistrate and another took hold of Brother Webber, and dragging him from the stage, delivered him, with Brethren Wafford, Robert Ware, Richard Faulkner, James Greenwood, and myself, into custody, and commanded that we should be brought before him for trial. Brother Wafford was severely scourged, and Brother Henry Street received one lash from one of the persecutors, who was prevented from proceeding to further violence by his companions. To be short, I may inform you that we were carried before the above-mentioned magistrate, who, with the parson and some others, carried us one by one into a room and examined our pockets and wallets for fire-arms, &c., charging us with carrying on a meeting against the authority of the land. Finding none, we were asked if we had license to preach in the county; and learning we had not, it was required of us to give bond and security not to preach any more in this county, *which we modestly refused to do;* whereupon, after dismissing Brother Wafford, with a charge to make his escape out of the county by twelve o'clock the next day on pain of imprisonment, and dismissing Brother Faulkner, the rest of us were delivered to the sheriff and sent to close jail, with a charge not to let us walk in the air until court-day. Blessed be God, the sheriff and jailer have treated us with as much kindness as could have been expected from strangers. May the Lord reward them for it! Yesterday we had a large number of people to hear us preach; and among others, many of the great ones of the land, who behaved well while one of us discoursed on the new birth. We find the Lord gracious and kind to us beyond expression in our afflictions. We cannot tell how long we shall be kept in bonds; we therefore beseech, dear brother, that you and the church supplicate night and day for us, our benefactors and our persecutors.

I have to inform you that six of our brethren are confined in Caroline jail, viz., Brethren Lewis Craig, John Burris, John Young, Edward Herndon, James Goolrick and Bartholomew Choning. The most dreadful threatenings are raised in the neighboring counties against the Lord's faithful and humble followers.

Excuse haste. Adieu.

John Waller.

331

Letter to N. Saunders, while in Culpeper Jail, from David Thomas

To Nathaniel Saunders, a Minister of Christ, now in prison in Culpeper for preaching the Gospel there, by Mr. Eaton:

Dear Brother,—I hear you are put in prison for preaching the Gospel of Jesus Christ. Perhaps you may think it hard. But O, what honor has the Lord put upon you! I think you may be willing to suffer death now, seeing you are counted worthy to enter a dungeon for your Master's sake. Hold out, my dear brother! Remember your Master—your royal, heavenly, divine Master—was nailed to a cursed tree for us. O, to suffer for Him is glory in the bud! O, let it never be said that a Baptist minister of Virginia ever wronged his conscience to get liberty, not to please God, but himself! O, your imprisonment (which I am satisfied is not from any rash proceedings of your own) is not a punishment, but a glory! "If you suffer with Him you shall also reign with him."

Dear brother, the bearer is waiting or I should have enlarged. This is only to let you know that I can pray for you with great freedom. Give my kind love to your fellow-prisoner, though I know him not. I hope he is a dear child of God. Pray for me, for I need it. I remain, dear brother,

Yours in our dear Lord Jesus,

David Thomas.
Fauquier,
September 26, 1778.

N.B.—Let me hear from you the first opportunity.

Address to President George Washington by the Committee of the United Baptist Churches in Virginia, assembled in the city of Richmond, August 8, 1789

To the President of the United States of America:

Sir,—Among the many shouts of congratulation that you receive from cities, societies, States and the whole world, we wish to take an active part in the universal chorus by expressing our great satisfaction in your appointment to the first office in the nation. When America on a former occasion was reduced to the necessity of appealing to arms to defend her natural and civil rights, a Washington was found fully adequate to the exigencies of the dangerous attempt, who by the philanthropy of his heart and prudence of his head led forth her untutored troops into the field of battle, and by the skillfulness of his hands baffled the projects of the insulting foe and pointed out the road to independence, even at a time when the energy of the Cabinet was not sufficient to bring into action the natural aid of the association from its respective sources.

The grand object being obtained, the independence of the States acknowledged, free from ambition and devoid of a thirst for blood, our hero returned with those he commanded and laid down his sword at the feet of those who gave it to him. *Such an example to the world is new.* Like other nations, we experience that it requires as great valor and wisdom to make an advantage of a conquest as to gain one.

The want of efficacy in the confederation, the redundancy of laws and their partial administration in the States, called aloud for a new arrangement of our system. The wisdom of the States for that purpose was collected in a grand convention, over which you, sir, had the honor to preside. A national government in all its parts was recommended as the only preservative of the Union, which plan of government is now actually in operation.

When the Constitution first made its appearance in Virginia, we, as a society, had unusual strugglings of mind, fearing that the liberty of conscience (dearer to us than property and life) was not sufficiently secured; perhaps our jealousies were heightened on account of the usage we received in Virginia under the British Government when mobs, bonds, fines, and prisons were our frequent repast.

Convinced on the one hand that without an effective national government the States would fall into disunion and all the consequent evils; on the other hand it was feared we might be accessory to some religious oppression, should any one society in the Union preponderate all the rest. But amidst all the inquietudes of mind, our consolation arose from this consideration, the plan must be good, for it bears the signature of a *tried, trusty friend;* and if religious liberty is rather insecure in the Constitution, "the administration will prevent all oppression, for a Washington will preside." According to our wishes the unanimous voice of the Union has called you, sir, from your beloved retreat, to launch forth again into the faithless seas of human affairs, to guide the helm of the States. Should the horrid evils that have been so pestiferous in Asia and Europe—faction, ambition, war, perfidy, fraud, and persecutions for conscience sake—ever approach the borders of our happy nation, may the name and administration of our beloved President, like the radiant source of day, scatter all those dark clouds from the American hemisphere.

And while we speak freely the language of our own hearts, we are satisfied that we express the sentiments of our brethren whom we represent. The very name of Washington is music in our ears; and although the great evil in the States is the want of mutual confidence between rulers and the people, yet we all have the utmost confidence in the President of the States, and it is our fervent prayer to Almighty God that the Federal Government and the government of the respective States, without rivalship, may so co-operate together as to make the numerous people over whom you preside the happiest nation on earth, and you, sir, the happiest man, in seeing the people whom, by the smiles of Providence, you saved from vassalage by your martial valor and made wise by your maxims, sitting securely under their vines and fig trees enjoying the perfection of human felicity. May God long preserve your life and health for a blessing to the world in general and the United States in particular; and when, like the sun, you have finished your course of great and unparalleled services, and you go the way of all the earth, may the Divine Being, who will reward every man according to his works, grant unto you a glorious admission into His everlasting kingdom through Jesus Christ. This, great sir, is the prayer of your happy admirers.

By order of the committee.

Samuel Hariss, Chairman.
Reuben Ford, Clerk.

Letter from President George Washington to the General Committee representing the United Baptist Churches in Virginia:

Gentlemen,—I request that you will accept my best acknowledgments for your congratulation on my appointment to the first office in the nation. The kind manner in which you mention my past conduct equally claims the expression of my gratitude. After we had, by the smiles of Divine Providence on our exertions, obtained the object for which we contended, I retired at the conclusion of the war with the idea that my country could have no farther occasion for my services, and with the intention of never entering again into public life; but when the exigencies of my country seemed to require me once more to engage in public affairs, an honest conviction of duty superseded my former resolution and became my apology for deviating from the happy plan which I had adopted.

If I could have entertained the slightest apprehension that the Constitution framed in the convention where I had the honor to preside might possibly endanger the religious rights of any ecclesiastical society, certainly I would never have placed my signature to it; and if I could now conceive that the General Government might ever be so administered as to render the liberty of conscience insecure, I beg you will be persuaded that no one would be more zealous than myself to establish effectual barriers against the horrors of spiritual tyranny and every species of religious persecution.

For you doubtless remember I have often expressed my sentiments that every man conducting himself as good citizen, and being accountable to God alone for his religious opinions, ought to be protected in worshipping the Deity according to the dictates of his own conscience.

While I recollect with satisfaction that the religious society of which you are members have been throughout America, uniformly and almost unanimously, the firm friends to civil liberty, and the persevering promoters of our glorious revolution, I cannot hesitate to believe that they will be faithful supporters of a free yet efficient General Government. Under this pleasing expectation I rejoice to assure them that they may rely upon my best wishes and endeavors to advance their prosperity.

In the meantime be assured, gentlemen, that I entertain a proper sense of your fervent supplication to God for my temporal and eternal happiness.

I am, gentlemen, your most obedient servant,

George Washington.

Extract Giving an Account of the First Separate Baptist Association

Went for the Association about 18 miles (Saturday morning, May, 1771). Got to the Association about one o'clock. Brother Hargitt was then about to preach to about 1,200 souls, from 40th chapter Isa., 11th verse ("He shall feed His flock like a shepherd; He shall gather the lambs with His arm, and carry them in His bosom, and shall gently lead those that are with young.") Brother Burris got up immediately (after) and preached from Isa., ch 55, 3d verse ("Incline your ear and come unto Me; hear and your soul shall live; and I will make an everlasting covenant, with you, even the sure mercies of David") with a good deal of liberty, set the Christians afire with the love of God; Assembly praising God with a loud voice; Brother Waller exhorting till he got spent; Brethren Marshall and E. Craig both broke loose together, the Christians shouting and they speaking for the space of half an hour or more; then ceased. Intermission for about one hour, then the delegates associated themselves together; a moderator chosen, which was Brother Hariss; clerk nominated, which was Brother Waller. Then the letters from several churches were read. Then concluded for that night....

Sunday Morning:... Went to the meetinghouse; Brother William Webber was about to preach from Second Tim., 2d ch., last clause of 19th verse ("The Lord knoweth them that are His"); Brother Walker preached immediately (after) from 5th Micah, 15th verse ("For now shall He be great unto the ends of the earth; and this man shall be the peace.") Brother Lewis Craig exhorted. Brother Hariss preached from 5th Isa., 5th verse ("And now go to; I will tell you what I will do to my vineyard. I will take away the hedge thereof, and it shall be eaten up; and break down the wall thereof, and it shall be trodden down.") Brother Lewis (Craig) exhorted. Brother William Marshall preached from 14th chapter, First Epistle to Corinthians. Present that day (supposed to be) 4,000 or 5,000 souls....

Monday Morning: Monday fast-day among us. The brethren delegates met at the meetinghouse by three hours b[efore] sun. Brother Lewis Craig opened Association by divine service. Brother Hariss gave the delegates a very warm and melting exhortation.

Then proceeded to business. We went on very well about one hour and a half, then a dark cloud seemed to overshadow us concerning a plan, Brother Walker for independency and great part of the brethren against it.... Sermons preached that day: Brother Lewis Craig preached first from 8th chapter Romans, last clause 38th verse, &c., ("For I am persuaded that neither death nor life, nor angels, nor principalities," &c.); Brother John Young preached from 14th chapter John, 6th verse ("I am the way, the truth and the life"); Brother Nathaniel Saunders, 3d chapter John's first Epistle, 13th verse ("Marvel not, my brethren, if the world hate you"); Brother Reuben Picket from Isa., 66th, 15th verse ("For behold the Lord will come with fire, and with his chariots like a whirlwind," &c.) About 1,000 people to hear preaching that day.

Met the delegates about three hours b[efore] sun, and after divine service proceeded to business. Went on very smooth and brotherly for about two hours, then there raised a dreadful contention among us concerning church covenants. However, we got over it, I hope, to the mind of God. Went on then very calmly for a while; came a petition from out of doors that there was a great company of people—500, I suppose—that came to hear preaching. Brother Lovell and myself were set apart by the Association to preach. We went. I preached first, from fifteenth of John, second verse: "Every branch in Me that beareth not fruit he taketh away, and every branch that beareth fruit he purgeth it that it may bring forth more fruit." Brother Lovell preached from sixteenth Revelation, last clause of ninth verse: "And they repented not to give Him glory." A good deal of exercise among the people.

Intermission about fifteen minutes. Brother Burris then set apart and preached to the people, from tenth Numbers, the last part of twenty-ninth verse: "Come thou with us and we will do thee good, for the Lord hath spoken good concerning Israel."

Intermission for half an hour. Then Brother Joseph Craig preached to the people, from twenty-fifth chapter of Matthew, last verse: "And these shall go away into everlasting punishment, but the righteous into life eternal."... Brother Bartlett Bennett exhorted and concluded meeting.

But to return: I went to the Association after I preached, and oh, what appeared a dismal, gloomy sight—the Association breaking to pieces concerning the Sabbath! Great arguments. At last

Brother Walker declared no fellowship with Brother Hariss and Brother Chiles. After long debating, they referred the query till the next Association. Then I thought we had gotten over our difficulties, but what appeared dreadful, shocking —query concerning preachers getting license—a dreadful contention about it, and once I thought that everyone that had obtained license would absolutely be censured. But the majority was in our favor. After a great debate; we agreed to refer it to the next Association... I begged a dismission, which I obtained with a good deal of difficulty, took my leave of the brethren, and pushed for home.

Petition to Preach to the Revolutionary Troops

Petition of the Baptist Association, convened at Dupuy's meetinghouse. Cumberland County, to the Virginia Convention, for liberty to preach to the troops in the army of the Revolution, August 14, 1775.

To the Honorable Peyton Randolph, Esq., and the several delegated Gentlemen, convened at Richmond, to concert Measures conducive to the Good and Well-being of this Colony and Dominion, the humble Address of the Virginia Baptists, now Associated in Cumberland, by Delegates from their several Churches:

Gentlemen of the Convention,—While you are (pursuant to the important Trust reposed in you) acting as the Guardians of the Rights of your Constituents, and pointing out to them the Road to Freedom, it must needs afford you an exalted satisfaction to find your Determinations not only applauded, but cheerfully complied with by a brave and spirited people. We, however distinguished from the Body of our Countrymen by appellatives and sentiments of a religious nature, do nevertheless look upon ourselves as Members of the same Commonwealth, and, therefore, with respect to matters of a civil nature, embarked in the same common Cause.

Alarmed at the shocking Oppression which in a British Cloud hangs over our American Continent, we, as a Society and part of the distressed State, have in our Association consider'd what part might be most prudent for the Baptists to act in the present unhappy Contest. After we had determined "that in some Cases it was lawful to go to War, and also for us to make a Military resistance against Great Britain, in regard of their unjust invasion, and tyrannical Oppression of, and repeated Hostilities against America," our people were all left to act at Discretion with respect to inlisting, without falling under the Censure of our Community. And as some have inlisted, and many more likely so to do, who will have earnest Desires for their Ministers to preach to them during the Campaign, we therefore deligate and appoint our well-beloved Brethren in the Ministry, Elijah Craig, Lewis Craig, Jeremiah Walker, and John Williams to present this address and to petition you that they may have free Liberty to preach to the Troops at convenient Times without molestation or abuse; and as we are conscious of their strong attachment to American Liberty, as well as their soundness in the principles of the Christian Religion, and great usefulness in the Work of the Ministry, we are willing they may come under your Examination in any Matters you may think requisite.

We conclude with our earnest prayers to Almighty God for His Divine Blessing on your patriotic and laudable Resolves, for the good of Mankind and American Freedom, and for the success of our Armies in Defence of our Lives, Liberties and Properties. Amen.

Sign'd by order and in behalf of the Association the 14th August, 1775.

Sam'l Hariss, Moderator.
John Waller, Clerk.

Actions of the Virginia Convention

Agreeably with the objects of the above petition, the Convention, as appears from the Journal, under date of "Wednesday, August 16, 1775,"

"Resolved, That it be an instruction to the commanding officers of the regiments or troops to be raised that they permit dissenting clergymen to celebrate divine worship, and to preach to the soldiers, or exhort, from time to time, as the various operations of the military service may permit, for the ease of such scrupulous consciences as may not choose to attend divine service as celebrated by the chaplain."—Page 17.

The subjoined extract from the Journal of the Virginia Convention of 1776 indicates the tenor of the petitions which were circulated for signatures by resolution of the General Baptist Association at their meeting at Dupuy's meetinghouse, August, 1775:

> *Thursday, June 20, 1776.*
>
> *A petition of sundry persons of the Baptist Church, in the county of Prince William, whose names are thereunto subscribed, was presented to the Convention and read, setting forth that at a time when this Colony, with the others, is contending for the civil rights of mankind against the enslaving schemes of a powerful enemy, they are persuaded the strictest unanimity is necessary among ourselves; and, that every remaining cause of division may, if possible, be removed, they think it their duty to petition for the following religious privileges, which they have not yet been indulged within this part of the world, to-wit: That they be allowed to worship God in their own way, without interruption; that they be permitted to maintain their own ministers, and none others; that they may be married, buried and the like without paying the clergy of other denominations; that, these things granted, they will gladly unite with their brethren and to the utmost of their ability promote the common cause.*
>
> *Ordered, That the said petition be referred to the Committee of Propositions and Grievances; that they inquire into the allegations thereof and report the same, With their opinion thereupon, to the Convention."* (Page 58.)

The Convention eight days prior to the consideration of the above-mentioned petition adopted *A Declaration of Rights*, the sixteenth section of which, as written by George Mason, and amended by James Madison, reads as follows: "That religion, or the duty which we owe to our Creator, and the manner of discharging it, can be directed only by reason and conviction, not by force or violence; and therefore all men are equally entitled to the free exercise of religion according to the dictates of conscience; and that it is the mutual duty of all to practice Christian forbearance, love and charity towards each other."

Preamble to Act Exempting Different Societies of Dissenters from Contributing to the Support and Maintenance of the Church of England.

October, 1776

I. Whereas several oppressive acts of Parliament respecting religion have been formerly enacted, and doubts have arisen, and may hereafter arise, whether the same are in force in this Commonwealth or not: For prevention whereof, *Be it enacted by the General Assembly of the Commonwealth of Virginia, and it is hereby enacted by the authority of the same*, That all and every act of Parliament, by whatever title known or distinguished, which renders criminal the maintaining any opinions in matters of religion, forbearing to repair to church or the exercising any mode of worship whatsoever, or which prescribes punishments for the same, shall henceforth be of no force or validity within this Commonwealth.

II. And whereas there are within, this Commonwealth great numbers of dissenters from the Church Establishment by law who have been heretofore taxed for its support, and it is contrary to the principles of reason and justice that any should be compelled to contribute to the maintenance of a Church with which their consciences will not permit them to join, and from which they can therefore receive no benefit: For remedy whereof, and that equal liberty, as well religious as civil, may be universally extended to all the good people of this Commonwealth, *Be it enacted by the General Assembly of the Commonwealth of Virginia, and it is hereby enacted by the authority of the same*, That all dissenters of whatever denomination from the said Church shall, from and after the passing of this act, be totally free and exempt from all levies, taxes, and impositions whatever towards supporting and maintaining the said Church as it now is or hereafter may be established, and its ministers.

Memorial of the Baptist Association at Sandy Creek church, Charlotte County, October 16, 1780

To the Honourable the Speaker and House of Delegates:

The Memorial of the Baptist Association, met at Sandy Creek, in Charlotte, the 16th day of October, 1780, in behalf of themselves and those whom they represent, humbly sheweth:

That a due Regard to the Liberty and Rights of the People is of the highest Importance to the Welfare of the State; That this heaven-born Freedom, which belongs equally to every good Citizen, is the Palladium which the Legislature is particularly intrusted with the Guardianship of, and on which the Safety and Happiness of the State depend. Your Memorialists, therefore, look upon every Law or Usage now existing among us, which does not accord with that Republican Spirit which breathes in our Constitution and Bill of Rights, to be extremely pernicious and detrimental, and that such Law or Usage should immediately be abolished.

As Religious Oppression, or the interfering with the Rights of Conscience, which God has made accountable to none but Himself, is of all Oppression the most inhuman and insupportable, and as Partiality to any Religious Denomination is its genuine offspring, your Memorialists have with Grief observed that Religious Liberty has not made a single Advance in this Commonwealth without some Opposition. They have been much surprised to hear it said of Things indisputably right and necessary, "It is not now a proper Time to proceed to such Affairs; let us first think of defending ourselves," &c., when there cannot, surely, be a more suitable Time to allow ourselves the Blessings of Liberty, which we have in our own Power, than when contending with those who endeavor to tyrannize over us.

As the Completion of Religious Liberty is what, as a Religious Community, your Memorialists are particularly interested in, they would humbly call the attention of your Honourable House to a few Particulars, viz.: First, the Vestry Law, which disqualifies any person to officiate who will not subscribe to be conformable to the Doctrine and Discipline of the Church of England; by which Means Dissenters are not only precluded, but also not represented, they not having a free Voice, whose Property is nevertheless subject to be taxed by the Vestry, and whose Poor are provided for at the Discretion of those who may possibly be under the influence of Party Motives. And what renders the said Law a greater Grievance is, that in some Parishes so much time has elapsed since an Election, that there is scarcely one who was originally chosen by the People, the Vacancies having been filled up by the remaining Vestrymen. Secondly, the Solemnization of Marriage, concerning which it is insinuated by some, and taken for granted by others, that to render it legal it must be performed by a Church Clergyman, according to the Rites and Ceremonies of the Church of England; conformably to which Sentiment Marriage Licenses are usually worded and directed. Now, if this should in Reality be the

Case, your Memorialists conceive that the ill Consequences resulting from thence, which are too obvious to need mentioning, render it absolutely necessary for the Legislature to endeavour their Removal. This is an Affair of so tender a Nature, and of such Importance, that after the Restoration one of the first Matters which the British Parliament proceeded to was the Confirmation of the Marriages solemnized according to the Mode in Use during the Interregnum and the Protectorate of Cromwell. And the Propriety of such a Measure in Virginia evidently appears from the vast numbers of Dissenters who, having Objections against the Form and Manner prescribed in the Book of Common Prayer, proceed to marry otherwise; and also that in many Places, especially over the Ridge, there are no Church Parsons to officiate. On the other Hand, if Marriages otherwise solemnized are equally valid, a Declaratory Act to that Purport appears to your Memorialists to be highly expedient, because they can see no Reason why any of the free inhabitants of this State should be terrified by a mere Mormo from their just Rights and Privileges, or censured by others on Suspicion of their acting contrary to Law. To these Considerations your Memorialists would just beg leave to add that those who claim this Province of officiating at Marriage Solemnities as their sole Right, undertake at the same Time to be the sole Judges of what they are to receive for the same.

Your Memorialists humbly hope that your Honourable House will take effectual Measures to redress these Grievances in such a Way as may manifest an equal Regard to all the good People of this Commonwealth, however diversyfied by Appellations or Religious Sentiments; and that, as it is your Glory to represent a free People, you will be as forward to remove every just Cause of Offence as your Constituents are to complain of them; and in particular that you will consign to Oblivion all the Relicks of Religious Oppression, and make a public Sacrifice of Partiality at the glorious Altar of Freedom.

Signed by order.

Sam'l Hariss, Mod'r,
John Williams, Clk.

Memorial and Remonstrance Presented to the General Assembly of Virginia, against the General Assessment, 1785, Written by James Madison

A MEMORIAL AND REMONSTRANCE.

To the Honorable the General Assembly of Commonwealth of Virginia:

We, the subscribers, citizens of the said Commonwealth, having taken into serious consideration a bill, printed by order of the last session of General Assembly, entitled "A bill establishing a provision for teachers of the Christian religion"; and conceiving that the same, if finally armed with the sanctions of a law, will be a dangerous abuse of power, are bound, as faithful members of a free State, to remonstrate against it, and to declare the reasons by which we are determined. We remonstrate against the said bill:

Because we hold it for a fundamental and unalienable truth, "that religion, or the duty which we owe to the Creator, and the manner of discharging it, can be directed only by reason and conviction, not by force or violence." The religion, then, of every man must be left to the conviction and consciences of every man; and it is the right of every man to exercise it as these may dictate. This right is, in its nature, an unalienable right. It is unalienable, because the opinions of men depending only on the evidence contemplated by their own minds, cannot follow the dictates of other men. It is unalienable, also, because what is here a right towards man is a duty towards the Creator. It is the duty of every man to render to the Creator such homage, and such only, as he believes to be acceptable to Him. This duty is precedent, both in order of time and in degree of obligation, to the claims of civil society. Before any man can be considered as a member of civil society he must be considered as a subject of the Governor of the Universe. And if a member of civil society who enters into any subordinate association must always do it with a reservation of his duty to the general authority, much more must every man who becomes a member of any particular civil society do it with a saving of his allegiance to the Universal Sovereign. We maintain, therefore, that in matters of religion, no man's right is abridged by the institution of civil society, and that religion is wholly exempt from its cognizance. True it is that no other rule exists by which any question which may divide a society can be ultimately determined but by the will of the majority. But it is also true that the majority may trespass on the rights of the minority.

Because, if religion be exempt from the authority of the society at large, still less can it be subject to that of the legislative body. The latter are but the creatures and vicegerents of the former. Their jurisdiction is both derivative and limited. It is limited with regard to the coordinate departments; more necessarily it is limited with regard to the constituents. The preservation of a free government requires not merely that the metes and bounds which separate each department of power be invariably maintained, but more especially that neither of them be suffered to overleap the great barrier which defends the rights of the people. The rulers who are guilty of such encroachment exceed the commission from which they derive their authority, and are tyrants. The people who submit to it are governed by laws made neither by themselves nor by an authority derived from them, and are slaves.

Because it is proper to take alarm at the first experiment on our liberties. We hold this prudent jealousy to be the first duty of citizens and one of the noblest characteristics of the late revolution. The freemen of America did not wait until usurped power had strengthened itself by exercise and entangled the question in precedents. They saw all the consequences in the principle, and they avoided the consequences by denying the principle. We revere this lesson too much soon to forget it. Who does not see that the same authority which can establish Christianity in exclusion of all other religions may establish with the same ease any particular sect of Christians in exclusion of all other sects? That the same authority which can force a citizen to contribute three pence only of his property for the support of any one establishment may force him to conform to any other establishment in all cases whatsoever.

Because the bill violates that equality which ought to be the basis of every law, and which is more indispensable in proportion as the validity or expediency of any law is more liable to be impeached. "If all men are by nature equally free and independent," all men are to be considered as entering into society on equal conditions, as relinquishing no more, and therefore retaining no less, one than another of their natural rights; above all are they to be considered as retaining an "*equal* title to the free exercise of religion according to the dictates of conscience." Whilst we assert for ourselves a freedom to embrace, to profess and observe the religion which we believe to be of divine origin, we cannot deny an equal freedom to those whose minds have not yielded to the evidence which has convinced us. If this freedom be abused it is an offence against God, not against man. To God, therefore, and not to man, must an account of it be rendered.

As the bill violates equality by subjecting some to peculiar burdens, so it violates the same principle by granting to others peculiar exemptions. Are the Quakers and Menonists[1] the only sects who think a compulsive support of their religions unnecessary and unwarrantable? Can their piety alone be entrusted with the care of public worship? Ought their religions to be endowed, above all others, with extraordinary privileges, by which proselytes may be enticed from all others? We think too favorably of the justice and good sense of these denominations to believe that they either covet pre-eminences over their fellow-citizens or that they will be seduced by them from the common opposition to the measure.

Because the bill implies either that the civil magistrate is a competent judge of religious truths, or that he may employ religion as an engine of civil policy. The first is an arrogant pretention, falsified by the extraordinary opinion of rulers, in all ages and throughout the world; the second, an unhallowed perversion of the means of salvation.

Because the Establishment proposed by the bill is not requisite for the support of the Christian religion. To say that it is a contradiction to the Christian religion itself, for every page of it disavows a dependence on the power of this world; it is a contradiction to fact, for it is known that this religion both existed and flourished, not only without the support of human laws, but in spite of every opposition from them; and not only during the period of miraculous aid, but long after it had been left to its own evidence and the ordinary care of Providence: nay, it is a contradiction in terms, for a religion not invented by human policy must have pre-existed and been supported before it was established by human policy; and is, moreover, to weaken, in those who profess this religion, a pious confidence in its innate excellence and the

---

[1] Mennonites.

patronage of its Author, and to foster in those who still reject it a suspicion that its friends are too conscious of its fallacies to trust it to its own merits.

Because experience witnesses that ecclesiastical establishments, instead of maintaining the purity and efficacy of religion, have had a contrary operation. During almost fifteen centuries has the legal establishment of Christianity been on trial. What have been its fruits? More or less in all places pride and indolence in the clergy; ignorance and servility in the laity; in both, superstition, bigotry and persecution. Enquire of the teachers of Christianity for the ages in which it appeared in its greatest lustre. Those of every sect point to the ages prior to its incorporation with civil policy. Propose a restoration of this primitive state, in which its teachers depended on the voluntary rewards of their flocks, many of them predict its downfall. On which side ought their testimony to have greatest weight, when for or when against their interest?

Because the Establishment in question is not necessary for the support of civil government. If it be urged as necessary for the support of civil government, only as it is a means of supporting religion, and it be not necessary for the latter purpose, it cannot be necessary for the former. If religion be not within the cognizance of civil government, how can its legal establishment be said to be necessary to civil government? What influence, in fact, have ecclesiastical establishments had on civil society? In some instances they have been seen to exact a spiritual tyranny on the ruins of civil authority; in more instances have they been seen upholding the thrones of political tyranny; in no instance have they been the guardians of the liberties of the people. Rulers who wished to subvert the public liberty may have found an Established clergy convenient auxiliaries. A just government instituted to secure and perpetuate it needs them not. Such a government will be best supported by protecting every citizen in the enjoyment of his religion with the same equal hand which protects his person and his property; by neither invading the equal rights of any sect, nor suffering any sect to invade those of another.

Because the proposed Establishment is a departure from that generous policy which, offering an asylum to the persecuted and oppressed of every nation and religion, promised a lustre to our country and an accession for the number of its citizens. What a melancholy mark is the bill of sudden degeneracy. Instead of holding forth an asylum to the persecuted, it is itself a signal of persecution. It degrades from the equal rank of citizens all those whose opinions in religion do not bend to those of the legislative authority. Distant as it may be, in its present form, from the inquisition, it differs from it only in degree; the one is the first step, the other the last in the career of intolerance. The magnanimous sufferer under the cruel scourge in foreign regions must view the bill as a beacon on our coast, warning him to seek some other haven, where liberty and philanthropy in their due extent may offer a more certain repose from his troubles.

Because it will have a like tendency to banish our citizens. The allurements presented by other situations are every day thinning their number. To superadd a fresh motive to emigration, by revoking the liberty which they now enjoy, would be the same species of folly which has dishonored and depopulated flourishing kingdoms.

Because it will destroy that moderation and harmony which the forbearance of our laws to intermeddle with religion has produced among its several sects. Torrents of blood have been spilt in the old world by vain attempts of the secular arm to extinguish religious discord by proscribing all differences in religious opinion. Time has at length revealed the true remedy. Every relaxation of narrow and rigorous policy, wherever it has been tried, has been found to assuage the disease. The American theatre has exhibited proofs that equal and complete liberty, if it does not wholly eradicate it, sufficiently destroys its malignant influence on the health and prosperity of the State. If, with the salutary effects of this system under our own eyes, we begin to contract the bounds of religious freedom, we know no name that will too severely reproach our folly. At least let warning be taken at the first fruits of the threatened innovation. The very appearance of the bill has transformed that "Christian forbearance, love and charity," which of late mutually prevailed, into animosities and jealousies which may not soon be appeased. What mischiefs may not be dreaded should this enemy to the public quiet be armed with the force of a law?

Because the policy of the bill is adverse to the diffusion of the light of Christianity. The first wish of those who ought to enjoy this precious gift ought to be that it may be imparted to the whole race of mankind. Compare the number of those who have as yet received it with the number still remaining under the dominion of false religions, and how small is the former! Does the policy of the bill tend to lessen the disproportion? No; it at once discourages those who are strangers to the light of truth from coming into the regions of it, and countenances by example the nations who continue in darkness in shutting out those who might convey it to them. Instead of leveling, as far as possible, every obstacle to the victorious progress of truth, the bill, with an ignoble and unchristian timidity, would circumscribe it with a wall of defence against the encroachments of error.

Because attempts to enforce by legal sanctions acts obnoxious to so great a proportion of citizens tend to enervate the laws in general and to slacken the bands of society. If it be difficult to execute any law which is not generally deemed necessary or salutary, what must be the case where it is deemed invalid and dangerous? And what may be the effect of so striking an example of impotency in the Government on its general authority?

Because a measure of such singular magnitude and delicacy ought not to be imposed without the clearest evidence that it is called for by a majority of citizens; and no satisfactory method is yet proposed by which the voice of the majority in this case may be determined or its influence secured. "The people of the respective counties are indeed requested to signify their opinion respecting the adoption of the bill to the next session of the Assembly," but the representation must be made equal before the voice either of the representatives or of the counties will be that of the people. Our hope is that neither of the former will, after due consideration, espouse the dangerous principle of the bill. Should the event disappoint us, it will still leave us in full confidence that a fair appeal to the latter will reverse the sentence against our liberties.

Because, finally, "the equal right of every citizen to the free exercise of his religion according to the dictates of conscience" is held by the same tenure with all our other rights. If we recur to its origin it is equally the gift of nature; if we weigh its importance it cannot be less dear to us; if we consult the "Declaration of those rights which pertain to the good people of Virginia as the basis and foundation of government," it is enumerated with equal solemnity, or rather with studied emphasis. Either, then, we must say that the will of the Legislature is the only measure of their authority, and that in the plenitude of this authority they may sweep away all our fundamental rights, or that they are bound to leave this particular right untouched and sacred; either we must say that they may control the freedom of the press; may abolish the trial by jury; may swallow up the executive and judiciary powers of the State; nay, that they may annihilate our very right of suffrage and erect themselves into an independent and hereditary assembly; or we must say that they have no authority to enact into a law the bill under consideration. We, the subscribers, say that the General Assembly of this Commonwealth have no such authority; and that no effort may be omitted on our part against so dangerous a usurpation, we oppose to it this remonstrance, earnestly praying, as we are in duty bound, that the Supreme Lawgiver of the universe, by illuminating those to whom it is addressed, may, on one hand, turn their councils from every act which would affront His holy prerogative or violate the trust committed to them, and on the other guide them into every measure which may be worthy of His blessing; may redound to their own praise, and may establish most firmly the liberties, the property, and the happiness of this Commonwealth.

Act to Establish Religious Freedom, by Thomas Jefferson (Adopted December 16, 1785)

Be it enacted by the General Assembly, That no man shall be compelled to frequent or support any religious worship, place or ministry whatsoever; nor shall be enforced, restrained, molested or burthened in his body or goods, nor shall otherwise suffer on account of his religious opinions or belief; but that all men shall be free to profess and by argument to maintain their opinions in matters of religion, and that the same shall in no wise diminish, enlarge or affect their civil capacities."

Reply of Thomas Jefferson to Congratulatory Address of the Buck Mountain Baptist Church

Several congratulatory addresses were sent to Mr. Jefferson on his retirement from the Presidency by different Baptist bodies in Virginia. The spirit of his replies is well expressed in the following letter to the Buck Mountain Baptist church:

Monticello, April 18, 1809.

I thank you, my friends and neighbors, for your kind congratulations on my return to my native home, and of the opportunities it will give me of enjoying, amidst your affections, the comforts of retirement and rest. Your approbation of my conduct is the more valued as you have best known me, and is an ample reward for any services I may have rendered. We have acted together from the origin to the end of a memorable Revolution, and we have contributed each in the line allotted to us our endeavors to render its Issues a permanent blessing to our country. That our social intercourse may, to the evening of our days, be cheered and cemented by witnessing the freedom and happiness for which we have labored, will be my constant prayer.

Accept the offering of my affectionate esteem and respect.
Th. Jefferson.

9 798330 320769